Teaching in the
British Primary School

Teaching in the British Primary School

VINCENT R. ROGERS

The University of Connecticut

THE MACMILLAN COMPANY
COLLIER-MACMILLAN LIMITED, LONDON

PREFACE

My first exposure to the sort of school described in this book came in 1966. I was a Fulbright scholar engaged in a study of British education, and it made obvious sense to try to get inside a school or two. My English friends and advisers guided me initially to Oxfordshire, where I visited the Bampton, Brize-Norton, and Tower Hill primary schools. I have not been quite the same since. Seventy-two schools later I still find myself wondering if what I saw was real, if such schools and teachers do exist. Four cartons of notes taken on 3×5 cards give material support to the fact that these schools do indeed exist and that they are becoming increasingly influential, not only in Britain but in the wider world as well.

I must note here that only about 25 per cent of Britain's primary schools fit the model described in this book. Perhaps 40 per cent can be described as quite traditional, whereas another third or so are in various stages of transformation. Nevertheless, 25 per cent is a significant number of schools, when one looks at the total size of the educational enterprise in Britain. Even more significant is the obvious movement *toward* this new kind of education among schools that cannot as yet be included among the exciting and innovative 25 per cent.

What is so unusual about these schools? In a few words, one might say that they are schools designed and organized *for children*. Those teaching in them seem committed to the idea that children are the most important component, the vital raw material, of a primary school and that they are to be heard, cared for, consulted, and respected.

v

What happens when teachers and headmasters accept and believe in this point of view is really the essence of the body of this book.

Of course, it is difficult to estimate in any precise way the extent to which educational practices in one country may be transported to another. Many Americans would agree, however, that our public schools are in serious trouble. John Holt, Jonathan Kozol, Herbert Kohl, Paul Goodman, Joseph Featherstone, and a host of others have made searching, often bitter comments on "the way things are" in American education today—particularly, but not exclusively, in our cities. Perhaps Charles Silberman put it as powerfully and as briefly as anyone when he said that our schools tend to be, on the whole, "grim, joyless places that are needlessly authoritarian and repressive— not because teachers and principals are stupid or venal, but because nobody ever asks *why: Why* the rules? or, *Why* the curriculum?"

Those who have helped develop the modern British primary school have indeed asked, "Why?" And the kinds of schools that have grown out of this search for an educational rationale are neither joyless, grim, nor repressive. On the contrary, they appear to be stimulating, challenging, happy places for children to learn. One should add immediately that the philosophy and methodology that permeate these schools seem to be effective for suburban, rural, and urban children. Some of the best primary schools are in the heart of London's slums, while others are in small, rural villages.

Is it possible, then, that a careful examination of the British primary school by American teachers, principals, superintendents, those working in teacher education at colleges and universities—and American *parents*—might reveal an educational point of view that is both relevant and, at least in part, transferable to American education? Those of us who have seen these schools have become more and more convinced that the answer is a resounding "yes." But others who have not had this privilege need a substantial, firsthand, detailed description of the emerging British primary school if they are to make an intelligent evaluation of what *is* in Britain and what *may be* elsewhere.

Assembling the kind of descriptive material that would bring the reader inside the walls of these remarkable schools seemed to call for an editing rather than an authoring job. Although I have spent considerable time in Britain and look forward to spending a good deal more, the detail I was seeking forced me to the conclusion that this book should be written *by* English teachers and headmasters *for* Americans. I think it quite fair to say that the contributors to this volume are a virtual *Who's Who* of British primary education. Each author has been intimately involved in the movement towards a freer, more child-centered primary school and writes out of years of experience *with* children, *in* schools. I feel confident that these educators have presented not only the philosophy behind the British primary school but also its day-to-day classroom practices and activities, in a way that should communicate effectively to American parents and teachers.

V. R. R.

CONTENTS

1. The Philosophy Underlying the British Primary School

EDITH MOORHOUSE

EDITH MOORHOUSE, *O.B.E., was Senior Advisor for Primary Education for Oxfordshire L.E.A. for 22 years. Before taking up her appointment in Oxfordshire, she taught for many years in a variety of schools in the West Riding of Yorkshire and in Hertfordshire, where she was Head of an All Age Rural School; she then became an Education Lecturer at Wall Hall Training College in Hertfordshire.*

Teaching in the Twenties

Forty years ago the emphasis in teacher training was on the techniques of holding the attention of a class of children: the question at the appropriate moment when attention began to lapse, the raising of an eyebrow, the quick drawing on the blackboard. It was believed that the span of attention was short, as indeed it was if the teacher had no histrionic ability or the lesson had no relevance to the interests or experience of the children. The teacher stood in front of the class of children of one age-group who sat in straight rows facing the blackboard and talked to and questioned the children for much of the day; the children copied notes from the blackboard or answered questions

1

in writing. The teacher was concerned with a class of children and had therefore to aim at the average, so that gifted children were held back and the less able children floundered and lapsed into laziness or naughtiness. Of course, there were always some gifted teachers who inspired children by their own enthusiasm and helped along the lame ducks. Playtimes, midmorning and midafternoon breaks were necessary, because children had a static life and in many schools they would rush on to the flat stretch of unchallenging asphalt playground, knocking and pushing and generally "letting go." Drill, drawing, and handwork were considered somewhat as frills or relaxation and demanded little imagination or creative ability. In fact, the timetable was very subject conscious and was divided into half-hour and hour periods. Every day, by law, had to start with worship and was followed by scripture (R.E.) and then arithmetic. English was divided into reading, composition, handwriting, spelling, dictation, English grammar and comprehension, literature and poetry, and in that order of importance. In addition, there were periods of drill or physical training, history, geography, nature study, drawing, handwork, and singing. On the whole, each subject was treated in isolation and the emphasis was on instruction. This "method" did not adequately cater to the mixed abilities in each class, consequently many head teachers "streamed" their schools; the brightest children were put together in one class and slow learners in another. Big schools had A, B, C, and D streams, and class teaching was then thought to be possible. Some teachers, however, held fast to the view that streaming children had many disadvantages and thought that segregation was bad socially; the A-stream children tended to be priggish, the D-stream ones felt rejected. There was a tendency towards assigning the best and brightest teachers to the brightest children and the ordinary, uninspired teachers to the slow learners.

Presentday Family or Vertical Grouping

However, a big change has taken place in many parts of Britain and is spreading rapidly. Not only has streaming been largely abandoned, but children of two, three, or more age-groups have been deliberately organized into parallel classes. This is known as *family* or *vertical grouping*, and you will find in a primary school of 560 children for example, six parallel classes of children from five to seven years of age, four parallel classes of seven-plus to nine-plus, and four parallel classes of nine-plus to eleven-plus, instead of two classes of children in each of the seven age-groups in A and B streams. Of necessity, the family-grouping pattern is traditional in the rural schools, but the smaller number of children in each class is an added advantage.

One finds on entering many primary schools today that for most of the day a number of different activities will be going on concurrently in each classroom or group of rooms. One group of children may be painting, another doing craftwork; some children may be reading for pleasure, some doing research on a particular interest from books; other children may be writing; some may be cooking, others using clay; some painting, some making books; some may be doing mathematics, and some working out a scientific problem. Children are getting their own materials and equipment as required and putting them back. The teacher cannot be seen at once, for there is no longer a "front" of the class and he/she may be somewhere in the room, sitting by a child discussing his work and giving it further impetus. One is struck by the initiative of the children, by their participation and involvement, by their sense of responsibility and self-discipline. To the uninitiated the impression is that the children can get on without a teacher, for they are working in a purposeful way; but, in fact, this engrossment is because the teacher has prepared a stimulating environment and because she knows each child and his achievements and can see who is needing help at any particular moment—a word of approval or sign of interest will be sufficient to encourage many children to work out their own ideas.

In this situation there is a completely different atmosphere; an entirely different relationship exists between teacher and child from that in a formal teacher/class situation. Formerly, the teacher depended on histrionic ability, force of personality, or projection of fear to discipline his class; today, there is mutual respect between teacher and child, and between the child in relation to other children and adults. Of course there are times when the teacher calls the class (family) together for discussion, to share poetry, stories, to sing and make music together, to do movement and drama. On other occasions, classes (families) join together to watch a television program or see films; sometimes the whole school gathers together to worship, to celebrate something good, to experience togetherness, so that the pattern is changing almost imperceptibly from an individual to group situations of varying sizes, according to the needs of the moment.

Fundamental Principles Behind a Teacher/Child Relationship

Two fundamental principles underlie these changes from a formal teacher/class relationship to a teacher/child relationship—from teaching to learning. First, there is a *real* appreciation and deep understanding of the uniqueness of each child. (Although much glib talk centers around individual differences, in many schools age is still sacrosanct and intellectual, emotional, and social differences are ignored.) The second principle is that children learn from experience, from exploration, and from active participation in discovery.

FIRST PRINCIPLE: APPRECIATION OF INDIVIDUAL DIFFERENCES

We are very aware of the differences of children who come into our schools at five years of age. Home backgrounds may vary enormously from the private house with a big garden offering many challenges to the isolated cottage, the council house, the soulless estate, the high flat —from city, urban or semiurban, to rural surroundings. Some children arrive at school socially adjusted and with a great facility in using language, because their parents have talked with them, shared their interests, encouraged contact and communication with their peers and with other adults. Such children appear intelligent and ready to meet the challenge of school. Other children arrive shy, timid, and tongue-tied, for they have been overprotected, shielded from physical contact and communication with other children. Others arrive aggressive, physically virile, but with a very limited vocabulary, for they have had to fend for themselves and are accustomed to such expletives and commands as, "Come in!" "Go out!" "Shut up!"; they appear less intelligent, less knowledgeable, because language as we teachers use it has not been developed. Children of farm workers are brought up in isolation and are often speechless for weeks and even months; for them, going to school and being one of many in an enclosed space is a traumatic experience. The real ability of these children is not apparent immediately. It might well be that the child deprived of preschool language could go further ultimately than the socially adjusted, verbose child. We are all aware of the consequences of illness, of hospitalization, of broken homes, of homes that lack harmony, of parents that are neurotic, overindulgent, or negligent. We know that the innate potential ability of each child varies enormously; but what that potential is cannot be assessed too early in a child's development, because of the socioeconomic and emotional influences that act upon him. Children learn in different ways and at different rates, so that age is by no means the criterion for a stage of development. If we think of children learning to walk we know that there is a wide variation in the age at which they achieve this skill. We do not expect every child to walk at a given age. We also know that they achieve this skill in different ways: some children crawl using hands and knees, others hands and feet, some children push themselves with one leg outstretched—the other tucked under. In fact, the child wants to move and finds its own way of doing so. Some children stay at this stage for a long time, others for a short time; then they stand and finally walk. But some children seem to cut out the preliminaries and concentrate their efforts on standing and then walking. The same is true of children learning to talk. The age at which this skill is achieved varies enormously, as well as the way in which the skill is achieved. Some children follow what to us seems a logical sequence of sounds, words, phrases, and sentences; but other children talk in a language of their own and may be two or two-and-a-half years of age before they talk the language we understand—and then talk quite fluently! If we think of children learning to read, we know that some children see and recognize patterns early and need little help in acquiring the skill, but others at a later stage seem to benefit by the use of a logical sequence of techniques. Because the rate of growth and development of children before the age of five is so terrific, individual differences and reactions to learning situations are very apparent in school. We need to appreciate that these differences continue beyond childhood and that we must accept and provide for them in our primary schools.

It follows from these considerations that there is no real purpose in organizing children into age-groups, for in a class of children who are six chronologically there will be children who are four, five, six, seven, eight, or nine intellectually and children with an equally wide scatter of social and emotional maturity. It is possible to cater to these differences in a class of six-year-old children, for example, if the work is planned on an individual basis, but there are many advantages in a family or vertically grouped class. Let us look at a class with children of five, six, or seven-year-olds in it. In such a class there is a wider scatter of intellectual differences, but children are not so acutely aware of them; the gifted five-year-old can stretch his intellectual ability alongside a six- or seven-year-old, and yet satisfy his emotional needs with the younger children, whereas the less gifted seven-year-old can work at the five-year-old level intellectually but with his age-peers in practical and creative work. If the teacher's attitude is right in accepting each individual for his true worth, then feelings of superiority or inferiority do not arise. If a teacher has a class of children of five to seven-plus, then he naturally collects materials and equipment to cover and more than cover that age-range, so that children are more likely to satisfy their intellectual needs. If one is concerned with the development of the whole personality of a child and not only with the learning of basic skills, then much of the education is absorbed and cannot be measured and passed on to another teacher, so that it is an advantage if the children are at least two years with one teacher. So often at the end of a school year teachers deplore the passing up of their children, for they know them well; they know how to get the best out of them and are sure that they could take them so much further if only they had them longer. I have heard even beginning teachers say, "Thank goodness I shan't have a sea of new faces next term. Half of my class will know me, know what I expect and where the equipment is, and I shall know them."

SECOND PRINCIPLE: CHILDREN LEARN FROM EXPERIENCE

The second principle underlying primary education is that all children learn through discovery. Learning is as natural as breathing, for each child is born with an urge to investigate and find out. A baby is thrust into a world with which he has to come to terms; he needs to find out his own powers, the nature of the world around him, and eventually how his own powers can influence that world. The baby's world is a small one concerned largely with mother or substitute mother, who satisfies his cravings for food, comfort, warmth, and love. At the same time the baby is finding out what his own limbs and body can do—with, what seems to us, aimless waving of arms, grasping of hands, kicking of legs, and bouncing about with sheer joy of physical satisfaction and awareness of its growing powers and strength. The child's world gradually extends: there are more people to come to terms with, the family, neighbors, and friends; the physical world widens, becomes something more than cot and pram. There are bigger spaces to be explored and more objects lying about. A busy mother pops her child in the playpen with a variety of things to play with while she gets on with her household chores. What does the child do? Picks up each object, handles it, pokes it with a finger, bangs it on the floor, shakes it (for it might make noise), puts it in his mouth (for it might be tasty), sniffs it (for it might even have a smell), inspects it (for brightly colored objects attract attention). The child is learning about things through his senses. He is not consciously aware that he is learning, nor perhaps is his mother, but he is absorbing qualities of these objects and discovering his own powers over them. From his many and varied experiences the child comes to appreciate hardness, softness, sharpness, roundness, weight (heaviness and lightness), and size (big and little). He perceives that *this* material conforms, and *that* resists, that colors vary, and so on. The adult will occasionally share these experiences with the child and add another dimension, namely that of words, which the child will imitate and eventually associate with an object or action. We know from experience that children vary widely in their reaction to this use of words and in their powers of retention. There is no need to teach a child to move if he sees an object he wants; the natural urge to find out motivates the child to get the object in his own way. Through his own powers and by his own experiences a child will find that he can pull himself up and, after many bumps, find he can stand and eventually walk. Adults provide the right environment, stable objects for the child to use (so that there are not too many failures) and, of course, they smile and speak encouraging words of approval. The child responds and tries again and again until he finds he can take his weight on his feet and make a few steps. In the early stages an adult hand is offered, then a finger, until the child suddenly feels his power to walk and revels in his independence. This moment is truly wonderful for us—to witness a child's body rejoicing in its freedom and success.

The child's world is now very much extended—a wider world to be explored. What happens if you go for a walk with a toddler (I put it this way advisedly, for so many adults take the child, who then has to concentrate on the act of walking in order to keep the pace)? It takes a long time to go a short distance, if the child takes charge. I recall going once with Kersteen who picked up a twig, looked at it, rubbed her hand along it, tapped her left hand with it, and then toddled on dragging it with her. There had been a storm and sand had collected in the gutter. Quite by accident her stick made a mark on the sand. Kersteen became aware of this, she stopped and drew patterns. Then her eye caught sight of a grate in the gutter, she looked at it, crouched and looked more closely, stamped on it, then poked her stick through the bars, when she managed to find the space. Having explored that situation she moved on. I steered her off the road into a lane, but there was a field gate that had to be climbed with great effort and strange antics and some frustration until, finally, a helping hand was accepted. Jumping off the gate she became aware of fallen leaves and had a glorious time kicking them and enjoying the movement and crackling sound. We finally returned to see an anxious mother who thought I must have walked her miles, but in fact we had been not many yards from home.

Resources of School Community

There is no sudden change in the growth and development of children at five years of age, when children in England are required to attend school. The need for children to explore and discover is still fundamental to learning, and the advantage of attending school is that the environment can be contrived, both in and out of the building, to meet this need. Many children are deprived of space, materials, experiences, freedom, and companionship in their home background; but all these needs can be provided at school.

MATERIAL OPPORTUNITY

Materials of every kind should be available: basic materials, such as sand, water, clay, and wood; a collection of junk, boxes, containers of every size and shape in wood, cardboard, and plastic; a wide variety of cardboard and paper in different shapes, sizes, thicknesses, and colors; paints (water, oil and emulsion), pens, charcoal, pencils, a variety of brushes, crayons, in fact all kinds of media for making marks that a child can explore; a variety of pastes and glues that do the job expected of them; scissors that cut; benches, a vice, and tools; an assortment of materials to stroke and use—velvet, silk, satin, wool, cotton, linen, fur, nylon. Each item has a different quality that can only be fully appreciated by handling and using and coming to terms with the discipline they impose. All these materials may be used at the child's own stage of development and maturity; one child might be at the stage of pitting his own strength against boxes and planks and yet be able to join in with a group of children of varying ages and abilities who are constructing a telescope or a space ship—that will hold several children—imaginative, constructive work which is the basis of mathematics.

Some children explore paint, finding out what it does, what happens when colors are mixed, what are the effects of thick and thin paints, while other children of the same age have reached the stage of recognizing pictures in what they have done, and still others know from the outset what it is they want to paint. The needs of these individual children cannot be met, therefore, by demonstration or instruction, but only by their own choice and experiences. These early experiments with materials will lead to work of quite a high degree of mastery and skill by the time the children are eleven years of age—skill in modelling, pottery, sculpture, in printing and dyeing of materials, of lino-cuts and wood engraving, of spinning, dyeing, and weaving, of book making, and many other crafts. Provision must be made for children to live through an adult world, whereby they may cook, dress up, have their clinics and hospitals, tea parties, shops, and plays. There must be tables where children can go to write and chairs available in the book bays for those who want to come to terms with books.

CHALLENGING ENVIRONMENT

Life itself is a challenge, and from the day they are born children are exposed to challenges that have to be met and overcome. The skill of teaching is to present each child with the right challenge at the right time; too great an expectation of what a child is able to do can discourage the child, make him withdraw mentally from the struggle and become lazy or rebel in an aggressive attitude. I know of a child of brilliant parents who arrived at school socially adjusted and with a great command of language. In the first two or three years he seemed to be what everyone expected him to be—a brilliant boy. However, as he passed through the school he gradually lost interest and was considered idle, because he was not living up to what was expected of him. In desperation he was given a test that revealed that he had by no means inherited the innate ability of his parents and that the hard struggle to respond to challenges beyond his ability had become too great and he had withdrawn and put on an attitude of laziness. His early success has been because of his socioeconomic background and interested parents. On the other hand, we have all met individuals who are not stretched to capacity, who are not challenged, and who become bored and troublesome. This need for the right challenge was brought home to me when sitting on a drive one hot day with a baby at the crawling stage who found enjoyment in pulling out grass from amongst the gravel. If he had to tug hard and succeeded, his whole being oozed satisfaction; but if he could not pull the grass out in spite of his effort then he showed intense displeasure, and I stepped in to help. I found that if I loosened the sod too much and he could pull it out without effort he was completely frustrated and unsatisfied. I had to loosen it just sufficiently for him to have to use effort and to feel his own power. It is impossible to meet this individual need if a *class* of children are being instructed. A group or class of children can be inspired and share enthusiasms and experiences with a teacher, for much of what is valuable in education can be taught and absorbed; but a learning situation that demands understanding must be personal and individual.

PHYSICAL CONDITIONS

The school building itself can either be a help or a hindrance, depending on whether it was built long ago, when instruction was the order of the day, or planned to meet the present philosophy. However, teachers who believe in discovery transform old buildings, exploit all the advantages of wall space and, by skillful use of furniture, create work areas for reading, for writing activities, for mathematical and scientific experiments, for practical experiences, and for music so that children know where to go and where to find equipment for the particular job in hand. But this is only the shell; it is what the teachers put into these areas that makes the difference, what materials and objects they display and celebrate—things for the children to look at, to hold, to smell, to become aware of in all facets, texture, form, pattern, color, and use. Teachers need to be very aware of their own background and recognize the possibilities of extending the children's background by their own contributions.

OPPORTUNITIES FOR EXPLORATION

Making discoveries about the things in school is only one aspect of learning; there is a world outside to be explored, be it rural or urban. So often we look for the spectacular when, in fact, children choose what seems to us insignificant. For example, one teacher took a group of children to a bridge; to the left was a woollen mill and to the right were the grounds surrounding abbey ruins. His intention was for the children to study and draw comparisons but, in fact, a snail attracted the attention of one boy. His interest and questions aroused the interest of the group, and snails became the topic that snowballed into an intensive study, to which the help of the British Museum was drawn. Books were made and snail patterns appeared on paper and material. What was important was not so much the information about snails which the children had gleaned, but their attitude. Here was a challenge, a field for exploration. They had to discover where and how they could find answers to their questions and then communicate their experience orally, in writing, in creative and practical work, using all their skills and learning new ones.

It becomes necessary to extend the environment to be explored still further, for children as they grow older need experiences for which transportation is involved: perhaps a visit to a museum, a church, a theatre, a fire station, bus or railway station, a library, a place of historical interest, a different natural environment, or a busy built-up city or port. Most primary schools hire buses for these journeys, but recently in Oxfordshire groups of rural schools have been provided with a mini-bus for their common use. Sharing this equipment has brought the schools closer together, they have been able to share resources and their teachers' skills and have been able to go further afield for their explorations.

COMMUNICATION MEDIA

One must always be aware that children have their own specific interests; they might have had some experiences at home or found something on the way to school that can be exploited by the teacher who is ready to discuss and lead the child on to an exploration of his own. Mass media at home and in school make an impact that cannot be ignored. It might well be that a television program or a film can be utilized because *that* is a burning interest to one or more children at the time. When children's interests are stimulated they become completely involved and need to communicate in some form and extend their knowledge. They might turn to books for further information, or for identification. Some need to write about their experiences; it might be a factual and a logical description, it might be a piece of imaginative writing, poetic prose, or verse. Some might need to set up an experiment, some, to formulate data they have collected. Others may want to communicate their experiences in some creative form in paint, wood, clay, wool. Children can find natural materials in their journeys of discovery and by using them discover the qualities and discipline of the materials they use. Some children may find inspiration in the sounds they hear and return to experiment in poetry or music making.

It is obvious that children bursting with enthusiasm can not all be interested in the same thing at the same time, hence a variety of activities go on at the same time in the classroom and its environment. Some children know exactly what they want to do and get on with it. Hence the teacher is free to listen and give guidance to those less sure of themselves and, through questions and discussion, lead those who are ready first to a deeper and wider consideration of their task.

BOOKS

Although firsthand experiences, which stimulate interests and the need to communicate, aided and developed by the acquisition of basic skills, are the basis of primary education, a very important extension of the child's own environment is through books. A child may find a fossil that can be identified and described, drawn and written about—an activity that might well be perfectly satisfying for a child at one stage of development. However, the fossil's exciting story and significance can only be fully appreciated by knowledge of its origin, for which the child needs to turn to books. Therefore books—*not in sets but individual books*—on every kind of subject and aspect of the world around us, past and present, and at every reading level, must be at hand for immediate reference.

But another world of books is of the greatest importance, namely that of literature—the world of story and poetry. Here is another environment in which the child can live in imagination, a world in which personal problems can be resolved and understood, a world of rich experiences of the past, present and, indeed, of the fictional future, a world of gods, goddesses, heroes and heroines, explorers, discoverers, adventurers, great people, ordinary folk, children, animals, and toys. Through literature the children meet good and evil, justice and injustice, kindness and cruelty, love and hate. An appreciation of these values throws a grave responsibility on the teachers in their choice of books and the balance of virtues and vices, the values of which the child will absorb.

This world of literature may be shared by teachers and children, for we all love somebody to read to us. A teacher can choose books written in language rich in sound and content beyond the capabilities of the fumbling reader and so enrich and extend the language of the listeners. One does not teach children to write poetry but rather one exposes them to experiences and language and love of words so that the only adequate expression of a given experience is through poetic writing. At times, of course, children need to withdraw from the activities going on around them into a private world of books and read for themselves, so that a wide variety of stories at all levels of reading matter must be at hand for them to enjoy.

In selecting books, quality of content, language, illustration, and production is of great importance and should not be entirely sacrificed to quantity; there should be some books that the children get sheer pleasure in handling, whether they can read them or not. I have seen children stroke the photograph of an animal as though it were real. Finding sufficient books used to be our problem, but today thousands of children's books are produced each year; the process of selection therefore, has become more and more important. Publishers are anxious to provide what teachers want, but so often the joy of discovery is taken away from the child. We teachers cannot take for granted that all children's books published are right for our children. Books, supplemented nowadays by slides and tapes, cannot take the place of experience but add to and enrich the child's own personality.

ANIMALS

Opinions vary about the keeping of animals in school, but I personally believe that children need to come into contact with living things. How else can they become aware of the wonder of creation, of the cycle of life, of birth, and of death? This contact has an important effect on attitudes toward life, to creatures and people. Many emotional problems are solved through handling animals, particularly for the children who desperately need to love and be loved. If animals are kept, they must be cared for, properly housed, cleaned, and fed, which is a discipline in itself. Animals can also be the source of very interesting work at all stages of development. I have seen the attitudes of boys change towards creatures. I recall one boy saying, "Dragon flies! I kills 'em." Later, when guinea pigs were introduced into the school, he became closely involved with their care and his attitude changed. I recall Fred, a boy who was a bully and twisted smaller children's arms; he was, in fact, E.S.N. (educationally subnormal), and obviously felt inadequate. Goats were introduced to the school community. Fred, whose one achievement was that he could knock nails into wood better than anyone else, constructed the goat house and manger. He took an interest in the goats, both on school days and at weekends and holidays, under some supervision. As a result, Fred found his place, and his bullying stopped. Problems are attached to the keeping of animals, but none are insoluble; and the effect on attitude towards living things is worth trouble, time, and patience.

PLANTS

The care of living plants, indoors and outdoors, the close observation and sustained study of what the children see happening before their very eyes will inculcate the scientific attitude, which is desperately important—an accumulation of predigested scientific facts do not help a child to come to terms with his environment, nor with his life. Life is to be lived, not taught.

Developments in other aspects of education, in movement, physical education, and drama are based on the same principles: the uniqueness of each child and the need for each child to discover himself and come to terms with the world around him. We teachers are more concerned with a balance of experiences—literary, scientific, creative, aesthetic, practical, and spiritual—than with subjects, and more with the wholeness and harmony of growth—physical, intellectual, social, and emotional—than with instruction and academic learning.

TEACHERS (HUMAN RESOURCES)

When children *have* been freed from the limits of achievement that teachers in a formal situation imposed, their accomplishments at times have been amazing and surprising. Hidden talents, potentials, and powers have been revealed, not only in learning situations, but in the way they conduct their affairs. They are able to assess situations and react with spontaneous good sense and with proper pride and dignity. If teachers are to help children to grow up in this way, they must be acutely aware of what is in their environment and indeed within themselves and discover the creative element in all learning. So many teachers were taught and trained in a purely academic way. Now they must try to welcome the new philosophy: that is, only by sharing creative experiences, in painting, drawing, poetry, in making music, in movement, or dance can they themselves find fulfillment and confidence and so become sensitized enough to be able to recognize the hidden graces and latent talents of their children.

2. How Children Take Responsibility for Their Learning

MARIE MUIR

MARIE MUIR received her Diploma in Social Studies at the University of London and was tutor to the course for Mature Students at Coventry College of Education. She has had fifteen years' experience in studying, visiting, and working in independent progressive schools. She has lectured on Social Sciences seven years in a teachers' training college and twelve years in the Education Department of Coventry College of Education.

"What matters is not what we learn but how we learn it." This statement is familiar to those who discuss and read about contemporary developments in educational theory and practice and it seems relevant to the subject of responsibility for learning.

In the early days of English primary-school education, ends were (in official eyes at least) more important than means. Teachers were paid according to the results they obtained, not according to their methods of teaching. Results were assessed in terms of how much children had learned at regular intervals in their schooling, in the areas of reading, writing, and arithmetic. *How* this learning had been acquired did not seem to be a pertinent matter for investigation. In this century, and particularly in the past twenty years, the means by which learning has taken place are held to be at least as important as its end products.

Like most challenging statements, the one quoted here needs careful scrutiny. What children learn is never unimportant; but if we take the view that the attitudes, beliefs, and values that are learned during the years in school count for more than the facts acquired and memorized, if we think that the ability and the desire to go on learning beyond those years are valuable criteria of the worth of the educative process, then how children learn is inextricably bound up with what they learn. Thus, helping them to take increasing responsibility for their learning becomes a major consideration throughout their years in school.

Just to say that it is a good thing to make children responsible for their learning does not take us far. We have to determine what responsibility for learning involves and define the areas in which such responsibility seems appropriate. Do we mean responsibility for what to learn, how to learn, when to learn—or all of these? And what is the teacher's responsibility? In this chapter I shall describe under each of these headings the interpretation that a growing number of British primary schools are putting upon the concept of responsibility for learning.

Responsibility for What To Learn

Responsibility for what children learn in school (or perhaps it would be better to say "responsibility for what *can* be learned," because we are all aware that it is one thing to provide opportunities for learning certain things and another to ensure that these things are learned) has traditionally been shared by administrative bodies and teachers, in varying proportions. English teachers are fortunate in having a large share in this responsibility. The idea that children should be more than sleeping partners in the decisions that have to be made about the content of their learning is not new to educationists: it is implicit in doctrines of education through play, through interest, through experience —in any theory that postulates that children themselves are good judges of what they need to learn. Our nursery schools were the first part of the English educational system to put this principle into practice. Now, a growing number of infant schools for children aged five to seven years are paying increasing attention to this idea, and in recent years it has penetrated into our junior schools, for children of seven to eleven.

Responsibility for deciding what to learn takes different forms at different stages of the primary-school years. One condition is essential at all stages: there must be opportunities for choice in what can be learned, because none of us can exercise responsibility without choice. In English infant schools, opportunities for choice between different kinds of learning began in a small way. I remember my mother once telling me that the highlight of my own infant-school days (now fifty years behind me) was the occasion when I rushed home to tell her that a great treat was in store: on the following Friday afternoon we were to be allowed to choose between drawing with colored crayons and cutting out fancy doilies from newspapers. (She told me, too, how the agony of exercising this unaccustomed choice kept me awake half the night.)

From the 1930's on, some of our infant schools were including in their day a "basic skills" period that allowed children a certain amount of choice between reading, writing, and arithmetic. The same schools—and sometimes others—also introduced the "activity" period, in which the choice of what to do was defined not by the teacher but by the materials and equipment available in each classroom. The same years saw the introduction into a few junior schools of "centers of interest" or "projects" combining work in several subjects and pursued over a period of weeks or months, for part of every day or every week. Responsibility for what to learn, in this kind of work, was usually shared by teachers and children: sometimes the choice was made by teachers, based on their knowledge of the interests and background of a particular class of children; sometimes content and organization were formulated by joint discussion between teachers and children, with children making the final decisions. This approach involved collective rather than individual responsibility.

Today, an increasing number of infant and junior schools are working along lines that encourage and develop individual responsibility for what is learned. Areas of choice have been widened in two ways: by the provision of a larger variety of stimulating materials that call for children's own decisions about how to use them and what to do with them, and by an increase in the proportion of time spent in school during which such choice may be exercised. New buildings planned to meet the new kind of organization contribute to this freedom, as well. A primary-school building that makes it possible for children and teachers to move from one activity to another or from one classroom to another with a minimum of trouble enables us to provide greater variety of activities. Thus, we can make more effective use of equipment and teachers' individual interests and contributions than in an older building, in which it is less easy to deviate from the "one class, one teacher, one classroom" idea. But, in old buildings as well as new, primary-school children now find opportunities for pursuing in their own way and at their own pace kinds of learning that traditionally have depended on teaching by adults rather than exploration by children; tables, corners, or alcoves are stocked with materials that invite handling, looking, listening, using, experimenting, and questioning.

Now, to choose what you do in school does not inevitably mean, of course, taking responsibility for what you learn. Before you can be responsible for something, you have to become aware of its nature and understand it. Children take time to become aware of "learning" as a conscious pursuit. In the earliest primary-school years, the kinds of learning that teachers wish to encourage often happen incidentally, in the course of pursuing other ends. For instance, the problems that face two six-year-olds using building blocks of various sizes to make a model garage can help them toward an understanding of the concept of area; attitudes of cooperation can begin to grow from the desire to accomplish something beyond the capacities of one seven-year-old on his own. But the extent to which these concepts and attitudes develop and are understood well enough to be applied to other situations depends on their teacher's ability to provide materials, suggest problems, and ask questions that encourage such development and understanding. It is difficult to say, therefore, that choosing what they do always results in children's taking responsibility for their learning. Sometimes they know not what they have learned until adults help them to relate particular instances to general principles. When, however, they begin to perceive what they need to know in order to solve new problems, to understand that trial-and-error is not the only nor the most effective way, and to appreciate that certain techniques and skills can make them increasingly independent of adult help, then responsibility for what they learn can become feasible.

A growing number of our primary schools now consider the fostering of this responsibility as one of their most important functions. This has meant a new approach to curriculum planning, to methods of teaching, and to resources for learning.

Children can exercise responsibility for deciding what to learn only if they are consulted in advance about the content of their learning—and only if the purpose of the proposed learning is explained to them. In schools that try to encourage this responsibility, we find frequent consultation between teachers and children about plans for future work. With the under-eights these consultations usually take place informally as teachers move around listening to and observing problems about current work and suggesting possible solutions and new developments to individual children or small groups.

As a result of these observations and discussions, from time to time, a teacher selects common difficulties or deficiencies and arranges a "helping time" for dealing with them or for sharing suggestions about further possibilities of extending work in hand. Helping times may be used to explain techniques of handling materials, suggest ways of finding out information, give information that is not available to children from other sources, or improve achievement in reading, writing, or mathematical skills. One helping time may be given to demonstrating different ways of making booklets, another to explaining the way in which reference books are classified in the class library, a third to giving the historical origins of a local event or visit, a fourth to demonstrating the way to use a simple dictionary to help with the spelling of unusual words.

Children are left to make their own decisions about whether to learn or not to learn what is offered in helping sessions. Those who choose to disregard these sessions are free to do so. It is thought that learning of this kind will not be effective unless or until children perceive its usefulness for themselves.

With junior classes (aged eight to eleven) joint consultation and decision making take on a more formal aspect. Discussion centers around work for the next week, the next month or, sometimes, the next term. Children's suggestions for the content of future work are listened to, their views treated with respect; teachers encourage further suggestions by questioning, comment on the feasibility of proposals, point out considerations that children have failed to see or could not be expected to see for themselves, and make suggestions of their own. At times they will indicate that the proposed unit of work is too wide in scope to be tackled adequately in the time available: a proposal from nine-year-olds to study "All the inventions in the world" was narrowed down, during the course of discussion with their teacher, to the study of "The ten most important inventions in the world." (Choosing the ten proved to be a task that involved a high degree of responsibility!) Another time a teacher's contribution may help children to understand that the information available about a particular subject is insufficient to justify spending several weeks' work on it. "What it is like on other planets" comes into this category, although in the very near future this may no longer be true. Another teacher function is to help children to assess the comparative value of topics they have suggested. Recently, I listened to a group of ten-year-olds discussing the relative merits of "canals" and "famous battles" as topics for study and thought that the arguments put forth would have delighted the heart of a professional philosopher. Adult expectations about the content of learning and the requirements of the next stage in the education system are also factors that can be discussed and evaluated. The following comments recorded during a planning session with nine-year-olds illustrate that children who are treated as active partners in the business of learning rather than as passive recipients of its products are capable of appreciating and accepting that immediate interest is not the only consideration in deciding what to learn:

DANIEL: I think we should learn to do long division next.

GERALD: What's that?

DANIEL: Well, I don't really know but they're always asking me at home if I have learned it yet. My brother can do it, so I expect I could if I tried.

AUDREY: How long would it take us to learn it, Miss X?

MISS X: I should think most of you would manage it in about two weeks, if you worked at it for a little while every day.

JOHN: Supposing we worked at it *all* day? Would we learn it in about two days then?

MISS X: I think you might get rather tired of it if you did it *all* day. Wouldn't it be better to do a bit each day?

GERALD: Oh no, if we really made up our minds we could do it all the time and learn it quickly.

CHRISTINE: What use is it—what do you do with it when you know it?

GERALD: I don't know, but I expect Miss X knows.

JOHN: Well, things you learn aren't always useful just when you learn
them. Sometimes you have to wait and find out when they're useful.

ROBERT: Perhaps it's useful for when you do exams for 11+.[1]

CHRISTINE: Is it, Miss X?

GERALD: I think we should find out all the things we should know
for 11+, and make sure we know them, even if they are not very
interesting. Then we shall see how much time we have got for
interesting things.

Parents and teachers sometimes fear that children who are given a
good deal of freedom about what they learn and how they learn it will
neglect the fundamental skills of reading, writing, and mathematics.
Sometimes schools that encourage initiative and choice in learning
make a certain amount of work in these three areas compulsory, or try
to use other activities to give meaning and interest to these three. But,
in those primary schools where reading, writing, and mathematics are
not unduly emphasized to the detriment of other kinds of learning
this compulsion becomes unnecessary. Primary-school teachers no
longer think that basic skills have to be learned first and then used to
acquire knowledge or develop understanding. They find that children
learn these skills more easily and effectively in the context of investigating aspects of their physical environment, recording those investigations, communicating their ideas and experiences to others, trying to
find answers to the problems that they encounter from time to time.
When children spend their school lives in an environment that offers
intellectual, aesthetic, and physical stimuli and challenges, we find
that some of them learn to read and to write and begin to comprehend
mathematical relationships. Moreover, this learning happens in a way
that requires little direct instruction from their teachers, and in what
seems a minimum of time compared with that needed by children in
schools where the three R's figure prominently in timetable and curriculum. Other children take longer and need more direction and individual help from their teachers. But when these children can see for
themselves from the outset the context in which these skills are useful
and illuminating, and when they are given the opportunity to experience the joy of successful learning in other directions before they begin

---

[1] The common phrase for the competitive entry to grammar schools at the age
of eleven.

on the mysteries, both literal and numerical, they settle down happily to the regular, consistent work necessary to become proficient readers, writers, and calculators. Extending the choice of what to learn does not detract attention and interest in what were once regarded as essential preliminaries to other kinds of learning; rather, it seems to enhance this attention and interest and to lessen anxiety about possible failures in areas of learning, which when compulsory tend to be accompanied in children's minds by fear of losing adult affection or approval.

The value of children's exercising some choice about what they learn depends largely on the possibilities of worthwhile learning open to them. In the past, the only choice often was either to learn what teachers decided to teach or to be thrown entirely upon your own resources in school. But primary-school teachers no longer look upon themselves as the sole or even the chief mediators of knowledge. For one thing, they now recognize that the kinds and extent of learning of which primary-school children have proved themselves capable are too many and too varied for any one adult to deal with adequately. For another, they and the children now have new media of teaching and learning at their disposal: books that children can use themselves, equipment for programed learning, tape recorders, TV and radio sets, all of which contribute to an increasing diversity of worth-while learning opportunities. The teacher's own personal resources of learning no longer define the area within which children can exercise choice: children can have direct access to reference information: books, catalogues of programed learning units, details of forthcoming television and radio programs, lists of films and filmstrips. Study and discussion of all these sources provide new possibilities for learning as well as aids to pursuing subjects already chosen.

Deficiencies (real or imagined) in existing sources of learning sometimes provide an objective for a new unit of work. Recently, I observed a class where a group of ten-year-olds was organizing a "travel agency." This project involved, among other activities, compiling a series of travelers' guides for display and consultation. The children had visited the local public library to arm themselves with books useful for this purpose. Things went well until they found that there were no suitable books about one country on their agency's list. The first suggestion to meet this difficulty was that this country had better be omitted from the holiday attractions offered. Then one boy who had shown little inclination to contribute until that moment said firmly, "No, you can't leave it out just because there isn't a guide. That's the country we should write a guide to ourselves, if nobody can find out much about it." Accordingly, a new school-made guide was eventually presented with pride to the local library. Its compilation engaged eight children for about two hours a day, over a period of six weeks; it involved reference to adult books and publications, inquiries to an Embassy, finding and talking with people who had visited the country in question, and long discussion (amounting to heated argument at times) about what should be included in the guide. It is doubtful whether a teacher-initiated, teacher-directed study on the same subject, spread over an equivalent period of time, would have produced the quantity and quality of intellectual effort demonstrated here: the comparison of information from different sources, careful scrutiny of material collected, and almost passionate concern about the accuracy of the contents of the handbook, which was finally produced. It would have been equally difficult for any other course of study on the same subject to have resulted in the real thrill of achievement made manifest when the new guide was donated to the children's department of the local library and accepted to make good a deficiency in its own supply of books about other countries.

This example illustrates another aspect of responsibility involved in "choosing what to learn." Primary-school children are pragmatic creatures: they like to see a practical purpose for at least some of their learning. This pragmatism can take several forms, but one of the greatest inducements towards taking a responsible attitude toward your own learning is to be in a position of being responsible for what somebody else learns from you. Organizing an exhibition, giving a series of talks, making a book to be read and used by others—any of these results in concern about finding and giving accurate information, deciding what is essential and must be included, what is peripheral and may be omitted, investigating the reliability of sources and verifying facts, perceiving questions that cannot be answered as well as answering those that can. There can be no more intellectually valuable pursuits than these, and they seem to be more in evidence in this combination of learner-teacher role than in most other school situations.

Responsibility for How To Learn

How children or adults learn is still something of a mystery, in spite of the years of experimental work. No one theory of learning seems to embrace all varieties of human activities that go on in the name of learning. To say that children themselves should take some responsibility for how they learn, therefore, seems rather a tall order. How to learn is not a conscious problem for children until they understand that not all the things they want to learn (or we want them to learn) can be acquired solely by exploration, by trial-and-error. When these methods which served well enough for most of their purposes in the preschool years fail in the face of new kinds of learning, children are bewildered and assume that some sort of magic accounts for the success others have achieved in these directions; they have only to find the right formula to break the spell, they think, and the secret will be theirs. "My daddy sits like this with his legs crossed, and he holds a book in front of him, then he can read it," a six-year-old told his teacher. "Well, I sit with my legs crossed, and I've held the book up like this for a long time but nothing happens. What must I say to the book to make it work?"

It takes quite a long time for most primary-school children to understand that there is no magic, that some kinds of learning do not suddenly reveal themselves to the initiated, that effort and practice are required from them and sometimes help from teachers. Only as they begin to realize this does how to learn become a meaningful problem.

Those of us who teach are tempted to think that it is our responsibility to solve this problem, as far as we can. So we study appropriate ways of presenting mathematics, natural science, or music to children at varying stages of development and with varying abilities, and when what we are trying to teach appears to have been learned, we feel that we have chosen successful methods. But our anxiety to teach well sometimes leads us to forget that learning is not a commodity to be handed over to the consumer already processed, packaged, and labeled but an activity, the nature of which can be communicated only by the initiated looking at the problems together with the uninitiated, investigating difficulties and discussing possible solutions rather than demonstrating and instructing.

This principle is well established at the highest levels of English academic education. Its relevance to the primary-school level is now beginning to be recognized. The following summaries of two class discussions (one in a class of ten-year-olds, the other with eight-year-olds) illustrate how some primary-school teachers now are attempting to help children toward an active responsibility for how they learn as well as for what they learn.

The previous week, after suggesting and considering with the teacher several possibilities for the next unit of work, the first class had decided to make a study of rivers. All those wishing to join in were asked to prepare suggestions about what this piece of work might include, how the study was to be made, and presented for discussion in this period.

After everybody had made their suggestions, a provisional list of those aspects of the topic it was thought useful or interesting to study was agreed upon. This was the list:

> How rivers begin and end
> Ways of traveling on rivers
> The most important rivers in the world
> Famous explorations of rivers
> River animals
> People who work on rivers
> Bridges.

The teacher, Mr. H., then asked for ideas as to how they should set about this study. Not unexpectedly, the first proposal was that they should hire a boat big enough to take them all on a trip from the source to the mouth of the nearest river. The teacher pointed out that the practical possibility of this trip would depend on how long it would take, how much it would cost, and whether a suitable boat was available. Offers were made to investigate such matters as the length of the river in question, how much of it was navigable by a large vessel, and how many miles per hour it was possible to travel on a river; and they were accepted.

Mr. H. then asked if it would be better to make this trip, or as much of it as proved to be possible, right at the beginning of the study, in the middle of it, or toward the end. The subsequent discussion on the merits of observation before information versus information before observation would have done credit to some more professional investigators. Initially, majority opinion was in favour of starting off with the trip—"to see what we find"—but this was swayed by the comment, "We might miss some of the best things, if we didn't know they were there." But how would you find out, then, what not to miss? Well, you could ask people who knew. Did anybody know anybody who had journeyed all the way up and down the river? Nobody did. Then could we find people who knew parts of it well? How? Put an advertisement in the local paper, ask the police, and send a letter to all the parents associated with the school were among the suggestions offered here.

Other sources of information were then discussed. Somebody knew there was a Canal Museum; was there also a River Museum to write to or visit? Could we write to the BBC and ask if there were any television or radio program about rivers scheduled for the near future? Where could we find out about films or filmstrips? What kind of books should we look for in the school library and the local public library?

Everyone agreed that the subject of the tangible results of this piece of work—the production of books, friezes, models, the possibility of holding a River Exhibition—could be left to the next meeting. The question of how work was to be organized seemed to be more urgent. Should everybody set out to find out all they could about the topics chosen, or should there be division of labor among groups? Would it be best to have the same number in each group? Supposing nearly every class member wanted to join the same group? How would each group let the rest of the class know what it was doing? Should everybody produce his or her individual book about rivers, or should we aim at two or three books containing contributions from those who wanted to offer them?

Finally, Mr. H. said he would like to know what his function in all this was to be. It was made clear that he would be expected to suggest sources of information, help with difficulties, answer questions, and settle arguments.

The second example of the class-discussion approach involved eight-year-olds who had reached the stage of realizing that the speed of their numerical calculation was being slowed down by their having to work out some parts of the multiplication tables or look them up on a chart. Their teacher, Miss T., had suggested that it would be worthwhile to give some time to memorizing these tables, that there were different ways of doing this, and that it would be useful to exchange ideas and then let everybody make his or her plan of work for accomplishing this task.

Miss T. then asked the children to suggest the kind of problems they needed to think about in their planning, and from their suggestions and her questioning the following points were listed:

How to identify those answers that you couldn't remember, or
frequently got wrong

Ways of helping yourself to memorize these answers

How often it would be useful to practice them—and for how
long at a time

How to test your own progress.

Each of these headings was discussed in turn. The first brought
suggestions from the children for making their own individual lists of
items they failed to recall or made mistakes about in the course of their
work. One or two saw that there could be deficiencies in this system
and put forward the idea of making a test by which all items could
be checked. Miss T. said there were ready-made tests of this kind
which she would make available. (But it was interesting later to find
that most of the children preferred to make their own.)

Suggestions for practice methods fell into two categories: those that
one child could use on his own, and others to be used by children
joined together in pairs or small groups. These children had been accustomed to a good deal of choice about how they worked and with
whom they worked, so from the beginning they assumed that everybody would tackle this particular learning problem on his own or with
others, as he pleased.

The issue of how many items it was useful to try to memorize at
a time was introduced here. Arguments for concentrating on one or two
items or for spreading their attention over a dozen were put forward
and considered in a way that would not have disgraced experimental
psychologists who have interested themselves in problems of memorization. Plans for making simple games (mostly variations on the basic
patterns of Bingo, Snakes and Ladders, and Snap) were discussed, and
it was agreed that everybody should contribute toward a "lending
library" of games useful for this purpose.

There was much difference of opinion about problems that we
adults would have labeled *frequency and distribution of practice.*
Some children advocated the policy of "the longer you spend on it,
the sooner you will learn it." Others thought it likely you would get
bored easily and waste time if you tried to do too much at once. At
this point, the teacher indicated that for this kind of work adult experience on the whole supports the policy of "little but often" and sug-

gested that a few minutes at odd intervals in each day might prove more profitable than half an hour at a stretch.

Ingenious suggestions for progress tests and methods of recording achievement were forthcoming, and several children undertook to incorporate these in a loose-leaf book, and they stated magnanimously, "Everybody could borrow it, even if they haven't suggested anything for it." Perhaps the fact that none assumed the teacher would test progress was the most telling evidence that they themselves had accepted responsibility for this particular learning task.

There were times in the following two weeks when certainly this classroom could have been called a *learning laboratory*. Each child conducted individual experiments in memorizing multiplication tables, compared results, offered advice to others, checked his own progress, and dealt with his own difficulties. To an onlooker, it was clear that something of the involvement, interest, and satisfaction of achievement which we regard as characteristic of learning at its best had gone into what is for some children in other circumstances a boring mental chore.

Responsibility for When To Learn

School timetables planned on traditional lines assume two things: that there is a time for work and a time for play; and that these times should be the same for all children in the same class. Teachers in the primary schools described in this book will quarrel with these assumptions on two grounds: first, that since one man's work is another man's play, the distinction between the two is not always easy to make; and second, that since we respect individual differences in the capacity for learning and the rate of learning, we should also respect differences in the rhythm of learning. To these teachers the principle of dividing up the school day into clear-cut work and play periods and assigning "basic" learning (mostly reading, writing, and mathematics) to those times when it is assumed all children's energies are at their best disregards these different rhythms. Not all children are at their best in the early part of the morning, nor at their lowest level in the last part of the afternoon. Nor do these primary-school teachers consider it to be true that young children can be expected to concentrate on one activity only for a very limited period of time. At almost any time any day, visitors to their schools can see children in the same class pursuing different activities, which some adults would label work, others play.

In this situation, *when* to learn (which is meaningful to children only to the extent to which they themselves differentiate between work and play) becomes largely the responsibility of individual children. In some schools, teachers set daily or weekly assignments of work to be carried out in the children's own choice of time and at their own pace. These assignments usually offer some choice of work and allow some discretion to be exercised about the amount of work to be done. On average, they are intended to take an hour to an hour and a half to complete, leaving the greater part of the day for self-chosen activities (although we often find children voluntarily exceeding the amount of work set). Sometimes visitors observe children continuing assignment work in periods when other apparently more attractive occupations are available, and it is difficult to convince them that this really is the youngsters' choice. Perhaps I did not manage to convince one visitor who found a nine-year-old in one of my classes concentrating on long division at the end of a hot July afternoon, when he could have been playing outdoors—even though I informed him that this *was* his choice and not my punishment. But in schools where the three R's are not emphasized to the detriment of other types of learning, children bring to them the same interest and concentration that they bring to other activities.

Other primary schools find daily or weekly assignments of work unnecessary, on the basis of the experience of some teachers. Given an environment that stimulates learning in educative directions and an atmosphere that fosters confidence and initiative, most children achieve and some exceed the standards of literacy and numeracy that are considered satisfactory in the later years of the primary-school stage. In the earlier years, some of them may seem to lag behind children whose teachers regard it as their own responsibility to ensure that their children acquire the basic skills of reading, writing, and numbers as quickly as possible. In the new kind of primary school this discrepancy occurs because decisions about when to begin learning certain subjects or skills is a matter for joint consultation. For instance, "reading readiness" is determined by children rather than by teachers; beginning to read may come later when a child decides when to begin rather than when his teacher makes the decision. But once children make it—because they have felt the desire or recognized a need to learn to read—then they have made that first step toward their accepting responsibility for planning their own learning in this direction and working at it consistently. We sometimes see children (once they have started reading when *they* felt ready for it) spending almost all their time in school on this activity for two or three weeks—and accomplishing in this time as much as children who have been regularly "learning to read" over a period of months, or even years.

Some may object that we primary-school educators are not helping children to acquire the regular disciplined habits of concentration necessary in adult working life by our yielding to and even encouraging individual idiosyncracies of effort and idleness in the early years. To this objection I would reply that children learn to concentrate by having the opportunity to concentrate for as long and with as much absorption as they are capable of on activities they have chosen or agreed to undertake. When they themselves have some part in deciding when they learn, as well as what and how they will learn, opportunities for concentration are at their best.

Sometimes, children in schools that allow and encourage their responsibility for learning can be seen apparently doing nothing at all. To critics, this is an outward and visible sign that to ask children to organize their own time is wrong; they will waste it. We should be sure before we endorse this view, that time *is* being wasted. The classic answer of the child accused of doing nothing—"I'm not doing nothing, I'm thinking"—may have something in it. Even if no productive thinking is going on, who are we to criticize? How many adults could claim that they never waste a few minutes or half an hour in the course of their working day? Indeed, our more creative thinkers are well aware of the necessity and value of their apparently fallow periods. Yet if we see children in school not gainfully occupied, we tend to think there is something wrong with them or with the educational policy that permits this to happen. We expect schools to be places where children are always going forward, but there is a case for regarding them as places where children can sometimes go backward: in our kind of society the degree of physical and emotional control we demand of children at an early age is such that sometimes in self-defense they *need* to go backward for a little while, in order to recover their balance. If we grant them the wisdom of deciding for themselves when to learn, we should also grant them the wisdom of deciding when *not* to learn.

They are sometimes better judges than we are of their need to stop
and catch up with themselves.

The Responsibility of the Teacher

Helping children to accept and exercise responsibility for their learning
does not mean that teachers abdicate *their* responsibilities. Like adults,
children can be responsible only for what is within their capacity and
control, and teachers must retain responsibility for determining the
areas within which children's decisions are desirable and effective.
Unless the adults with whom they learn set limits to these areas, children of primary-school age are likely to feel insecure. In order to experiment confidently and usefully with making their own decisions about
what to learn, how to learn, and when to learn they need to know that
in the background are adults who are willing to help but ready to point
out considerations children may not be aware of themselves. Adults
can help by preventing mistakes that might have serious consequences
and if necessary should be prepared to uphold the needs of a minority
against the wishes of the majority.

Sometimes, too, teachers make it clear that those who teach (as
well as those who learn) need to establish certain conditions, if their
work is to be productive. For instance, they will stipulate that if children choose to join a group for the purpose of learning a foreign language, they must work regularly with the group, because spasmodic
attendance would make the teacher's task difficult and impede the
progress of the whole group. They will insist, if necessary, that the
principle of deciding for yourself *when* you want to learn has to be
modified, if your activities interfere with other children's freedom of
decision about when to learn, or if the cooperation of a number of
children at the same time is essential to the work in hand. Playing
orthodox or unorthodox musical instruments comes into the first category, dramatic work into the second.

It is in relation to *what* children learn that the responsibility of their
teachers needs clear definition. If all kinds of learning were of equal
value, no problem would arise: teachers could restrict their function
to suggestion, approval, encouragement, and help with children's own
proposals about the content of their learning. But the chief justification
for providing special people, places, and times for the pursuit of edu-

cation lies in the belief that some kinds of learning are more worth-while than others. Many of us maintain that the most important function of education is to help human beings to discriminate between the worthwhile and the worthless, and although we do not wish to underestimate the importance of *how* we learn, we could not happily agree that *what* we learn does not matter.

Therefore, a teacher's responsibility lies in trying to ensure that the choice of what to learn is offered to children in the context of that which is likely to be of enduring rather than ephemeral value: learning that will add to new understanding of vital issues of human living on all levels, learning that will foster an appreciation of those intellectual and aesthetic disciplines that interpret and transmit the raw material of experience into arts and sciences. This task is not easy, because it involves sensitivity toward growing human beings plus an awareness of the nature of these disciplines. Mediating between these two calls for a constant consideration of priorities.

Teachers who work in the primary schools described in this book are aware of the difficulties of this responsibility but do not shirk it nor seek to throw off the burden it entails by adhering to the view that "children should learn only what interests them." Instead, such teachers share with their children the considerations that sometimes lead them to reject children's proposals for the content of learning.

Because they themselves have had experience with the difficulties as well as the satisfaction that responsibility brings with it, children are more ready to recognize the validity of the responsibility than are children from whom responsibility has been withheld on the grounds that they are not yet ready for it. Children are more ready to go along with adult authority when they have been given opportunities for testing adult suggestions and advice.

3. | Vertical Grouping

MARY A. MYCOCK

MARY A. MYCOCK, M.Ed., received her Trainer's Diploma from the National Froebel Foundation and is Deputy Principal of the Manchester College of Education. Previously, she was a teacher and a head teacher in primary schools before becoming Principal Lecturer in Education at Hereford College of Education. She is Examiner in Primary Education for several University Institutes of Education, and she lectures extensively at teachers' conferences and courses throughout the British Isles. She has specialized in research on vertical grouping in the English Infant School.

Compulsory primary education in England covers two administrative stages:

1. The infant stage (4+ to 7+ years)
2. The junior stage (7+ to 11+ years).

These stages are provided for either in separate infant and junior schools or in combined schools that provide schooling for the whole age-range (4+ to 11+ years). Teachers in England have a high degree of freedom in organizing their schools, deciding on methods, and setting their own standards, therefore primary schools vary from the narrowly instructional through to the flexible, individualized situation. The infant school, however, is a uniquely English institution which has earned a reputation for lively pioneering work in educational practice. Junior schools (now largely freed from the strangulation of early selective examination) are fast developing a comparable reputation.

Traditionally, the large English primary schools have normally classified their pupils according to chronological age, the children progressing through several classes and moving from teacher to teacher according to age (and sometimes ability). However, in small schools mainly in thinly populated rural areas, mixed age-grouping with children of several ages in one class has been unavoidably customary, because of the small numbers of children in each age-group.

In recent years, in England there has been considerable interest in the relationship between school classification and the development of children. There is a growing belief that the system of school classification can be a significant influence on the whole development of each child; and this conviction has resulted in some large urban primary schools voluntarily adopting a system of vertical or "family" grouping— claiming that this classification is superior in many respects to the traditional grouping.

Vertical grouping is a method of organization in which individuals of different ages are placed together in the same class as a deliberate educational policy. At present, vertical grouping is more frequently to be found in infant schools. In these schools all classes are parallel with *each class* containing an equal proportion of children of all ages from four-and-a-half to seven-and-a-half years, the children remaining *throughout* their infant school stage *in the care of one teacher.* Each child's progress in such an organization is an individual one occurring within a stable and continuing community and guided by one teacher. In the junior schools where educationists have begun to question the whole notion of homogeneous grouping whether by age or ability, attention has been focused on problems of class organization with particular reference to streaming and nonstreaming. Nonstreaming like vertical grouping provides a new approach to the potentialities of children, a progressive trend directed toward the optimum development in many dimensions of each individual child, and many of the arguments in their favor are common to both fields of experimentation. Some junior schools have progressed from nonstreaming to vertical grouping, especially in the seven-to-nine age-range, and teachers speak enthusiastically of the opportunities that this grouping affords; but as yet, specific evidence from the junior stage is much less abundant than from the infant stage.

It is important to be clear about terminology. The full name for vertical grouping is *vertical all-age grouping* although the shorter name is more frequently used for the deliberate planning in which a child remains in the same class with the same teacher for a span of several years. Sometimes it is called *"family"* grouping because the escalated age-range is similar to that found on a smaller scale in the ordinary family and also because of the more intimate atmosphere that a vertical classification invariably generates. Sometimes, erroneously, it is thought that family grouping implies that all members of one family are in the same class, but this is not necessarily so. The needs of the individual child determine his placement in a specific class. Parental choice is another factor—parents sometimes want their children together in a class. Transfer from one class to another is easy if there is genuine incompatibility between siblings.

Wherever vertical grouping exists it implies a flexible school in which the organization has been so adapted as to facilitate and foster maximal learning in the widest sense—social, emotional, and intellectual. A vertically grouped class is not an amalgam of three distinct age-groups, e.g. the fives, the sixes, and the sevens, each with its separate and well-defined plans. It does, of course, contain roughly equal proportions of each age, and there is certainly some group work in the vertical organization, as well as individual and class work; but such groups as there are form and re-form on the basis of individual interests and needs, not on the basis of age. Groups are formed in relation to essential teaching points.

In the oldest educational institution undoubtedly pupils of various ages were gathered together under the guidance and direction of one teacher. Treatises on educational history contain many references to children of several ages being taught together, e.g. in the Dame schools of the eighteenth century, in the monitorial schools of Bell and Lancaster, and in Robert Owen's infant schools. The village school was one of the earliest educational institutions, and throughout its history it has made use of a mixed-age classification. But in all these schools, vertical grouping was the result of administrative convenience rather than because of the application of any educational principle.

The educational reformers Pestalozzi and Froebel both related organized learning in school to the family situation and recognized the value of the mixed-age group. Dewey emphasized the importance of the democratic social community where school groupings were not necessarily contingent upon age or ability. These educational reformers used vertical grouping as an integral part of their philosophies rather than as an administrative expedient, and their ideal has been revived and reapplied in the modern application of vertical grouping in English urban schools. Susan Isaacs' work at the Malting House, Cambridge, has been another important influence. She set out to foster in every possible way the child's joy in discovery. She recognized the reality and seriousness of a child's thinking in his play and the effectiveness of an educational approach based on the exploration of an abundant environment which also contained interested informed adults. Miss Isaacs demonstrated the utilization of play situations as a basis for more formal work, an approach which is an integral part of vertical grouping.

What has caused teachers to change their organization? Why have many teachers begun to question whether the traditional class based on chronological age fosters true learning? The Plowden Report on Children and their Primary Schools (1966) emphasizes that "the willingness of teachers to experiment, to innovate and to change has been one of the mainsprings of progress in the Primary schools" (para. 1151). The views of one such teacher are given:

The more I worked with classes of children grouped in the traditional horizontal way, the more difficult I found it to provide the individual attention that the children required. It seemed very unnatural to teach forty children of the same age together, all demanding the same kind of attention from me or from each other. I began to find this age-classification a hindrance and a frustration in meeting individual needs. When the opportunity arose for me to work in a vertically grouped school I found that this more flexible organization provided a more natural and relaxed atmosphere where the children of varied ages were able to learn from one another as well as from me, and where too they were able to work at their own pace and to their full capacity.

Another teacher writes:

My class contains twelve children in each of the three ages, five, six and seven, thirty-six children in all. The youngest have recently come to school, the eldest are now in their third year with me. I know them all as individuals. I teach them as such and seldom as a class although flexible small groups are organized frequently, and we all come together sometimes to share in music-making, literature, some special event or vital discussion. Yet group influence is strong. Ours is a stable, close-knit and unified little community with each individual making an important contribution to the motivations and standards within the group.

Whether the children are playing with toys and materials, mutually solving practical problems or working on self-chosen assignments and programs, I circulate among them, helping, guiding, watching, listening, teaching and acting as a "resource person" or a "source of reference!" Mine is a subtle task for I must plan and organize the environment in such a way that the children will explore its possibilities, utilize its opportunities and so learn more effectively. This makes heavy demands on my resourcefulness but it provides a climate in which many-sided and insightful learning is fostered.

Vertical grouping is not "the latest method" to be adopted hastily by the primary-school teacher anxious not to be out-of-date in her educational approach. It is not an educational method at all. It is the deliberate application of a type of school organization that some teachers find most conducive to the promotion of good living and good learning; its adoption springs from the conviction that it is right for the full growth of each individual child in a particular school. Some teachers find that they prefer to work with partial or transitional vertical grouping in which only two age groups are combined together in one class, whereas others feel that the full benefits of vertical grouping are only achieved when three or four age groups are contained within one class. One head teacher of a seven-class vertically grouped school comments:

As a staff it is difficult to define the point at which we began to contemplate the virtues of vertical grouping for our school. The necessity for it gradually took firm root in our minds and we became convinced that our existing free individual methods would be complemented and extended by a more flexible organization. We absorbed the idea through extensive discussion. The teachers were enthusiastic and over a period of two years we grew organizationally into this pattern combining the full age-range (4+ to 7+) in each of seven parallel classes. The time was ripe for change and we took a great deal of trouble to involve the parents in our thinking and planning. The benefits of the changeover are immeasurable and none of us has regretted it. We should find it difficult now to work in any other way.

Progressive work and personalized learning can be achieved by sensitive, thoughtful teachers in any form of school organization, but creative education with the fullest and most flexible use of physical and human resources seems to be found with greater frequency in the vertically grouped classroom. To quote another head teacher:

> *. . . organization in family groups seems to be the best way to ensure the full use of every opportunity provided by the school, the teacher and the children.*

Flexibility of organization cannot be separated from providing for the many-sided aspects of a child's development. It is a central factor in motivating children to learn, in the content of learning, and in integrating the curriculum. Over the last three or four decades there has been a gradual change in primary schools from formality to informality, as psychological knowledge of individual needs and differences increased. The more we learn about children the more we realize the immense range of behaviour at any age and the absence of any real *stages* except those of administrative convenience. This realization has bred doubts about the value of the rigid organizational patterns and narrowly fixed age-groups and instructional-groups that have so far been an integral part of schooling. It has forced us to look more closely at children, at their ways of learning and their schooling conditions. In the light of these observations fundamental changes in the whole concept of education are taking place. We recognize now that children grow and develop through interacting with their environment and that, therefore, the environment must be organized in such a way as to provide maximal conditions for learning and in this way to motivate children to become agents in their own learning. All teachers of young children recognize the tremendous influence of environmental experience, because they see it with great clarity when children enter school bringing with them the influence of their home backgrounds in their attitudes, prejudices, habits, ideas, and speech.

The utilization of studies from several disciplines (biology, psychology, sociology) have all revealed the impact of social phenomena upon human growth and learning, and recent research has concentrated on the differential effects of environmental influences in childhood. There is a growing body of evidence that environmental experience is of greater importance than had formerly been realized.

Research by many workers (e.g. Goldfarb, Baldwin, Bowlby, Douglas, Bernstein) suggests that the climate or atmosphere in which a child grows and learns can be a very important influence on that learning. Such research indicates that the school faces a far greater responsibility than was hitherto recognized in providing an environment propitious to the needs and potentials of each individual child, and experiments in more flexible school organization have their roots in this realization. In school, children learn not only skills and intellectual knowledge, but they also learn attitudes, feelings, habits, and ideas, both in relation to learning and to the people with whom and from whom they learn. Children must feel in harmony with their world and with the people contained within it, for the quality of learning depends heavily upon the relationships that are sustained both with the adults and the contemporaries who share it. Vertical grouping appears to provide the child with a greater sense of belonging, of support, and security as well as providing a wider range of relationships and social experience than can easily be found in the traditional grouping. Vertical grouping implies a climate in which there is opportunity both for guidance and for choice.

Educational Principles Behind Vertical Grouping

Let us look more closely at the educational principles that teachers are seeking to realize and implement more satisfactorily through vertical grouping.

THE NEED FOR CONTINUITY AND COHERENCE IN THE EDUCATIONAL LIFE OF THE CHILD

Teachers of young children have always recognized the importance of stability for good growth. One of the benefits of vertical grouping is that a child joins a settled and nurturing school group in which he remains for a prolonged period, and in which he is able to have a close continuous relationship with an informed, sympathetic adult. The classroom atmosphere is settled, the routines are well defined and maintained by children well habituated to their practice; in such a school situation bewilderment and uncertainty disappear. New entrants to school are fewer in number in any one class (for they are distributed throughout all the classes), and moreover they are quickly received into attentive groups of older children already well adjusted to school. Stability and coherence are further safeguarded by the elimination of "moving up" from class to class, from teacher to teacher. Discontinuity, stress, and disturbance are avoided in a vertically grouped situation where through prolonged association the teacher is able to ensure that a child's education both follows and harmonizes with his development as well as anticipates the course it will follow. Such conditions have a profound effect upon a child's capacity to learn.

A cooperative experience stimulated by baking equipment. The six-year-old girl in the center is reading the recipe while the other older and younger children have selected tasks and are participating at their own level.

THE NEED TO RESPECT THE CHILD AS AN
INDIVIDUAL IN HIS OWN RIGHT

Writing about schools for primary-school children, Van der Eyken declares that "our environment is all too often anti-child." When classes are organized in homogeneous groups which are taught according to specific plans initiated and carried through by competent teachers, then it becomes all too easy to frustrate or deaden a child's own thinking by forcing him to conform to an adult-dictated routine. Children's true learning and thinking can be suffocated by a benevolent captivity. A formal school routine is impossible in a vertically grouped situation for the wide age-range necessitates an individual approach. Children have characteristic ways of looking at their world and interpreting it to themselves. Teachers must have respect for the dignity of the individual and must provide for growth at an individual pace. Learning in young children often appears to the adult to be unsystematic, haphazard, and unstructured, although it is basically continuous, personal, and meaningful to the child. Piaget has supplied a new understanding of the ways in which children organize their experience at successive levels. He has shown that children need time to extend, differentiate, and correct their impressions; for they have their own ways of thinking, feeling, and doing. The school must provide an enabling atmosphere in which the teacher accepts each child in his own right, provides for individual motivation, tempo, and maturation, and thus facilitates maximal individual growth. Only by providing the widest range of human and material opportunity as well as the most flexible pattern of living-learning can this be achieved; many teachers find that a vertical classification provides this more adequately.

THE ACCEPTANCE OF THE CHILD AS THE
AGENT IN HIS OWN LEARNING

Children have a natural urge to explore and discover, and learning takes place most effectively when there is a permissive climate and where there is continuous interaction in a challenging environment. Here again, the work of Piaget is particularly helpful to teachers, because he has demonstrated that both reliable concept formation and language growth depend heavily on early experience and the ways in which children are given opportunities for repeating, systematizing, classifying, and coordinating such experience. Piaget's influence has been immensely beneficial to education, for he has shown how development can be inhibited by implanting ideas that are too fixed. If children learn facts and skills "in isolation," they often fail to grasp relationships and to develop insights into such processes as reversibility, comparison, and associativity.

Children need a school environment that promotes their own thinking, which involves them in the selection and/or rejection of ideas, in developing discrimination, and in forming value judgements. Ideally, the environment should always be in excess of a child's available mental structures and strategies so that he is constantly stimulated and required to reorganize his handling of situations. In order to learn to be good thinkers at their own level, children need to make choices, initiate inquiries, seek substitutions, and achieve trial-and-error solutions. The teacher must be able to encourage, guide, support, and extend children so that new avenues of thinking are constantly unfolded through personal effort and self-discovery. Real learning is based on insight, and we want children to propose hypotheses, to ask questions, initiate investigations, and test out ideas for themselves. This involvement in their own learning is a self-generating process. Activities are generated, they restimulate themselves, widen and are filled in and join up with larger wholes. Children follow and find more to follow; they watch and find more to watch; spiral progressions are set up that lead to new interests and new activities. Their learning emerges naturally through their play:

Janet was playing in the home corner on a snowy day, preparing a "meal" with three other children. She said, "I'll just go out for a pan of snow and boil it for some milk." She collected the snow and put the full pan on the radiator, then returned to lay the table. Later she went back to the radiator and found the pan partly filled with clear water. This was the beginning of a prolonged sequence of testing and experimenting with the qualities of snow, the effects of warmth, the degree of warmth needed to produce certain conditions, the effects of school heating on air and other substances. Janet was completely absorbed in a cumulative learning process, which lasted several days and which extended thought and language far beyond the point at which teacher-centered instruction would have carried her. This child was operational and not simply active. Other children were interested observers and commentators, and much real enquiry was generated.

PROVISION FOR THE FULLEST DEVELOPMENT OF A
BALANCED PERSONALITY

Children today live in a world of immense horizons, and school must be a place in which children are able to grow in many dimensions. School must concern itself not only with the wholeness of individual development but also with the fostering of attitudes, qualities, and abilities that will enable children to live happy well-adjusted lives in a complex and changing social environment where economic affluence and materialism confuse values. Children need tranquility and security, but they also need to learn to live dangerously—confronted by challenges, obstacles, uncertainties, and sometimes temporary failures. We cannot remove stress from children's lives, but we can strengthen their ability to cope by safeguarding the atmosphere in which they can produce their best effort. We can help them to gain satisfaction from their own efforts and from cooperating with others. The vertically grouped situation provides continuity, coherence, and stability; but its freedom also provides for more choices and for the development of more effective resources for coping with problems. Flexibility of organization of this kind allows for—even dictates—the growth of better attitudes, deeper understanding, and greater confidence. There are absence of strain, a wide range of available social roles and experiences, extensive opportunity for both leading and following, constant practice in the establishing and maintaining of good relationships. Such growth also acts as a greater stimulus to intellectual development, through introducing a wider range of interests. Throughout, the teacher has a vital function in servicing and maintaining and contributing to this dynamic school situation, as well as in safeguarding against persistent failure and excessive fatigue.

Consider several teachers' comments on their work:

My class is not simply an administrative unit, it is a genuine democracy. The best preparation for future living is a full and rich life now, each class a microcosm of the world.

The children have really taken over the classroom. They have great pleasure in this and a very high sense of responsibility. I spend much more time in direct teaching of individuals or small groups and less time on routine matters, for the younger children absorb these naturally from the older ones. Freedom from routine work enables me to give much more time to individual help and attention. When I first began with a vertical group I feared that work would suffer but the reverse is true. The children are not tied to an authoritarian adult and they can organize themselves. I learn from them all the time as they work harmoniously together or alone, relaxed, interested, confident and full of zest for their activities.

The right climate of a school is one of its imponderables, but the vertical classification in the hands of convinced and enthusiastic teachers appears to make a reality of providing for the whole child. Not all teachers like or want this way of working, and many fear that the wide age-range brings greater problems than those to be found in traditional grouping. Some teachers change to vertical grouping, find it unsuccessful, and return to the earlier pattern; but most of those who adopt it do so as an expression of their personal philosophy, not just as a whim. Those who try it tend to make it their own and are eager to bear witness to its opportunities and advantages.

Changeover Procedures from Horizontal to Vertical Grouping

How do these teachers make the changeover from an established horizontal classification to a flexible vertical classification? Clearly, this process is one of gradual evolution and not an administrative exercise with a date deadline. Changes in the concept of the school have been taking place within the last few decades, and in general teachers have come to accept the principles underlying an education based on children's needs and interests. This changeover has resulted in friendlier relationships, a more permissive school climate, and provision of a more stimulating environment. Teachers with traditional class groups working in this freer atmosphere have become more and more immersed in active learning, and in many schools this gradual metamorphosis has taken place:

1. At first, teachers worked on a narrowly fixed timetable with short lesson periods.
2. The narrowly defined timetable was superseded by three broad blocks of time covering the three main areas of learning:
   A.M., before break: Activities
   A.M., after break: Mathematical experience
   Afternoon: Language and literature
3. Gradually, teachers found that children could plan their own time and experiences and achieve a balanced integrated whole under the guidance of the teacher—all three aspects of the curriculum going forward simultaneously. In this way an integrated day evolved. The transition to vertical grouping could be made gradually and naturally from this point, allowing a period of time for the reorganization of materials and equipment.

One head teacher describes changeover to vertical grouping:

*Vertical grouping must grow out of the existing pattern and every-
one needs TIME to absorb the idea and to prepare for it organizationally. The process cannot be hurried. Children and parents must be
prepared. After more than two years of working an integrated day with
traditional grouping we moved gradually into vertical grouping. We
have no timetable and the traditional playtime has completely disappeared.*

A class teacher described her "family":

*My group functions as a family. The children help each other, take
an interest in each other's efforts, and have great pride in the achievements of their companions. All seem to recognize their obligations and
their rights. They are fully stretched and developing at their own rate.
There is always legitimate regression for children who often need to
relax after self-imposed strenuous effort.*

PARALLEL GROUPING OF INTELLECTUAL PEERS

In a vertical organization, intelligent children are able to be with
their intellectual equals irrespective of age, while slow children are
not made to feel lost or dull competing unsuccessfully within their own
age-group. The children become accustomed to working in a class surrounded by other children who have reached more mature levels of
sociability, emotional stability, and intellectual achievement. These
circumstances enable the children to gain more realistic views of themselves and also provide valuable guide-ropes, enabling them to live in
"today" and also to move forward confidently into the "tomorrow" of
experience. Also, there is more scope for leadership experience, because
all the children in turn become the "elder statesmen" and more experienced members of the class community.

PROLONGED TEACHER/CHILD RELATIONSHIP

There are many gains for the teacher who can work happily and
successfully in a vertically grouped situation. In England at present,
new entrants to school are admitted to school terminally so that at the
beginning of the year all vertically grouped classes are smaller in numbers and are even in size. The teacher never faces a whole class of

strangers, nor is absence of pupils a worry because she is not taking the class stage-by-stage through a set syllabus. Moreover, she knows the children well and the classroom climate is such that the children work through concentration and interest. Problems of discipline are minimal, because the children are absorbed in their learning and because the atmosphere generates personal responsibility. Also, the prolonged teacher/child relationship is less frustrating for the teacher, for the children remain with her long enough to consolidate progress and to bring the fulfillment of her efforts. The unity of the staff and therefore of the school is more genuine, because all are sharing common purposes and common problems. Interclass jealousies are diminished and mutual responsibility increased.

UNSTRUCTURED DAY

The *integrated* or *unstructured* or *unscheduled* day is essential to the successful working of vertical grouping. The day is stripped of artificial divisions as far as the space and the amenities of the building render this possible. In practice, schools experiment freely with their plans and arrangements, and there is no set pattern for vertically grouped schools. A few schools start the day with a time for religious assembly and for discussions, leaving the rest of the day unspecified for all kinds of individual or group work, including some teaching periods. Often the day culminates in a quiet communal half hour at the close of school. Some schools find that a simple act of corporate worship comes most naturally at the end of the morning; [1] others leave the class teacher to decide the point at which any corporate activity shall take place. The close and continuous association with the children means that teachers really *know* their children and can make decisions in the light of changing needs and circumstances. There is an optional period of play outside for those children who wish to have it. Children have their milk when they are ready for it; and teachers either have coffee in the classroom or take a short break at a convenient point, in liaison with another teacher.

Within the vertically grouped classroom there is always a great deal of purposeful work in progress, but the atmosphere is usually one of calm concentration and absorption with the task in hand. Here are some happenings that went on in one classroom:

[1] Religious Instruction is required by law in British schools.

1. *David (7) is an advanced and enthusiastic reader, and when he goes into the library area he is invariably followed by one or two other children who ask him for help. Today he spent the whole hour helping a six-year-old and then reading some captions on pictures for the youngest children before settling down to seek some sources of reference for himself.*

2. *A few of the youngest children spread out the floor model of the farm and began to identify some of the animals as baby cows, baby sheep, and baby horses with their mothers and fathers. The group was joined by a six-year-old girl who provided the correct terminology in a friendly, acceptable fashion—calf, lamb, foal, mare, and so forth. This stimulated further questions and books were brought out. The conversation turned to shapes and sizes, and soon the group was absorbed in making sets and series. At this point they were joined by the teacher who brought solid geometric shapes and templates in order to feed this growing point. Later the children began to record their observations in drawings.*

3. *After a visit to the seashore the teacher created an "interest table" with things she had collected. It contained:*

coral	sea coal	dried spawn
shells	driftwood	bits of rock
seaweed	pebbles	fish scales
sea water	a crab shell	reference books and pictures

A great many children gathered around the specimens, and a short time was spent with a big group, identifying the materials and posing problems. Reference books were identified. Some of the children were greatly attracted by the collection and it was well used throughout the day by a number of children, although for others the initial handling was sufficient for the time being, and they took up other tasks. Those who continued with the interest table worked in a number of ways:

1. Two young children were absorbed in finding out the properties of the materials:
    the wetness of water
    the grittiness of sand

the intractability of wood
the saltiness of sea water.

2. A few six-year-olds were identifying and labeling the materials by comparison with pictures.
3. Two seven-year-old boys made extensive use of the microscope, and hand lens. They discussed their findings and then worked on written descriptions and some creative writing.
4. One boy decided to compile a catalogue, another to begin a model of a harbor.

The children helped each other, discussion was lively, but everyone was industrious and highly organized, yet relaxed and concentrated.

STRUCTURED ENVIRONMENT

An unstructured day is only made possible by having a highly organized classroom, and the success of vertical grouping rests to a

A library bay meeting the needs of all abilities.

large extent on a highly structured environment. Space and opportunity to spread out are very necessary, and whatever the type of building it is essential to make use of every corner. Because there are no formal class lessons and the teacher works only with small groups in desk work it is possible to dispense with some of the traditional furniture (tables or desks and chairs) and to divide the room space into working areas:

> One-third, mathematical activities
> One-third, language activities
> One-third, creative activities.

It is a great advantage to have part of the room carpeted for quiet activities and part of it covered with a washable dirt-resistant surface. Ideally, the classroom should be a workshop with its own sink and running water as well as its own storeroom. In actual practice, almost any classroom—however inconvenient—can be rearranged to provide minimal conditions for vertical grouping. Teachers surmount the most daunting obstacles in various ways: by creating alcoves with a judicious rearrangement of cupboards; by using open shelves to save space; by utilizing corridor and cloakroom areas; by saving space through extensive use of the floor as a work area; by the utilization of pegboard; and, where necessary, by persuading school managers to insert a convenient French window to enable easy access to the playground.

One child, Diane (6), came into a rearranged classroom and exclaimed, "What a lot of space! Where did it come from?" (A germinating point for further development!)

ORGANIZATION OF MULTI-PURPOSE EQUIPMENT

Every good infant-school teacher is familiar with the range of equipment and material needed by children during their infant-school years, and the requirements of the vertical classification do not differ much from these. In the vertically grouped school this essential basic equipment and material must be available in *every* classroom in order to meet the needs of the extended age-range, but in smaller quantities because there are fewer children of any one age in each class. Much of the equipment should be capable of being used in many ways. Everything must have a properly organized and identified place, for the children must be able to get for themselves the things they need and must take responsibility for general care and tidiness.

Indispensable equipment include:

1. A pleasant clean home corner in which to feel secure, with equipment for cleaning, cooking, eating, washing, coping with "the baby," and telephone; a variety of materials for extending home play, e.g. nurse and doctor uniforms, stethoscope, folding bed, postman and policeman outfits, equipment for road safety play, and so on; shops and shopping equipment. Not all this equipment is out at once, but it is available. Children of different ages use the home corner differently according to their needs.
2. A simple dressing box or wardrobe accessible to the home corner with a mirror.
3. A comfortable library area, containing well-displayed books for enjoyment and for reference. (It is helpful sometimes to have a "reserved" bookshelf for the older children.) Not too many books should be displayed at once, but there should always be reading material available that is related to what is going on in the room, or serves as a stimulus to some new development. A writing area should be included, giving children access to paper of several kinds and sizes, colored pencils, thick lead pencils, crayons, felt pens, "magic markers," picture dictionaries, word books, alphabet books, templates, and tracing materials. There should be writing and drawing books of various sizes and shapes containing approximately four to 12 pages stapled together within varied interesting cover papers.
4. A mathematical area with tools and equipment for a wide range of experiment and experience: Materials for sorting, grouping, and comparing. Materials for balancing. Scales and weights. A wide variety of weighing materials. Spring balance. Letter scales. Rules, tape measures, string, ribbon, cord, tape, scissors. Trundle wheels. Clocks and clock stamps, clock templates. Money (real and cardboard), purses, bags; bottles, spoons, containers of all sizes, bowls, small bath, buckets, sieves, funnels, and so forth. Bricks, tiles, mosaics, quantities of 1-inch cubes, materials for shaping and pattern making, fraction apparatus. Construction toys. Structural

apparatus (e.g. Stern, Cuisenaire, Deines). Square-ruled paper in many sizes and rulings. Number games, challenge cards, and assignment cards in relation to each aspect.

5. A constructional area with a variety of materials and joining substances: Sand, water, clay, dough. Classified materials such as leather, cones, fabrics, buttons, sequins, tins, reels. Paper of all sizes and colors. Paints and easels. Junk materials. Bench and tools for woodwork. Sink with running water. Junk boxes and cartons of all kinds.

6. An interest table that the teacher uses as an important channel for "feeding the environment." It should be planned and organized by her to provide aesthetic pleasure and intellectual stimulus. Its purpose is to extend the children's ideas, to open up possibilities, to encourage thought and investigation. A good idea is to have this table near the classroom door so that the children have to pass it regularly.

Here is an account of some extensions based on an interest table:

Thomas (6) brought in a dead mouse and buried it in our little garden. He asked what would happen to it, and a group discussion arose on "What is a skeleton?" Here was a germinating point for further growth. The teacher put out a model of the human skeleton, a sheep's skull, a horse's leg bone, some models of birds of different sizes and wing spans, some fossilized coal, and ammonites. Several reference books were put on special display in the library area, and out of all this grew great interest in "living and being." For weeks the children, individually, in pairs, and in groups explored seeing, smelling, hearing, tasting, and feeling. This necessitated a great deal of counting, recording, and reading at several levels, and the content of the interest table changed as investigations developed.

Within the carefully prepared and structured environment vertically grouped children find both skilled guidance and stimulating opportunities for choice. There is always a wide range of work going forward, and because of this the educational climate is both richer and more stimulating than that in the traditional classroom. There are no arbitrary limits to learning; verbalization and symbolization are correspondingly greater. The output of effort and achievement is impressive, but the children are not in competition with one another;

they are absorbed in maximum personal effort. Experience in a community of this kind makes an important contribution to the moral development of the children—through cooperating, sharing, making mistakes without being a failure, taking responsibility, and using sympathy and imagination in dealing with others.

Here is an observed classroom situation in a vertically grouped school:

A few five-year-olds are playing with sand and water, talking together with great vigor. The two youngest children are taking part in highly serious home play with two older children. The library corner is in full use, and the teacher is working with several children who are either reading, recording their findings with a tire and pulleys, or working on graphs of the largest, smallest, and similar family sizes to be found in the group. Everyone is busy yet none of the teacher's time is being given to the obvious control and administration of routine matters. Three older boys who made kites the previous week had watched the weather for a strong wind. They learned about the Beaufort Wind Scale from the teacher and had also studied cloud formations. A weather station has developed from this situation. Ten children are engaged in various aspects of this interest, the three boys who made the kites acting as leaders. The teacher is frequently consulted, or is an intervener in:

Preparing a weather report
Telephoning the weather center
Making a compilation of weather rhymes and proverbs
Writing about a recent storm
Experimenting with blotting paper and cobalt chloride for weather signs
Using the world globe to discuss winds
Making a rain gauge and recording findings
Using a weather vane and recording changes
Using reference books on meteorology
Keeping records of experiments
Looking at newspaper weather reports and relating these to the globe and atlas
Finding out about temperatures
Recording sun hours.

Three other children are busy completing a classroom opinion poll on favourite desserts. Everyone has time to deal courteously with their inquiries. There is some reading and writing developing around this and a good deal of number work. Four other children are beginning to find out all about castles, using adult guidebooks. Two are doing some construction work, one is measuring for a "massive arch," another is collecting materials. The teacher is "a source of reference." A great deal of discussion and 3-R work goes in to this interest and they gain a great fund of authentic information. The children have been reading stories about fairy tale castles and this is reflected in their creative writing.

In another classroom:

Every facility in the room—and in the corridor—is being used by the children—math area, library corner, writing table, interest table. In the construction area a bridge and fortification are arising, involving experimentation with sound, pattern work with floor tiles of various shapes and sizes, building up a wall frieze; recording, consulting the teacher, watching, discussing, helping. All these things are going on and the children are deeply involved.

The home corner has been extended to form part of the Baby Clinic, and a boy in a white doctor's coat and two girls in nurses' uniforms are busy dealing with the welfare of dolls, Teddy bears and children. The patients are weighed and their weights recorded, there is much measuring of "medicine." Two children are arranging and selling "baby foods" and toilet preparations, while one child is concentrating on accurately filling a baby bottle with a measuring gauge on its side. The doctor's hours are posted, and record cards of patients and treatments are being kept. A simple medical dictionary, books on first aid, home nursing, and diet are all available for reference. Some of these have been made by the children, others by the teacher. There are reference charts and lists of essential words to consolidate the learning. The eye-testing chart has two variations—i.t.a. (initial teaching alphabet) and traditional orthography. Following this interest through creates a strong need for the tools of the 3-R's and the teacher uses every opportunity to foster skills. The children get a great deal of practice because of the demands of the interest, and the teacher has no need to depend on educational devices to arouse or hold interest and attention. The children acquire skills without strain in a highly social setting, and have ample opportunities for necessary practice.

And in another room:

BOY *(looking at a picture of merchant ships):* Why do ships have cranes on them?
GIRL: They lift the parcels onto the ships. *(The teacher supplies the term 'cargoes.')*
BOY: I should like to make a crane for my ship.
The teacher suggests that he look for a book. The girl volunteers to help. Both spend a long time on a book about machines.

THE TEACHER AS A RESOURCE

The role of the teacher in the vertically-grouped situation is a complex and subtle one. She is responsible for establishing and maintaining an appropriate and flexible environment in which children can learn through their own activities, an atmosphere free from tensions, full of good will, tolerance, and mutual understanding. To do this adequately she must have both sound knowledge of and imaginative understanding of how children grow and develop. Such a teacher must be able to hold herself in readiness for the moment when the children need help and at the same time must anticipate the path that development will follow. She must be able to organize the classroom as a workshop capable of long-term provision for a variety of experience and be ready to adapt, improvise, and augment when required, in order to exploit to the full "moments of readiness." In traditional classrooms it is possible to lose and waste a frightening number of opportunities, because school organization is too rigid to allow a growing point to be nurtured or an individual level of aspiration raised.

At all times, the teacher must encourage the children to go forward, to progress, to assimilate, and to accommodate in their thinking. She must intervene productively in their activities and, in order to be able to foster these processes, must therefore know how children think and learn. She must have accurate and detailed knowledge of how to help children to acquire and use the basic skills. All this implies an extensive knowledge and real understanding of curriculum

development as well as the ability to interpret and apply this knowledge in the service of the individual child.

The teacher must recognize the needs of each child and must see
that these special needs and aptitudes are catered for. Her role is one
of helping each individual to develop to his fullest potential. Her
relationships with the children must be friendly and sympathetic.
Learning does not flourish without the warmth, the interest, the encouragement, and the support of the adult acting not as an authoritarian figure determining in advance what shall be done but as a
leader alive to the possibilities of every situation—active and observant,
watching for opportunities to give help and instruction where needed.
In all this she will be aided greatly, if she has enlisted the allegiance
and trust of the parents, especially the mothers. The prolonged teacher/
child relationship can provide a bridge between home and school,
thus harmoniously uniting the two major aspects of a child's life.

The teacher must be a source of reference and inspiration. This
task is demanding and continuous, requiring a wealth of experience,
wide interests, considerable mental and physical energy, sound academic knowledge, resourcefulness, tenacity, receptivity, and sympathy.
She must challenge, stimulate, and open up new vistas. When the
need arises, she must be able to teach skills, techniques, and information very thoroughly, but in the main her teaching will be with
individuals and small groups.

Through all the work the teacher must be able to evaluate individual effort and progress and must be able to record them satisfactorily. Any program of free individual work demands careful scrutiny
of individual progress, and the teacher must devise records that will
enable her to do this with economy of time and effort. Many interesting experiments in appropriate individual record-keeping are taking
place at present in vertically grouped schools, for records play a vital
part in the realization of the aims and principles implicit in this
flexible organization. Lack of goals and lack of planning can bring
progressive educational thinking into disrepute.

When teachers are asked about the disadvantages of vertical grouping, they often reply that they are not so great as those of traditional
grouping or that such problems as occur are capable of being resolved. But some teachers are anxious about the cooperative activities
of music, story, poetry, and physical education, fearing that children

might be starved of experiences in these subject areas. Teachers in a vertically grouped situation overcome this problem in a variety of ways. An immense amount of material is available that is a child's literary heritage, and teachers often avoid any tedious repetition by using a richer and wider range of appropriate material than is normally found in the chronologically grouped class. Other teachers tell stories and share poems with small groups at one time, or they prepare material for different maturational levels and make listening optional. The children can decide to do other things but must respect the need of the story group for quietness. Sometimes the head teacher of the school has a "listening time" for poetry, story, and music, and children of different ages are invited to participate; sometimes two teachers work at these activities together, each offering material at a different maturational level. Occasionally, the older children can make a contribution by reading to the younger children. It has to be remembered that children enjoy repetition of favourite material, and the vertically grouped organization can facilitate this. However the problem is tackled, the need for careful records of the material presented to children must not be overlooked by teachers.

Musical experience presents little difficulty in the vertical organization. There are usually group facilities for creative music making and experimentation with sounds, and in this it is helpful to have some older and more experienced children working with younger ones. Singing and listening to music are an integral part of classroom life and are enjoyed as a class or a group with great frequency. The teacher takes class lessons if she wishes. After all, choirs in real life are seldom organized on the basis of age! Younger members are helped by older ones.

Music is a natural part of spontaneous dance, and children often work together to provide the music for a group who want to develop some creative movement. The modern approach to physical education is one of emphasizing individual growth and tempo, and lessons are organized to encourage personal expression and development. All the classes in a school usually share the large agility apparatus. They come in groups or as individuals, and sometimes as classes to use the equipment according to interest and need. The head teacher sometimes takes special responsibility for the supervision of this operation, setting tasks at different levels, where appropriate.

Evaluation of Results of Vertical Grouping

Critics of vertical grouping often raise the problem of standards. They fear that some children may underfunction in a school situation not definitely systematized to follow a syllabus or may lack the stimulation of a change of teacher at the end of each school year. Research undertaken by the writer indicated that there was no evidence whatsoever of lower standards of attainment in a vertically grouped situation. Furthermore, there was evidence that the vertical organization was productive of better work attitudes, of higher levels of aspiration, and of less discouragement in failure.

Opponents of vertical grouping also point to the dangers of over-possessiveness or overprotectiveness on the part of a teacher who might become too attached to a group with whom she sustains a relationship over a period of years. Vertical grouping demands great maturity on the part of teachers, and it would be unwise to change over to it, unless teachers are ready for it and understand all the implications of the changeover.

Research by the writer into the effects of lengthened teacher/child relationship revealed more highly integrative relationships in the vertical group and therefore greater emotional security for the children.

Certainly, vertical grouping is not the universal panacea for all school problems and inadequacies, and any educational enterprise depends on the quality of the teachers who are implementing it. We cannot separate organization from teachers. The quality of the teacher is of crucial importance in a vertical classification, but it would be idle to suggest that this is not also true of the traditional classification. The quality of an environment depends on the adults who provide it, and the Plowden Report on primary education suggests that teachers and their attitudes might possibly outweigh all other considerations and influences. Every school has to face the problem of the really poor teacher and has to decide upon an organization best for all the children committed to its care. Head teachers report that in a vertically grouped school discussion is easier, the teachers learn more freely from one another, and the less-than-average teacher can get maximum support and help from colleagues who are facing the same kinds of situations. Vertical grouping eliminates the "closed classroom," utilizes corridors and adjacent working spaces, breaks down barriers, and in so doing exposes children to a range of additional influences and opportunities. Sometimes head teachers find that it is helpful for teachers to pair themselves so that the maximum support and encouragement can be arranged, particularly for inexperienced teachers.

Indeed some teachers are already combining vertical grouping with "open planning" whereby a small group of teachers (two or three) work together in order to pool their strengths and abilities. In this situation children remain with one teacher for a span of years but have access to the strengths of other skilled adults at certain times and in certain situations.

The educational environment as a functional variable has received little systematic attention so far; but the results of a small piece of research into the effects of vertical grouping appear to demonstrate that in several important directions the vertical classification can be more beneficial to primary school children than the horizontal classification. If the educational viewpoint is maintained that social and emotional learning are as important as intellectual learning, then the adoption of vertical grouping for a more effective realization of this ideal would appear to be worth consideration, provided that this is a way of life chosen by the teachers as the expression of their educational beliefs, and provided also that the teachers are able to apply their principles to sound educational practice. Where this is done, the children are superbly provided for. At present our knowledge largely rests on the evidence of dedicated and sincere teachers who have proved the value of vertical grouping with the children they teach. Such evidence is sincere and convincing, but it could be strengthened by further research providing more comprehensive data on the effects of school environment.

4. | Cooperative and Team Teaching

DON SKINNER

DON SKINNER is head teacher at Michael Faraday Junior School, Southwark, London. He has a diploma in Child Development from the University of London and is a part-time lecturer at Goldsmith's College of Education. His school has been the subject for many press articles including the London Times *and* Daily Telegraph. *He himself has written for educational journals on developments in primary education in Great Britain.*

Michael Faraday Junior School stands in a socially deprived area in Southwark, some two miles from the center of London. The community is predominately lower working class—if one can still use this antiquated term—containing few, if any, professional or artisan workers. Apart from the social characteristics of the community, its physical character is now changing completely as the neighborhood around the school is first demolished and then replaced with blocks of tall apartment houses, which are both functional and in an odd way beautiful. I have been head teacher at the school for nearly three years, in which time we have moved from a very formal, rigid type of education to one where the intellectual and social needs of the child predominate.

At present, the school is growing toward an integrated day, in which a child develops his own interests working in an undefined time structure. To enlarge upon this, the children in many of our eight classrooms now begin the day by selecting from any of four areas of curriculum development in which they may be interested. Selection usually occurs within English, Mathematics, topic research, and craft studies.

The classroom is divided into four working areas, a carpeted quiet bay, a mathematics bay, an art and craft work area, and a research-writing corner. Each bay is separated from its neighbor by white storage units in which relevant books and other apparatus are stored; and each bay is fully functioning in material that will be used by children while working in it. Movement and speech are encouraged, and desk arrangements are planned to stimulate "talking to" rather than "talking at" other children.

The child is assisted in developing his interests by the teacher who advises (even at times, structures) solo investigation on the part of the child. Because of its special problems mathematics is partially structured, although an active discovery approach is used. In other areas of the curriculum integration is almost complete.

We do everything we can at school to involve our children's parents, both in and out of the classrooms, in the developing intellectual and social maturation of the children.

It is interesting to note the contribution parents do offer when deepening a child's intellectual experience. Recently, one of my parents took a child (not her own) who was working on the topic of ships to the Maritime museum. For the child who was writing a book about ships and carefully constructing a Viking boat this visit was a significant experience. For the mother it was an enjoyable opportunity, not only to help the school but also to get to know a child from a different home. In fact, many of our mothers help the children by working alongside the teachers in the classrooms.

From time to time, a class is brought together for a topic, a shared experience in Creative English or combined with other classes for a team approach to a learning problem, which is the theme of this chapter.

When I first suggested to the staff that we might try team action as a development in our teaching, to my surprise considerable hostility was aroused. It was pointed out that team teaching with its structured approach was contrary to our philosophy of development of the child in his choice of learning. The opinion that team teaching with its emphasis on the acquisition of imposed knowledge in formal teaching situations was more appropriate to the secondary school (eleven years plus) than to a progressive primary school was also voiced. To convince the staff of the values of team teaching one needed to show its effectiveness in developing educational techniques and in satisfying a child in the learning situation. To rationalize my position, I prepared a paper for staff discussion. This paper outlined developments in team teaching in America, with its emphasis on a hierarchy within the team, a multiplicity of electronic aids, and adequate secretarial help. I pointed out that this costly and complex approach was not only impossible for us but, perhaps, undesirable in a British primary school. Subsequently, I dwelt at length on the advantages of joint planning and the necessity to leave our classroom boxes so that children could mix freely and cooperate with others from different classes. I reminded them that team teaching contained a fundamental principle of the division of labor, drawing on the talents that each teacher brings to his profession.

For me, the problem of team teaching was a more personal one:

Team teaching calls for group teaching and learning . . .

. . . *and* for individualization.

How could I as head teacher enlarge the horizons of my staff and children? Not, I felt, by feeding in techniques, because however good these may be they tend to limit the initiative of the individual. I had the feeling that to create opportunities and place materials in strategic points would encourage and stimulate both staff and children to experiment for themselves. As an observer, I felt I must isolate intrinsic growth from the mediocre and commonplace and communicate these discoveries to the staff. Now, this is not always easy to do. Teachers often fail to put their discoveries in the shop window and sometimes are even completely unaware of that exciting moment when a growth point needs exploiting and communicating within the school. After all, what for some people may be a revelation in terms of curriculum development, for others may be an aesthetic experience to be appreciated in the context of the occasion. For me, then, team teaching was essentially a matter of communication and the bringing together of creative vitality in active learning situations, preserving as far as possible the child's desire to follow his own interests.

Within this definition and after long and patient argument we agreed to try the experiment. Basically, as I have indicated, team teaching is only used now and then, cropping up perhaps once or at the most twice a term, depending on the strength of the stimulus that sparks off the joint venture.

Let me concentrate on three stories of team-teaching ventures, not only because to analyze in depth a team approach will help you, the reader, in your evaluation of its merits, but also because the themes undertaken appeared significant to us in the understanding of our children. The joint study on Violence concerned nine-year-old children. The Zoo visit was made by seven to eight-year-olds. And children in the 10 to 11 age-group made the Environmental Study. While reading these themes I think you will begin to understand the problems, hopes, and joys of working with these delightful Southwark youngsters.

Joint Study on Violence

Unfortunately, as in so many socially deprived communities, violence tends to be endemic in the area. Many staff discussions and a paper on discipline produced a working policy on this thorny subject. The staff and I were agreed on the basic truth that if we used violence as a solution to our disciplinary problems, then the child (who imitates to learn) could only draw one conclusion. Force may control violent impulses in school, but if our aim was to create conditions so that much of the frustration and deprivation within the community could be diverted into more creative forms, other solutions were needed. Drama, in which such emotions as terror, fear, anger, and misery were unlocked into fantasy play proved very helpful. However, the staff felt that violence could be made into a study theme for children and we chose our nine-year-old group for this project.

The teachers agreed that the children should be made aware of the aggressive forces at large in the neighborhood and that violence should be seen as isolated, indiscriminate reactions to environmental frustrations, rather than as an acceptable way of life. Accordingly, we divided our classes into groups, and with the assistance of volunteer university students we searched the community for evidence of antisocial disorder; but with little success. Staff, students, and groups trailed back reporting just the odd reflection of neighborhood turmoil. A child screaming its dissatisfaction in East Lane Market and a woman shouting at her baby for throwing his Teddy bear out of the carriage we felt were reactions typical of any working or middle-class area in the world. One interesting, and rather perceptive comment came from a little girl, "Mr. Skinner, why do our mothers sweep rubbish into the gutters when we have a dustbin (refuse) collector?"

Closer examination began to isolate unconscious aggressive forces that tended to trigger off public acts of violence. For example, a child in a neighboring class was continually fighting—fighting to show that he did not care about his body odor. In discussing his violence it emerged that this boy's home (like so many others) lacked a bath-room. We discussed this type of frustration and its possible conse-quences; the groups agreed that possibly the forces rejecting the boy's smell came from children who had recently been rehoused. From this growing point we set out to examine other influences within the home that exploded into antisocial reactions. Some children complained of rotting wood on staircases that caused twisted and fractured ankles from time to time. They told us of attempts to redecorate their houses with paper that immediately peeled off because of damp walls; they complained of rats that made them frightened to fall asleep. [Did you ever try being mature and calm when your body was longing for sleep?] They spoke of outside toilets. One child said, "I can't go to the toilet in the night because I am frightened someone will jump out on me in the back yard." By the way, this child was receiving treatment for bedwetting. I wonder if anyone probed deeply into his background for more natural causes? And of course the usual ghost stories emerged, inevitable in houses of this antiquity. Faced with this type of social frustration, little wonder that neurotic and unstable reactions occurred. In middle-class areas we tend to resolve such instability in words; in an area where the spoken vocabulary is so limited, fists and feet have to compensate.

After a staff meeting concerned with this now rather complex study, we decided to reject a neighborhood housing research project as being too dangerous. I might explain here that our children's parents are sensitive (as I presume so many other parents are) to questions concerning home and family conditions. One volunteer student suggested that perhaps we were so busy looking into causes of violence, that we were neglecting the children's fantasy life, which might help them to formulate acceptable solutions to their problems. Agreeing to this suggestion we broke up our project on Violence into these theme headings:

1. **The Ideal Home in the Ideal City.**—We correctly judged here that the children would treat their community as a city.
2. **My Mother and Father.**—Here we suggested that they would have to go forward in time and it was *their* children writing about them.
3. **Fear.**—The causes and consequences.
4. **Mental Health.**—As you can imagine there is a great deal of nervous and psychotic breakdown in our area of Southwark.
5. **Murderers and Their Victims.**—The North Peckham area of Southwark has more than its fair share of gangster activity.

We divided the children into five groups allowing one adult to be responsible for each group. We agreed that as in all creative writing visits and drama would be important features of each of the themes. As some of the themes would obviously prove more attractive than others, we structured each group to obtain a balanced intake both in boys and girls and levels of intelligence. As coordinator for the groups I assisted in group discussion, in supervision of visits, and as a communication link (liaison) to enable each group's work to be brought to the attention of the other groups. I was also responsible for the resulting exhibition.

THE IDEAL HOME IN THE IDEAL CITY

The Ideal Home theme provided a very moving general discussion, particularly where it revealed the expectations of socially deprived city children. Sharon said that her ideal home would have a garden, "not a large one, Sir," in which a tree surrounded by grass would be the main attraction. Deborah wanted a front garden and a gate "to stop dogs doing their mischief." [It must be explained here that most of the old houses in the Faraday area open onto the street.] Tony said his ideal home would have a space for a dustbin—his mother for convenience' sake kept theirs in the hall and Tony was always fighting when provocative statements were made about the smell in his house. As expected, high priority was given to indoor toilets, gardens, bathrooms, and "enough bedrooms so that you could have one to yourself."

Again, stable relationships seldom develop in a family when the need for privacy can rarely be satisfied. My guess would be that Pam, a very intelligent and sensitive girl, would place at the top of her priorities a room where she can devote her time to reading, freed from the background noise of television and conversation. The written work was rather disappointing. The perfect home ranged through science fiction—robots to do all the work—to the limited dreams of a deprived community. Significantly, nobody in the group thought his ideal city should be composed of apartment buildings. As in most high density areas, London over the last twenty years has begun to invest in "flats," leaving houses for the grassier suburbs. John anticipated a city that was underground, giving more room for rural pastimes. Unfortunately, no visits were arranged for this group and very little drama emerged. A pity about the visits because the opportunity of viewing completed, furniture-equipped show houses might have raised the children's expectation levels.

MY MOTHER AND FATHER

The Mother and Father theme proved more promising, mainly because most children are optimistic about developments within the family. Running through their work was a rich vein of home; their children did not complain about overcrowding, punishment, lack of play amenities, and so forth. Instead, they concentrated on visits to country and seaside, comfortable viewing positions for television, and exotic foods. A touching note was struck by Maureen, who is fatherless. Her ideal, half-remembered father was given substance, for on Christmas Eve he was pictured as coming back from a long journey, providing gifts, food, a new house, clothes, furniture, and "a nice, warm face."

The injustices they resolved not to visit on their children included *violence*, "My Mum and Dad never hit me, even when I deserve it"; *want*, "I have thirty-eight new dresses in my wardrobe, I give away a lot of my clothes to poor children." [Other people are poor, not them]; *lack of social amenities*, "My Mum took me to the park round the corner and we played all day." [This from a girl whose mother works too hard at office-cleaning and housekeeping to indulge in the luxuries of play.]

FEAR

Fear (the richest and most intriguing symptom in an unstable community) gave us a wealth of background material on the children. Rather than look at their irrational manifestations of uncertainty, somehow we had to link the deprivations our children had to cope with in their daily lives to the cultural and intellectual experiences they were likely to encounter in such a neighborhood. For example, the existence of ghosts is widely accepted among our children, and this belief is nourished and sustained by parental doubt and immaturity on the subject. Without a doubt in a community that is dark and primitive in a cultural sense, complete reality tends to be shallow and somewhat uncertain. In short, it may well be (as a psychologist claims) that adult belief in the supernatural is sometimes necessary to compensate for guilt feelings aroused by the deprivations they see around them.

Certainly, in the preliminary discussion and subsequent drama work, ghosts dominated the Fear theme. When talking on the subject, most of the children claimed to have had some experience, either first- or secondhand. The teacher who was leading the group did her best to relate apparent manifestations to the old, creaky houses, but the children would have none of it. "My Mum actually saw my Nan at the top of the stairs," said Anne.

John wrote:

> Walking down a dark alley, frightened
> Street lights flash, gone
> Suddenly I shiver,
> I hear footsteps, a white shape
> It is a ghost.

Janice wrote of her very dark, damp room:

> As I go to bed at night
> I see a shadow on the wall
> I sit there shaking, frightened,
> I can't open my mouth to scream,
> Ghosts can't be there, but I can see them.
> Cold as I am I run down stairs.

Linked with the unnatural is an associated fear of darkness. Actually the back streets of Walworth demand fairly strong nerves at night. Old, often abandoned, crammed together off narrow, dimly lit roads, the houses are frightening. Imagination can distort the shadows for a young mind. Christine wrote:

> I have a fear,
> It is walking down a dark alley,
> I hate the dark!
> Once I walked home
> A shape jumped out and ran after me
> I was alone
> I am cautious
> I keep looking behind me,
> It feels like being hunted down,
> The darkness is broken by a street lamp
> Then back into the night.

Carol described "the wind swishing the darkness into my eyes." Sandra told of "the darkness that will swallow me up with a cold feeling."

Jean wrote literally of a night experience, revealing a fear of ghosts,

I was walking down a street, it was gradually growing dark and I was alone. I walked past a solitary street lamp and my shadow grew longer. My footsteps echoed around me and I turned around quickly. No one there. The street was enveloped in darkness. I quickened my pace, I started to sweat. My house came in sight. I dashed to the door, glanced round and found my pursuer was a dog. Its lean body like some grey ghost.

Other fears springing from the environment dealt with falling. "I dream I am gliding down five hundred stone steps, I trip and fall, head over heels, tumbling." Many of the neighborhood houses have a flight of stone steps to the front door, which have been the source of many accidents. It was common for the children to express fears of bridges collapsing, especially nearby Tower Bridge that spans the Thames.

Linda wrote, "When I am half way over the bridge I have a frightening feeling it will open. I sweat with fear. Will my bus crash through the side?" Brian who lives at the top of a tall block of "flats" is terrified by elevators (lifts). "I am scared of getting stuck in a lift. When the light goes out I feel dizzy, hot! Help! Nobody comes, I suffocate, my spine shivers. All I see in my eyes is black." Incidentally, many fears of falling come from children who have suddenly been uprooted from small houses and placed in giant, twelve-story blocks of flats. Dreams apparently are quickly forgotten by our children, for they rarely appeared in the discussion or written work. The fears expressed either happened or were lying there in the imagination waiting to be told.

MENTAL HEALTH

Mental illness was dealt with imaginatively because of its personal nature and a high incidence rate within the community. Unlike the Fear theme, which produced much exciting and revealing drama and movement work, we decided to deal with mental illness in a quiet way, to facilitate understanding and compassion. Kate whose mother had a leucotomy wrote a moving, detailed account. She told of the slow drift into psychosis, springing apparently from a feeling of the utter hopelessness about life. She described the husband leaving home, the dirty house and unfriendly neighbors, lack of money, her mother's refusal to leave the bed and, finally, the sick woman's violence, so irrational and terrifying. As I understand it, this account is exactly how it happened to her mother. Naturally, Kate longed for release from childhood so that she might leave home. The volunteer student dealing with this theme suggested to the children that they should draw a face and then fragment the drawing to produce and suggest a distorted mind. Sharon produced a coiled face through circular cutting and wrote, "Coiled springs make her want to explode outwards at people." Keith said, "The man's mind was a whirl of thought. The blank expression had no purpose. But his problems wandered through his mind whirling and twisting." Billy wrote, "Unhappy, sad, alone, no friends. His mind fixed on another world. Nobody takes any notice of him." Perhaps the best of the written work came from Joseph, a boy who gives the impression that life is a battle he will never be able to win. He wrote:

Man his eyes small, sad,
His mind seeks comfort beyond his reach.
The weather-beaten face is gray.

[Joseph's face is black.]

MURDERERS AND THEIR VICTIMS

This theme produced the most exciting art work the school at that time had seen. Each child, either murderer or victim, produced a life-sized figure, which he mounted on a backcloth to suggest an appropriate mood or movement. The murderers were bold and vividly colored, their victims drawn in chalk on black paper. Murderers and victims were displayed on a staircase facing each other, the written stories providing a link on an adjacent wall. Against my advice, drama was attempted, but it became obvious at an early stage that many undesirable instincts were being set loose and it was decided that this aspect should cease.

The written work matched the art in its vitality. Through discussion the class examined the motives and mental stability of the murderer, presumably as a plea for tolerance. The results were encouraging. Steven wrote:

His mind is full of the hate and anger he feels for himself. He takes the greatest joy in harming delicate things. Perhaps it was because when he was younger men cut off his leg with an axe for not paying his gambling debts. Now he has no mercy for anyone.

Mary said:

The man is evil, insane and cruel. His mind needs turning round. He is like a hungry fox looking for its prey, but this animal kills with a knife and not claws. He is unhappy in the blood that surrounds him.

Donald surmised:

The blood-thirsty killer, killing for money and fun. His knife glitters in the moonlight. He hates every person in the world, especially the police. His guilty conscience makes him kill more and more. Blood drips off his knife and stains his hands. His mind is sick.

And so it went on, story after story dealing with hatred, blood, axes, knives, and revenge. A frightening and salutary reminder of the potential in a frustrated, deprived community. Perhaps the most telling sentence in this written work came from Pamela who in dealing with the murderer's reactions after stabbing his victim wrote, "His hatred drained away from him and he felt tired." You would go a long way to find a more classic statement on the release of tension following an act of violence.

Although as far as possible free choice was given as to whether the child should be victim or murderer, because of the popularity of the latter role some structuring had to be done by the team teachers. Naturally healthy children derive little pleasure from being victims, so enthusiasm here was lacking. However, if you are to be a victim, panic and blood must be the necessary accompaniment. Walking on the embankment of the river Thames, Fred heard footsteps, "He walks slowly towards me—I am scared, my body boils over. I freeze with fear. . . ." Then the inevitable knife is plunged in. Most of the murderers appear at night, nearly all come from the darkness of alleys or narrow roads, all of them are mad.

When the team study was completed, group themes flooded the hall and corridors, and special assemblies introduced other classes to the work that had been done. On the whole the results were impressive if not exciting. Each member of the team reported that interest and above all insight grew as the work progressed. At frequent intervals, meetings were held with both classes [1] in which they freely discussed their work. Teachers feel that the study on violence appears to have produced more positive reactions to cooperative effort, a tolerance toward hostility, and a keen interest in neighborhood planning and rebuilding. I regret to say it also exposed considerable tension and violent solutions boiling just beneath the surface of their day-to-day lives.

---

[1] Two-classes approach to team teaching. See next section, Study of the Zoo, paragraph 1.

**MURDERERS AND
THEIR VICTIMS** Theme

Joint Study of the Zoo

The weakness of team teaching is that it often predetermines the structure and the content of the learning, without significantly involving the interests of the child. To safeguard against this somewhat sterile approach we often combine two classes for a visit and then allow the children's interests to dictate the joint planning that follows. Such a visit occurred one summer when after much pressure from the children of the first year, the staff and I agreed to release valuable P-TA funds to rent a bus to visit Whipsnade Zoo in Hertfordshire. Whipsnade for Southwark children is what parts of New Hampshire would be to residents of the Bowery, in New York City— rolling downlands, green trees, hills, sun, and fresh air. On our last visit to Whipsnade the previous year, children rolled down the grassy slopes, climbed back up, and then rolled down again. The animals wandering in their natural state in open countryside were largely ignored. For staff members to carry along a sheaf of questionnaires that would involve the child intellectually from dawn to dusk would not only be a mistake, it would be educationally wrong. Far better to involve the child in all his senses and then on our return to isolate and study at team level those experiences that were meaningful to him. The main preparation preceding the visit was aimed to foster the sense of excitement growing in the children. However, animal books were left in conspicuous positions in the quiet bays, including some beautiful books by Brian Wildsmith; and a film on Elsa, the tame lioness was shown. The teachers also concentrated on collecting follow-up material that we were certain was going to be needed: chicken wire for large animals (an enthusiastic class request here), simple animal research books, handmade books for children's research, imaginative written work and so on. In discussion before the visit it was decided that one teacher, Chris, would specialize on craft aspects and Phil, the other teacher, with the help of a portable tape recorder would concentrate on speech, and they would both combine on the written work. I helped in the planning and with my camera attempted to keep a photographic record of the visit and subsequent work. The bus trip lasted just over an hour and predictably fascinated the children. Chris drew my attention to Joanne who was, as usual, isolated in the bus. Tactfully we drew her into a singing group at the back of it. Tony quietly gazed out of the window, "Look at those cows," he muttered, a sense of wonder noticeably absent from his voice. I guessed that for him Whipsnade was not only going to be too quiet but that the animals would be an unnecessary distraction from a day out of school.

In the Zoo the children immediately rushed to the elephant enclosure. They yelled encouragement at two elephants shooting sand at each other. "Look at 'im, Miss! Cor! I wish I could have a bath in sand." "Why do they use their trunk, Mr. Skinner?" Terry said, "I would roll over in the sand if I was them." Jane reminded him of the elephant at London Zoo who had recently fallen over and died. Edmund said that in a book he'd read elephants washed each other with water, so why didn't they give them a pool? Joanne wanted them to have a river to bathe in. I asked the children to keep their eyes open for a river. Later that day Graham said to me, "You can't have rivers on chalky soil, Sir, the water would soak through." The children drifted off toward the cat enclosure but found the sleepy leopards rather boring, so we took them to the kangaroo pen. They were fascinated with the babies peering out from their mothers' pouches. Girls immediately responded to the maternal scene with little cries of delight. Debbie queried, "Have they been born yet Miss?" Later, Stephen doggedly trailing a kangaroo on his stomach, replied wistfully to a threat that he would be picked up and carried away, "I wish it would, Miss, I just fancy a ride in that pouch."

By this time, young appetites had taken over from curiosity and we lunched with the indigenous marmots on the hillside. Raymond who earlier had won many admiring glances following his determined attempts to obtain peacock feathers from those rather large, bad tempered birds, now turned his attention to the marmots. At one point only his legs stretching out from the holes in the chalky soil could be seen. He would have cheerfully surrendered all his precious lunch, if he could have fed the marmots; yet, in school he rarely makes contact either with the adults or with other children; however, Raymond won many friends that day. At a later point he came up to me and said, "I don't like animals with big eyes, Mr. Skinner, they frighten me." [Incidentally, his mother who is alcoholic tends to be thyroidic.]

We used the dinner-hour break to record impressions of the children's reactions to the animals, but the children were so excited by the marmots and a group of kangaroos on the hillside that they tended to give monosyllabic replies to our questions. Afterwards, a transcript of these tapes showed them to be largely valueless. Tony told Phil how disappointed he was that "a zoo like this hasn't got a laughing hyena." Nicky did not believe that the puma in the Zoo was the same as those in the jungle—at least the television jungle!

The children had decided that one of their models would be a giraffe so we made a detailed study of this animal. The children were fascinated by the long neck swooping down to pick up food, and Stephen noticed the chewed bark and leaves at the top of small saplings. At the rhinoceros pen (another proposed model) everybody commented on the grey thick hide and horn. Lorraine said, "Oh my Gawd, the smell!" and wandered off. The highlight of the afternoon was the feeding of the seals—climaxed inevitably by Janet slipping in a muddy puddle, "My mum'll kill me," she cried and refused to be comforted for the next hour.

Toward the end of the afternoon the children had a sixpenny horse ride. It must have been a shock for some beautifully dressed children from a private school and a party of nuns nearby, to hear the healthy cries of eight-year-old cockney children inviting Lesley to, "Kick him, then you'll 'ave a longer ride." We took them home. Wearily we handed the children over to the parents and then checked that the classrooms would be ready for the work explosion bound to take place the following morning.

It had been decided to use Phil's classroom for the four animals while Phil could use Chris's room for the tape magazine being prepared on the visit. [Phil also supervised normal curriculum development for the children, when they were not engaged on work connected with the animal study.] For discussion purposes the children from both classes divided themselves into four groups to work on either the lion, giraffe, rhinoceros, or elephant. To secure an immediate response we decided to let all of them work on their wire models on the first day so that a recognizable shape would emerge and stimulate their interest. Unfortunately, the chicken wire proved obdurate and stronger wire cutters had to be secured. By dinnertime some sixty children, three adults, and four emerging six-foot-high giant animals were combining to produce anarchy. As only the adults appeared able to cut the wire, numerous scratches and tears were appearing all over us. The inevitable tin of powdered paint fell and added to the confusion. A quick conference after lunch produced a decision to

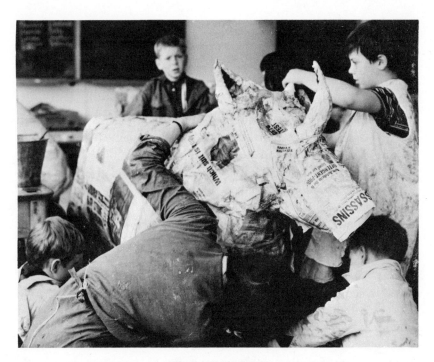

The animals grow.

work with two groups at a time. This division of work proved fairly successful and was adhered to for the remainder of the craft work.

By the end of the second day, four distinctly zoological wire shapes occupied a large area of the classroom. However, after an application of papier-mâché the elephant's legs buckled, the giraffe's head fell off, and the overweight rhinoceros kept toppling over. Only the lion maintained some show of dignity—the children had insisted on his lying down, as he had been observed at Whipsnade.

Although Chris and the children repaired the animals, quite obviously they needed help. To ensure that the papier-mâché, calico covering, plastering, and painting stages were supervised adequately and the work completed reasonably quickly, additional adult supervision was necessary. At that particular moment Mrs. Holder, Tony's mother, came over to see me about another matter, and I appealed to her. She is a warmhearted, generous woman, and her response was immediate, "Leave it to me, my ducks, I'll come over first thing in the morning."

She and other parents who were drawn in proved invaluable in assisting the children to mix plaster, cut calico, prepare paints, run errands for additional materials, and above all in helping them to clear up the classroom at the end of each day.

During the period of constructing the animals the children's insistence on detail quite surprised us. A strong argument arose within a group as to whether the rhinoceros should be the African or Indian species—apparently the African rhinoceros has two horns. On numerous occasions, all work was suspended while they scoured the school and local library for extra books that would give greater accuracy to their models; the rhino's tail was a case in point here.

The elephant's tusks were fitted incorrectly and only changed when a triumphant Gillian produced a photograph proving exactly where the tusks were sited in relationship to the trunk. The children worked from photographs to fit the lion's mane and tail, having decided on a lion rather than a lioness. Mrs. Holder provided two brand new mops, which the children dyed to produce the mane. When painting the giraffe, they discovered that the spots became more diffused around the legs.

In encouraging this type of accuracy through the use of books, it became easier for the children naturally to turn towards simple sources of reference when they began their written work.

Their research came from a fairly rich variety of simple animal books that we had acquired for the project. The children showed great enthusiasm in discovering how the animals lived, their homes, foods, weights, dimensions, and so on. An interesting point in the writing of the books was that many children made an index of information they had discovered and listed books they had used. In writing about the kangaroo Susan said, "They don't walk on four legs, but hop along and feed on grass, leaves, and fruit. Young kangaroos are very tiny, and they feed on their mothers' milk. They live in their mothers' pouches." Afterwards Susan admitted that much of what she had written she had observed for herself at Whipsnade. She also used three information books on kangaroos, one of which she had obtained from the local library.

Jane was concerned with the making of the giraffe and wrote that they "travel in herds and eat the leaves from young trees. They have very large eyes and long eyelashes." Graham discovered the weight of elephants, the hunting habits of the lion, and the meaning of the word *carnivorous!* As the investigation developed, it became obvious how interested the children became in factual knowledge, and how

The animals become part of the classroom environment.

they used this information in their imaginative writing. A great success was a small drama presentation in which each child became an animal and the stage bedecked with climbing ropes and ladders became part of the jungle. The children dressed as animals swarmed over ropes and climbed staging equipment, stopping at frequent intervals to introduce themselves to a delighted audience—a dramatic and stimulating end to a thoroughly enjoyable project.

Joint Environmental Study

In an area as rich in history and industrial development as Southwark, perhaps the main problem is to isolate those aspects that we can study in detail and link up to the creative drives within the school. For this environmental study, Joyce, a teacher of considerable intellectual resources linked with Barry, another teacher, whose dramatic talent will probably at some future stage lead him into the London

Theatre. This team was an extremely fortunate combination, for Joyce was able to concentrate her energies on writing a small history of Southwark (which may well become a standard source of reference for teachers in the Southwark area), while Barry was able to study in some detail developments in drama covering the Chaucerian, Elizabethan, Victorian (Dickens), and Modern times. Indeed it was within this framework of reference—except for a brief review by Joyce of developments within Southwark from Roman times—that the environmental study was made.

Their two classes divided into four groups and with the aid of two students began the project with a study of the immediate area surrounding the school. Children were asked to find their position from an ordinance survey map of the area (50 inches to a mile) but found this rather difficult. The accompanying questionnaires, however, restored interest and there was much discussion on types of building within the streets, the bricks that had been used, ages of housing, windows, garden space, among others. Sondes Street was described by one child as like being in the country, because it is distinguished from other roads in the area by having front gardens containing flowers, grass, and trees with little traffic noise.

The children questioned workmen on their road excavations, "Where are you taking the gravel?" "Why is the water gushing?" Later, Obeymi telephoned the Metropolitan Water Board and the Southwark Borough Council for information. After some half hour's conversations in which he jotted down facts given by some patient, good-hearted officials, he wrote an impressive account of why new drainage was necessary in nearby Portland Street. Other children sketched tall blocks of flats, which were used later in full-scale paintings. Linda and Janice investigated a small factory that specialised in the production of metal wheels and was linked to the ancient guild of tire-smiths. They were thrilled at the courteous reception they were given and the interest their questions aroused among the workmen.

A large measure of choice was given to the children for the development of neighborhood studies; these topics ranged through underground travel, Southwark Cathedral, and the activities of highwaymen in the 18th century. Involved beyond belief in his work Obeymi chose to study the London underground service. In nine pages of foolscap he gave a comprehensive and detailed account of our tube (subway) travel. From a variety of books, letters, and telephone calls he traced not only underground development, past and future, but established which lines were the deepest and longest and which had the fastest elevators and largest escalators. He also discovered that on the proposed new Victoria line "a mechanical shield armed with powerful sharp cutters has been developed to bite into London's blue clay." To complete his study, Obeymi made a model underground station with battery-operated electric light.

Christine wrote extensively on bus routes through Southwark. Using a map of the borough she traced bus routes and the different areas for which each service catered.

Quite a number of children selected to study London Bridge [and, incidentally, were highly critical of the decision to sell this famous landmark to America]. Fred traced the bridge from its first-century Roman use, through Viking attack to its misuse in medieval times by people starting fires and endangering wooden houses built on the bridge. Mario spoke of the architectural failures of our Norman ancestors who made the pillars of the bridge too thick, thus speeding up water flow to a torrent. A study of Clink Street aroused much interest because of its legendary prison—we still use the slang term *clink* for prison—and the discovery by children of some of the original cells. The Elephant and Castle study provoked an examination of the many roads converging at this London landmark, including the original Roman Road that ran through Southwark. The legend of the Elephant and Castle being named after the Infanta di Castello (a Spanish Princess) who stayed at one of the local inns was examined with much interest but evoked polite disbelief.

Lesley and Janice made a study of Southwark Cathedral, dealing in an intense and emotional manner with the greed, murder, and untimely death of Mary Overies' lover, which led to the establishment there of a nunnery in the seventh century. The development of the Cathedral at Southwark through Nunnery, Priory, and Church aroused less enthusiasm, although Janice wrote at length on Saxon name derivations. Other studies involved Southwark civic services, breweries, bridges, coaches, and highwaymen. Many interesting and complicated models were made by children as part of their research.

While these individual pieces of research were being pursued, Joyce gave a series of lessons to both classes tracing the development of Southwark from the first century A.D. to the present day. Through the use of the overhead projector many valuable manuscripts and maps were shown to the children. At the same time our copying machine provided exciting examples of these rare documents for the children's folders.

Investigation of the area west of London Bridge (which prompted and enriched many of the individual researchers through maps and questionnaires) provided the lead-in for an examination of drama developments in Southwark. Barry began by talking to both classes about inns and their function, both for entertainment and as coach stops in medieval travel. He examined in detail the Tabard Inn where Chaucer's travelers of the Canterbury Tales made their start and the importance of the George Inn as a coach stop. Visits were then made to the George Inn, and our children were able to see one of the Shakespearean plays, which are still regularly performed in the inn's courtyard.

An exploration of Bankside revealed the plaque of the old Globe Theatre. Barry was able to explain that because of their unpopularity in Elizabethan times many theatres had to be built outside the City walls, leading to the enrichment of drama developments on the south side of the river. The children were fascinated to discover that many theatregoers of that period arrived by barge, rather than use the inadequate road system of that time.

On their return to school a group was made responsible for a large-scale model of the Tabard Inn, which the children insisted on displaying at a certain height, so that viewing would be through the courtyard gates exactly as a traveler would see the inn on entrance.

Imaginative stories were then written by the children; as pilgrims they described their stay at the inn on the way to Canterbury. To our surprise they were very interested in Chaucer's tales, and many sensitive portraits of the leading characters emerged in their writing. In describing the Miller Michael wrote, "This kindhearted man, as ugly as a bull with a wart on the side of his nose, used his thick beard to tickle the wife of Bath's neck." Bobby said of the Merchant, "He had a gloomy face, with even gloomier eyes, yet through his honesty he could always hold his head up high." Stephen wrote as a traveler and described his reception at the inn: "A servant helped me off my horse and charged me a penny for his labors. It was a bad start, but I hastily paid him for I knew too well these rude little fellows. I got a drink, for the dust on the roads had given me quite a thirst."

By now a flourishing play began to take shape based on the

pilgrims' arrival at the Tabard Inn in which each told his tale. A film of Chaucer's England gave valuable background material when the children planned the shape and dialogue of the play. As each traveler told his story, strolling players dramatized it. Other groups provided entertainments for the inn's visitors, using medieval dance and song styles.

In their study of Elizabethan drama and in particular the work of the old Globe Theatre children were introduced to stage forms of that period in which the stage projected forward surrounded on three sides by the audience. Children wrote long and imaginative accounts of theatre presentations at the Globe. Christine wrote of her long journey by barge and the excitement she felt at hearing the trumpet sounds on the river indicating the start of the play. Pauline gave a vivid description of the theatre with thick oak doors, peeling plaster, and elaborate carvings on the stage. She wrote, "When the play started all was silent, then someone called across the theatre to his friend. Father thought the play was silly and began to throw tomatoes at the actors. Everyone left laughing." Drama developments in Victorian times and the present day also were examined.

They completed the study with an evening performance in which the children, acting as guides at an exhibition of work, discussed their research and presented part of Chaucer's Canterbury Tales for parents and friends of the school.

Conclusion

I feel that in evaluating the contribution these three team studies made to the intellectual enrichment within our school, we should not neglect the social developments emerging through relationships between children and adults in less familiar surroundings. There is much to be said for any scheme that encourages children and adults to leave their little "boxes" and to plan, cooperate, and work together for the greater good.

Less happy is the undeniable fact that relationships at times can and do break down. A teacher can become dissatisfied with the standards and efforts of a colleague, with whom a previous harmonious staffroom relationship had been established. [I heard of one teacher from another school who left the staff because of this.]

Positive gains were made in parental cooperation, and some very deep friendships have been formed through using our mothers in these team studies. Mrs. Holder gave strength just when it was needed in the zoo venture. Mrs. Morris took small groups to London Bridge for plaque rubbings. Mrs. Saker helped children in their researches at museums, and so it went. The use of a copying machine, overhead and film projectors, and tape recorders all played their part in realistic and meaningful studies. How far team teaching should be used in a school where the integrated day is such an important feature is a matter for conjecture. What cannot be denied is the success that greets the efforts of mature and professional adults who combine to enrich the intellectual and social life of their children.

5. Teaching Reading in the Infant School

ANN FRYER

ANN FRYER is Headmistress of Brocks Hill Infant School, Oadby, Leicestershire. Previously she was Head of Bell Street Infant School, Wigston, Leicestershire. She holds a Diploma in Special Education and taught slow learners for seven years, specializing in reading problems.

You who are reading this book are among the lucky ones. I doubt if most of us can even remember what it was like having to learn to read. Reading has become so much a part of our daily life that it is hard to imagine what it is like to be illiterate. We have broken the code of the written symbol, and a printed page is something we turn to quite naturally for pleasure and information.

The adult illiterate is denied this source of communication. He cannot read his mail, fill in forms, read the newspapers or public notices or transport timetables, look up what film is on the cinema or what programs are on radio or television; he cannot buy goods from a mail-order catalogue or read hire/purchase agreements or other legal documents. He has to ask what the destination signs on buses read and get someone else to look up a telephone number. How does he keep in touch with distant friends or relatives who are not on the telephone? or write a note to school about his child? An illiterate housewife cannot follow a cookery recipe or make out a shopping list. This lack of independence must be very humiliating and a constant reminder of one's own inadequacy and, of course, in a civilized society there is a severe limitation in the number of employment possibilities open to an adult illiterate. If he were blind he would meet with sympathy and understanding, but illiteracy is not a socially acceptable handicap; anyone suffering from it is made to feel inferior.

When we learn that one in ten students have left our secondary schools as nonreaders and many more have not achieved real fluency, we are confronted with the living proof that our traditional methods of teaching reading have failed.

Many believe that if children have not made some real progress in learning to read by the age of eight years, then their chances of ever being really fluent are diminished. This realization places a heavy responsibility on the primary schools for making a successful start in reading studies.

I worked with older nonreaders in schools for seven years and saw the demoralizing effect that an inability to read often had on these youngsters. By the time they were 10 and 11 years old, many of them had given up trying. An early enthusiasm they may have felt had been submerged by many factors: being pushed too early; being neglected when ready; being given unsuitable or uninteresting reading material; absence through illness or truancy; frequent changes of schools attended; emotional disturbance; poor home circumstances; having an undetected hearing or sight loss; being bored or unhappy in school; being badly taught with unsuitable methods; being a strong individualist in a heavily conformist society; being unfavorably compared with an older or younger sibling, and so on, endlessly.

Children can suffer from a multitude of problems and be the victims of unhappy circumstances, which make the interpretation of a "happy childhood" as being a carefree, untroubled period of growth a gross oversimplification.

However, with the knowledge we have gained from research into the ways children learn and the factors that can inhibit learning, together with the availability of modern materials, I like to believe that we can improve our teaching over the whole ability-range. Fundamentally, we should be able to change the attitude of our students and improve the lot of our next generation of parents.

In the modern British primary school there is a strong concern not merely with performance but with a child's attitude to learning.

In the past we have been guilty of overstructuring our schools and overorganizing our children so that they became too dependent on the adult stimulus and lost the ability or desire to cope with any responsibility for their own learning.

Early experiments with "group method" (where the groups were chosen by the teacher and their tasks allotted by her) were not really successful. One example of this is a class where the groups were given the names of animals—tigers, lions, kangaroos, and giraffes. At 9:30 a.m., directed by the teacher, the kangaroo group wrote their news, the tigers read, the lions built with structural apparatus, and the giraffes wrote their news. At a given signal from the teacher the groups swapped around. The kangaroos were now reading, the tigers building, the lions transferred to number activities, and the giraffes read books. This practice continued through all the permutations—despite the tiger who might be bursting with an exciting news event at 9:30 a.m., or the lion who might find himself with a complicated connector structure unfinished when the signal was given. The interest, span of concentration, and involvement of these children were given no importance in this relentless pursuit of a system centered around the teacher and frequently led to conflict between teacher and child.

This practice has now largely disappeared, and in the modern approach children mingle freely, grouping and regrouping themselves as interests and abilities meet.

One class I would like to describe to you met in an old building and contained 40 children between the ages of five and seven years in the care of Mrs. Bray, a gifted and experienced teacher. The large building bricks, the woodwork, and the sand were kept in a space beside the cloakroom and were shared with another class—children from both rooms could be found there at most times during the day. You could visit here on different days and not see precisely the same situation, but on one such occasion this is the sort of thing you might see:

Some children are writing, some sitting on a homemade mat reading, and some may be weighing, using Dienes or Cuisenaire mathematics materials. Some are in the Wendy House, perhaps one or two are painting or at the Discovery Table. Some children are watching and learning from the activities of others. A group may be playing a word game with the teacher, having milk at the lunch table, or visiting another class to experiment with musical instruments. The social benefits and language development are undeniable, for it is by working and communicating with others that understanding grows—common understanding between child and child and between children and teacher.

"Some children will be watching and learning from the activities of others."

There is no place for fear and boredom here. Nevertheless, with all this going on, the teacher can tell you without reference to her notes and records exactly how Andrew is progressing with his reading, which sounds are giving Elizabeth trouble, that Dennis is going through an insecure phase because of trouble at home and needs an extra boost to his confidence, that Kathryn is showing a feeling for design in two and three dimensions, and that Richard has had a renewed interest in number activities since he became friendly with Mark.

The equipment, which is easily accessible to all the children, has been carefully selected and is constantly under review in the light of what is needed as the children's interest and skills develop.

We no longer have rooms crammed with desks and tables at which an active five-year-old is expected to sit all day. Our apparatus is kept on open shelves and can be chosen by the children when needed. No artificial barriers are created between subjects, allotted set periods on a timetable. Usually the only timetable you will find is for the use of the assembly hall, and even this can be altered, subject to agreement between teachers.

"A group may be playing a word game with the teacher . . ."

Teachers have the same amount of furniture allocated to a classroom and arrange it according to personal preference. One typical arrangement of furniture in my school can be seen on the Plan of Class Furniture for 40 Children.

Key to Plan of Class Furniture for 40 Children

a Open waist-high shelves with equipment easily accessible for children to choose. The top surface can be used for displays, nature table, science exhibitions, and so forth.
b Bench surface for display or work in process.
c Low movable furniture units on castors, having twenty-four drawers and pegboard backing.
d Portable room divider with pinboard surface on one side and pegboard on the reverse.
e Book display unit.
f Wendy House with dressing-up box.
g Shop.
h Wall cupboards, floor to ceiling.

k Shaded area kept uncluttered, with furniture for children working on the floor and for gathering the children together for stories, poetry, class discussions, and other group activities.

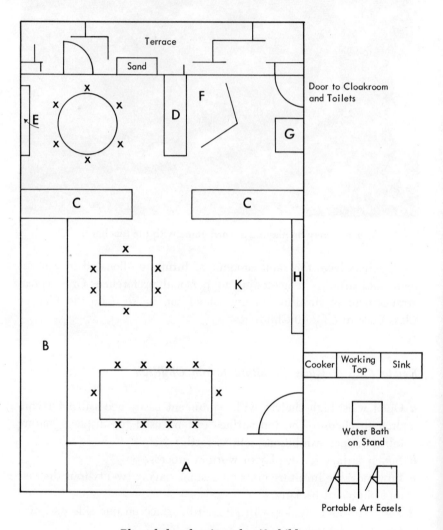

Plan of class furniture for 40 children.

In the plan of the classroom, note that there is seating space at tables for only twenty-two children. We find that this is ample in a free program as there are always some children who are working else-

"Shaded area kept uncluttered with furniture for children working on the floor . . ."

where: on the floor building with big bricks, "poleidoblocs," and other construction sets; or at the sand tray, water bath, or painting easels; or standing at the Science Table, in the Wendy House, or by the shop; sitting on the floor in the Book Corner reading; visiting the school library; or baking. This leaves us with a larger space for circulating and as a result fewer paint jars are spilled and a carefully constructed model is rarely knocked over.

In my own school we do not break for a midmorning or midafternoon playtime. Officially, school starts at 9:15 a.m. and finishes at 3:15 p.m., with a lunch period from 12 noon to 1:30 p.m. Most of the children are in school well before 9:15 a.m., some of them up to half an hour early. They may come in to their classroom or the library when they arrive and start on whatever they are interested in, whether or not the teacher is present. For example, they might have a story they are eager to write, or some mathematics left unfinished from the previous day. They keenly desire to have first choice of a popular piece of apparatus; or yet again they may want to visit a younger or older sibling's class to be shown something interesting. Maybe they want to feed the pets, listen to the tape recorder or sit and talk with their friends. There is no need to blow a whistle or ring a bell to signify the start of morning school because by 9:15 a.m. they are all in anyway. The teaching staff also arrive at least half an hour early, which gives time to chat, to mount pictures for the wall, to set out some interesting item brought from home, or to write up some notes, or discuss a problem with a colleague and get the benefit of her experience.

The teachers all get on well together and it is essential that they should. In a school where there is a deep interest in the individual personalities and development of children, discussions that are part of the scene before and after school bring a close sense of comradeship and cooperation between teachers. If someone has a good idea, it is shared with the rest of the staff; classes frequently combine for various purposes, and doors are rarely closed.

A feeling of friendship between the adults in a school creates an

"They may visit a younger or older sibling's class to be shown something interesting . . ."—like this collection of wooden objects.

atmosphere that brings out a better response in the children. When the nerve ends are not blunted by fear and repression, they can develop the sensitivity to absorb experiences and create exciting adventures of the imagination, which transform the mundane into the extraordinary.

The children are involved in what they have chosen and thus there are few discipline problems or conflict between adult and child.

Possibly the greatest change in our schools has been the shift of emphasis from the more "passive" passing-on of subject matter from teacher to children to the more "active" involvement of the child in the learning situation. We start with the child's natural curiosity about the world and provide a stimulating environment in which he can explore and discover for himself and be given expert guidance when needed. Nowadays we try to foster initiative, courage, enthusiasm, imagination, creativity, and compassion for others. Today, we take a wider view of the child than that based on measurable performance.

"Adventures of the imagination which transform the mundane into the extraordinary . . ."

I believe that children are educated more naturally and more effectively in a relaxed, secure atmosphere where self-discipline is widely
practiced than in a formal authoritarian situation where a child who is
not seen to be actively working is considered to be wasting his time.

The more varied and interesting the opportunities are in a school,
the more chance a child will have to discover and develop any talent
he may possess. In a modern school you would hardly find a rigid
scheme of what one might expect every five-, six-, or seven-year-old to
achieve. The achievement of any seven-year-old depends on what he
was capable of at two, three, four, five, and six; and his knowledge
will depend on what intelligence he has brought to his experiences.
It is part of the educator's job to offer the opportunity to develop the
senses, not to limit or inhibit a child's potential by concentrating too
narrowly on a predetermined curriculum geared to the average level.

If children are compelled to go to school, then they have a right
to be provided with experiences suitable to their present level of social,
emotional, and intellectual development—ensuring an even progress
at a rate suitable to their capacity. This belief does not mean that only
the right physical conditions must prevail; but of equal and possibly
greater importance is the human environment—something one can
only describe as "atmosphere." A situation where individual differences
and levels of ability are accepted, where the development of one talent
or skill is not overemphasized at the expense of others, where a natural
gift for early reading has no special virtue attached to it but is recognized as one of the natural differences between children like being
tall, having a quick number sense, or showing a gift for art.

Some children learn to read and write very easily and with little
prolonged assistance. Others who have been deprived of early experiences of books and speech often have poor language development and
require extra help and encouragement, through a longer prereading
period. Opportunities to increase vocabulary, a challenging and stimulating program of experiences, practices increasing visual and auditory
discrimination, activities building confidence in their own ability to
tackle skills thereby leading to greater independence, and the freedom
to develop at an individual rate remove much of the stress and tension
out of learning to read that so many children have had to suffer in the
past.

Reading is not something that every child can absorb through his
pores. Do not assume that if a child is placed in a cheerful environment with nice books at hand he will automatically become literate

in time. A negative attitude to reading can create unnecessary delay and sometimes dissipates a child's eagerness and expectations and results in a loss of confidence in his teacher. What we teachers must do is to become expert in recognizing the signs of reading readiness in a child so that we can give him the greatest possible chances of success.

When a child enters school it is important that a teacher does not have preconceived ideas about his stage of development based on his chronological age. (This is also true of children who transfer to your school at any age.) During the first few weeks in a free situation much can be learned by talking with the child and observing him:

What activities does he choose?
Does he choose easily or need guidance?
How long is his span of concentration?
Is he sociable and confident in his contacts with other children and teacher?
Does he show imagination in his drawing, or building, or conversation?
Is he able and willing to carry out requests and keep a message in his mind?
Does he have a good vocabulary and express himself fluently?
Has he good hand/eye coordination?
Can he listen with interest to stories and remember what he has heard?
Has he the ability to count events in sequence, e.g. his route to school?
Does he take an interest in books and pictures?
Can he share or participate in group activities?
Does he talk about his own drawings or paintings?
Is he dependent on adults or older children to instigate an activity?
Is he curious about the activities of others?
Does he belong to a children's library?
What do you know about his home background?
Has he been in hospital or suffered a serious illness?
Can he perceive differences between similar, but not identical pictures?

For example:

"Can he select from different but similar shapes the one which identically matches . . . ?"

Can he select from six or seven different but similar shapes the one which identically matches the one he is given? For example:

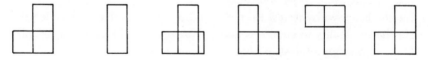

Can he do this with single letters or combinations of letters?

For example:

b:	d p q b d	cat:	act cat can cot cat eat
o:	d e p a o	boat:	boat beat about coat boat
ea:	eo ae ca ea ac	pbdg:	gbdp bpdg pbdg pdbg
on:	an in no oo on	wmnv:	wmvn wmnv mvwn mwnv

What do you know about his aural perception?
Can he pick out of a group of named objects those which have names starting with the same sound? Can he play "I Spy?"

Teachers of infants need to be skilled observers of children and have the ability to relate what they see to the professional knowledge

96

they have about different methods and materials. It is part of a teacher's job to know what the different approaches and methods are, what materials are available and to apply this knowledge to the picture she has compiled about an individual child. Some children may be ready for one method, some for another. An awareness of the different techniques that have been developed will better qualify you to select an approach that would offer a child his greatest chance of success.

If a happy and relaxed child whose development suggests reading readiness does not in fact seem to be making any progress, it might be wise to check on whether or not there is a medical reason for this. I am sure that many children who have been considered slow or backward are actually suffering from an undetected handicap. Early medical investigation of a suspected defect can save a child unnecessary difficulty and he can get the medical attention he needs.

We have lost the interest of numbers of children in the past by separating reading from the rest of the school curriculum, instead of letting it be an integral part of their daily experience to be enjoyed as much as the sand, water, Wendy House, or mathematics. Surely, when he wants to bake some cakes, the degree of child involvement and motivation in reading a recipe is higher than when his usual reading experience is reading a page of a set primer every day, if the teacher has time.

Contrary to popular opinion, I believe that the ritual hearing of one page a day from an early primer can positively inhibit progress, apart from being a waste of time for both child and teacher. In this situation reading becomes a chore for the child and a bore for the teacher. The meaning of the sentences and their relationship to those going before and those to follow in building up a story sequence are often lost by the disjointed way in which the book is tackled. I have seen this practice applied to quite fluent readers with the explanation that "they like me to hear them read and I can only manage one page a day." One possible explanation of the children "liking" this might be that if the teacher is anchored to her desk most of the day hearing children read, then they too want a share of her undivided attention. What other valuable reading experiences are being sacrificed and how much real progress is being made is questionable at best.

A fluent reader's comprehension of what he has read may be better judged by having a little talk with him from time to time and letting him tell you the gist of a story in his own words. Discuss any descriptive passages or unusual words used. Perhaps he can think of other sentences where these words might be used again. What about the personality of the characters in the story? Does he know of a similar character in real life or in another story? Does the sequence of events remind him of anything?

The less fluent readers still do not need to be heard every day if you are making the right provision of other material in your room. When they ask to read to you, then hear a meaningful series of pages so that the piece being read at least makes sense and provides a talking point.

With the beginners, it would be more valuable for them to be doing a hundred and one other reading activities, strengthening their readiness and development to the point where they too are able to read a sequence with meaning. It would be unwise to start a child on a graded reading scheme unless you were really confident that he will be successful with it as this can make such a difference to his attitude and self-confidence. If there is any doubt as to his ability, it is better to concentrate on other word games and pre-reading activities until confidence is established.

Children in a lively classroom are reading all the time, discovering the meanings of words and sentences as they are needed to pursue a chosen activity. Writing reinforces reading, and both complement each other—developing at a roughly equal rate and relating to the child's spoken vocabulary.

A page a day of reading is like insisting on a page a day of writing in a "news book." More often than not this becomes a sentence or few words rather than a creative piece of work. Some teachers used to choose one child's piece of news and write it on a blackboard to be copied by all the children. Copying a sentence from a blackboard demands quite an advanced step in coordination for a five- or six-year-old. Looking up to a blackboard, finding the letter he wants and keeping the pattern of it in his mind while transferring it to a page of a book on his desk can be quite an ordeal when he is really not too familiar with letters and words. There are far less laborious ways of helping a child to become familiar with letters and practicing writing them: tracing over letters and words that the teacher has written for him in his book; writing underneath the words; tracing sandpaper letters with a finger; writing words in candle wax and painting a color-wash over them; making letters in plasticine or dough that can be

"Children in a lively classroom are reading all the time—discovering the meanings of words and sentences."

baked in an oven; feeling under a cloth for wooden or plastic cut-out letters and trying to identify them without looking; making up words and sentences with letter tablets in a word-building box; drawing letters with a stick in sand; printing them with an ink pad and printing set; cutting them out of felt—these are just a few of the ways children are able to enjoy and learn.

I have seen whole news books from quite able children—books full of repetitive sentences that one might expect from beginners who are just gaining confidence in writing on their own. "I played ball with John" as a day's written effort from a seven-year-old fluent reader who can write displays a certain lack of stimulus and involvement in his work. It seems to me that many children lose what might be a genuine desire to write creatively in striving to think of a few simple sentences that will earn them a tick ($\sqrt{}$) or star in their book.

Surely it is much more relevant and enjoyable when a child tells you some item of interest for him to write it in his book "so that we

"Making up words and sentences with letter tablets in a word-building box."

don't forget it,"—perhaps a discovery made at a science table could be recorded, or an invitation to some friends to a tea party in the Wendy House, or a letter to a farm or railway station asking if he might visit, or a letter to a firm requesting information for a project, or a letter of thanks for a favor received, or a written contribution to a class book or newspaper. Every day there is the opportunity to write a poem, a story, or a play script; or there are labels that need to be written for wall displays and answers to a chosen assignment to be recorded. The quality of the content becomes of a much higher standard when a child is involved in what is written rather than just performing an expected habitual act, and the chances of his wanting to write and continuing to enjoy it are vastly increased.

Children who already have established the habit of writing only one line a day can often be encouraged to extend this by writing a question about what they have written; for example:

CHILD: I went to the seaside on Saturday.
TEACHER: What did you do when you got there?

CHILD: Here is my tortoise.
TEACHER: Has he got a name? What do you do with him in winter?

"Labels that need to be written for wall displays . . ."

This technique has a dual purpose: the child reads what you have written (either on his own or with your help) and extends his thoughts about his writing. Even when the pieces written are quite long stories, a question or a comment are more fun to receive than a tick (√). One of my young teachers, Caroline Laurance, is particularly good at this and her class books are always a joy to read. Two examples might serve as illustrations:

Robert (6) wrote a humorous story about "A Man in the Woods" who every day had a different adventure. One day's adventure read, "Once he went out into the woods, and he met a fox and he shot the fox and pulled the fox home. He had fox on toast!"

Beneath the story Miss Laurance drew a face with a smile from ear to ear and wrote, "I did enjoy your story, Robert. This is what my face looked like when I was reading it."

Another child, a small girl, wrote about a trip with her family. "When we got to Skegness we went on to the beach and when we had been there for about five minutes it began to rain. Then we had to hurry and get off the beach and it was horrible because I had taken my shoes and socks off, so when the wind blew, all the sand got on my feet and it stayed there because I had already had a paddle, and so when my mummy dried me the sand hurt me."

Comment: "Do you know, Lynsey, the same thing happened to me when I was a little girl. I can remember now the scratchy, gritty feeling of the sand between my toes. What a coincidence that it should have happened to both of us."

The children love to read these personal touches written in their books by the teacher, and incidentally learn new words, which they absorb into their own written and spoken vocabulary. How much more interesting than a dry tick, which is done in a moment and does not even prove that a teacher had read the piece. If you demonstrate your interest in their writing and express pleasure in reading it, it creates a greater enthusiasm in the children; and gives them an incentive to write something they want to share with you.

What is more natural than a child wanting to imitate adults—father working on his car or weeding the garden? mother cooking or doing the housework? Children also want to imitate the adults in their environment in respect to reading, writing, and talking. Spoken and written language is as much a part of a normal child's world as houses, windows, or food and as interesting to explore and investigate as paint, play bricks, or large cardboard boxes. Some say that teachers should always tell stories to children, not read them from a book, but I believe that children should see their teacher reading a story that they can all enjoy. Let the children select a story from the Book Corner sometimes, and they will enjoy it again privately as a self-chosen activity.

Encourage children to use books for pleasure and information. If you are seen doing this, they will follow your example. In your classroom place appropriate books near class collections and activities; for example, near the Nature Table you would place books on shells, stones, flowers, plants, leaves, trees. On the Science Table there would be books about magnets, light, sound, simple science experiments, electricity, the weather. In the Wendy House you would put books about going shopping, laundry day, people at work, comics, or children's newspapers. Near the dressing-up box a couple of books on historical costumes or fancy dress might spark off a few good ideas. In the cookery corner, books about food, hygiene, and cooking recipes are obvious choices. Near your stock of waste materials (junk) place your books on "Things to Make and Do," Paper Cutting and Folding, Model Making, and so forth. Measuring, weighing, counting, number-work cards, and a selection of number text books would be displayed near the scales, tape measures, rulers, Cuisenaire, Dienes, and other mathematical apparatus. With the musical instruments you would require books about famous composers, stories of such musical films as *Mary Poppins* and *The Sound of Music*, illustrations of instruments of the orchestra, and so on. These books are all in addition to those you would have in your class library or Book Corner.

What books should be found in the Book Corner? First of all, this corner must look attractive and welcoming, and the books must be well displayed. One or two chairs and some small carpets allow children to choose how they would like to make themselves comfortable when reading or looking at books. A wide range of books, fiction and nonfiction, should cater to all abilities. Some expensive books with lovely pictures, hard covers and, good quality paper are worth the initial cost; a sample of attractive books from a range of reading schemes; books made by other children for current and past interest topics; expendable "paperbacks" like *One Fish, Two Fish* and *Clifford, the Big Red Dog* [which I believe are American publications and are greatly enjoyed by our children]; myths, legends, folk tales, fairy stories; a well-illustrated encyclopedia, picture dictionaries; poetry books; books on topics of perennial interest such as planes, trains, ships, zoo animals, pets, ballet dancers, horse riding; stories about historical figures. If possible it is a good idea to have books with illustrations but no text, so that children can make up their own stories from the sequence of illustrations. Very few such books are available, but I consider them to be an important extra in any classroom; they can be easily homemade and greatly encourage both readers and nonreaders in making up their own stories, increasing their vocabulary, and fluency.

Illustrations can be obtained from a variety of sources—magazines, photographs, publicity material offered by manufacturers, airlines, and towns. Sort through your portfolio material and arrange a series of pictures in sequence. Trim and mount on colored cards, pastel paper,

"Checking a friend's spelling against a picture dictionary . . ."

or brown paper. Here are examples of the different types of picture books we have made:

The first book was made up of illustrations showing a typical local house and family of father, mother, son and daughter with their two pets. The family is shown taking a day trip to the seaside, having a picnic, collecting shells, looking at rock pools and sea birds, and finally returning home.

One possible story text for these pictures could be:

Leicester is a town in England, and here is number 46 Coombe Rise. Mr. and Mrs. Edwards live here with their two children Michael and Ruth. They have two pet dogs called Patch and Rover. Patch is a Dalmatian and belongs to Ruth. Rover is a Labrador and belongs to Michael. Mr. Edwards has got the car out of the garage because they are all going out for the day. The car is a Ford Zephyr, four-door sedan. Here they are arriving at the beach. It is a sunny day and the beach is crowded with other families. Michael and Ruth put on their swimsuits, and, after having a swim, they have a game with the beach ball and the dogs join in. After their game they are hungry so Mr. and Mrs.

Edwards spread out the cloth, plates, and cups ready for a picnic tea.
They have egg-and-cress sandwiches, ham rolls, crisps (brittle candy),
fruit cake, ice cream, and coca-cola. After the meal, the children explore
some rock pools and collect shells and seaweed to take home. The sea-
gulls are screaming overhead looking for scraps of food left from the
picnic. They are having such a good time that the day passes very
quickly, and before long the sun starts to set, and they have to collect
all their things ready to go home again. It grows darker on the journey
home and Mr. Edwards turns the car headlights on. When they get
home Michael and Ruth have a glass of milk before going to bed.
What a happy day they have had! I wonder if they will dream about it?

Children telling the story put their own interpretation into the pictures and often identify themselves with the characters. One child
might invent an adventure about the dogs running off with the ball, or
collecting gull's eggs, or tell you of a personal incident that happened
when he visited the seaside. Others might describe some of their
favorite beach games, tell you some of the things they do on car journeys, or recount a dream they think the children in the picture book
might have had. Some children use these books to make up a game;
in which one child tells about one page and another child carries on,
so that they build up a story together.

Other popular picture-book themes are Space, Cowboys and In-
dians, Castles and Princesses, Farms, Pirates and Treasure, A Visit
to Another Country, and so on. It depends on the interests of the
children.

A second popular illustrated book without words was made up from
actual photographs taken in and around the school. These portrayed
members of staff, the caretaker, and groups of children working in a
variety of situations (Wendy House, library, cookery corner), with
a variety of apparatus (sand tray, water bath, percussion instruments,
mathematics equipment). This kind of book can be as long or as
short as you like, but, as you may imagine, its interest as a conversation piece in the classroom is obvious. The expense is negligible
being only the cost of the rolls of film and the album to mount the
pictures. We find, too, that this type of book has inspired children
and parents to take interesting photographs while they are on vaca-
tion—pictures which they have then brought to school to share with
the other children. One parent who visited Canada on business,

"Groups of children working in a variety of situations . . . with a variety of apparatus."

brought in his color slides, which we projected while he gave a talk to the children. An enjoyable and informative experience for us all.

Children are very good at making these books from pictures they collect or draw for themselves. Long before they are capable of writing their own stories, they enjoy arranging a sequence of illustrations in an imaginative and creative way and recording their stories on a tape recorder. You might ask a child's permission to write his story under the pictures he has arranged, so that it can be chosen as a reading book.

All the while we are trying to establish the notion that books are fun. They give pleasure and interest to those who make them and to those who look at them. We try to demonstrate that writing and reading are as natural and enjoyable a form of communication as talking and listening. By learning to read we can enjoy more than just the ideas and thoughts of those people we can hear; we can also benefit from the wealth of knowledge and literature that has been recorded by people we can never meet.

There is no magical formula for teaching children to read. They travel many different paths to achieve the same goal and take varying lengths of time over the journey. We try to smooth the way by removing well-known obstacles with skillful preparation and by re-

"A well-trodden route is one taken through a child's natural interest in the pictures he has drawn."

lieving unnecessary stress by pacing ourselves to the individual. A well-trodden route is one taken through a child's natural interest in the pictures he has drawn. In talking with the child about his picture, a teacher can invite a child to choose what he would like her to write about his picture, and then they read it together. According to the child's ability he might then go and trace the words over the teacher's writing or copy the sentence underneath.

When children gain more confidence, they are encouraged to write the words they know without help and are given a personal word book. This is a small notebook, and the letters of the alphabet are written in sequence on the top right-hand corner, one letter per page, i.e. first page— **Aa**; second page— **Bb**; third page— **Cc**, and so on. In i.t.a. (initial teaching alphabet) we have one page for every sound symbol. This is used when a child needs a word he either cannot write for himself from memory or find by referring to a class word list, and after encouraging him to find the appropriate page according to the initial letter of the word the teacher writes it in his notebook. It is not long before each child compiles quite a substantial personal word list, and you will often hear one child ask another, "Have you got *circus* in your list? I need it, and Mrs. Bray is busy." All sorts of words are exchanged in this way. Another game they play with one or two friends is turning to a particular letter in their notebooks and checking their list of words against each other, asking in turn, "Have you got *elephant?* or *eggs?* or *every?* or *empty?*" And they use a self-devised method of scoring for words not in the other child's list.

This personal notebook works well in conjunction with a class set of homemade wall pockets—one card for each initial letter, one pocket for each card. On these cards are written those words most frequently requested by the children and regular additions are made to it during the term. It is surprising how quickly children learn to refer to the wall pockets before asking their teacher for a new word, and if they cannot find the one they need, they bring both their personal notebook and the card so that the word can be added to both simultaneously "in case someone else needs it." These wall pockets can save a busy teacher a great deal of time otherwise spent in writing out the most popular and frequently used words in each child's personal notebook and offers the children the opportunity of greater independence in looking up words for themselves. This activity is also good training for the later use of dictionaries and has a side benefit in that children often become interested in the other words listed on a card and ask the teacher or another child what they say, so that a lot of self-motivated incidental learning of new words takes place.

We use several graded reading schemes as one will have a more ready appeal to some children than to others. Whatever the topic of series might be we use a set of large wall pictures as an introduction to the characters in the books, and with a small group of children we discuss what words we might use to describe the picture. (The homemade books without words are excellent preparation for this.) The large wall pictures are similar to those illustrating the reading books, so that before a child chooses his book he is familiar with the contents. Another related activity might be to set out cardboard cutouts of the characters and their house, garden, trees, and so forth, along with matching words written on separate cards, to match the cutouts. The children often choose this activity, setting out a scene in different ways and making additional figures as the fancy takes them. This can be reinforced in various ways: with picture/word dominoes; making families in clay, plasticine, or pipe cleaners; houses from cardboard boxes; gardens by sowing grass seed on a tray lined with soil or blotting paper; furniture from matchboxes; Cuisenaire or color factor mathematics apparatus, and so on.

Words that cannot be illustrated like *come, is, to, play* can be introduced in another game which children enjoy. For this you need to make a set of instruction cards, e.g., "Go to the door," "Come here," "Play the piano," "Bring me a pencil," "Look out of the window," and so on. A small group is invited to play this game with you, and you show the cards to them reading aloud the instruction. The number of cards you introduce at any one time depends on the response you get from the children. Having read the cards with the children, you then select one card to hold up and ask if anyone can either mime the action (as in "Play the piano") or do what it says (as in "Go to the door"). This game is another that is available for children to choose as an activity, when you are not using it.

Another reading game is played by putting a picture with a sentence found in a reading book onto a display board or flannelgraph and by having a matching set of separate words in a pile nearby. Read the sentence with the group, e.g., "At the corner of the street was a house with a blue door." Then invite a child to offer to find the word *At*, another child to find the word *the*, another to find *corner* and match them under your sentence. Read the sentence again together when it has been built up. Now reverse the process. "Who can bring me the word *corner?*" "Now I want the color *blue*." When you have nearly all the words back again, see if anyone can tell you the words that are still left. These are group games that children like to play for themselves, and once you have introduced them to one or two groups, it is surprising how quickly the rest of the class catches on.

If a child becomes bored or restless when he is in a group playing these reading games, it is better to invite him to choose another activity as they are probably too difficult for him and he would be better employed doing something else. If his main reason for playing the game is that he wants to be with you, then give him an assurance that you will come and see what he has chosen when you have finished working with the group.

With some children it is necessary to write their reading books for them in order to capture their interest, particularly in the case of an older nonreader who would look and feel foolish with a book written for five-year-olds. I once had a seven-year-old boy called Andrew who was interested in numbers but showed little enthusiasm for books. His hobby was collecting car, bus, and train numbers, and this provided us with some obvious topics for his specially written books. From a motor sales showroom we obtained several advertising leaflets illustrating cars of different makes. We cut out one of each make and mounted them in a large book, one per page, allowing room beneath for some writing. A duplicate pocket-sized book was made for Andrew who was asked to spot the same make of car and record the number. The following day he brought his pocket book, and we started writing beneath the pictures of the cars he had spotted in his big book. For example: "Here is a Ford Popular. I saw one like this outside the paper shop last night. Its number was EUT 493." "There were two Cortinas in our street. One was my dad's, CUT 974, and the other belongs to Jane Williams' father, BEU 8." "I see a Rolls Royce, BBC 3, every morning at about half past eight going toward town. I wonder if the man driving it works at the BBC studios in town?"

Andrew obviously enjoyed making his book and said, "If I stand near the playground gate at dinner time and spot some more, can we do it again this afternoon?" This was very encouraging, and his enthusiasm captured the interest of other children in the class, who also started to make similar books. Soon, he could read not only his own book, but, in comparing his cars with the other children's, he learned their texts as well. From this we went on to buses and received a lot of help from the City Transport Department who sent us timetables, routes, and information about the recruitment of drivers and conductors. This information we read together and rewrote where necessary in Andrew's book. I do not know which of us was the happier when Andrew finally asked for a personal word notebook, "because I can do a lot of the words myself now, and I need only ask you for the hard ones."

It is easy to be concerned when a child takes a long time to achieve reading readiness, especially when anxious parents appear to place the responsibility for his nonreading on you, his teacher. But, if you can be confident that you are giving this child every opportunity and that in your professional judgment it would be wrong to try and rush things because of later consequences, then you can better reassure parents who are not trained teachers that you too have the best interests of their child at heart; and you can give them a picture of his present stage of development and how you are catering for it. This way both home and school can work together and you can relieve some of the natural anxiety that the parents feel, thereby taking any undue stress or pressure from the child.

There are so many pressures and circumstances working for and against children that it is only by knowing them as individuals, catering to their strengths and weaknesses of intellect and personality, that we can help make their time in school a creative period and not a destructive one.

Robert Frost wrote that "a poem, like love, should begin in delight and end in wisdom." What better aim can we in education have than that a child's journey through school should take the same path and begin in delight, continue in discovery, and end in wisdom?

6. Teaching Reading to Older Children

P. J. TANSEY AND DERICK UNWIN

P. J. TANSEY, *B.Sc., A.C.E. (Oxon), is a senior lecturer in education at Bulmershe College of Education, Reading, England. He has taught in schools in New Zealand and England for a total of fifteen years. With Derick Unwin he has published a number of articles on aspects of simulation in journals both in Great Britain and America, and their book,* Simulation and Gaming in Education *was published by Methuen in 1969. He has acted as educational consultant to the British Broadcasting Corporation.*

DERICK UNWIN, *M.A., B.Sc., is Senior Lecturer in New Media at the Education Centre, New University of Ulster, Northern Ireland. He is co-author of* Programmed Learning in the Schools, *Longmans, 1965, and co-editor of* Aspects of Educational Technology, *Methuen, 1967. For some time now he has been carrying out research into the use of new media in the teaching of reading.*

Introduction

The majority of children entering the English junior school (aged from seven to eight years) have acquired the basic reading skills in the infant school. For them the form that reading will take in their next

112

four years is the acquisition and reinforcing of phonic awareness through a series of graded readers. The acquisition of reading skill needs careful direction: this direction should be so designed to make reading a natural experience. Good teachers see reading as a fundamental communication art and integrate it with written and oral communication patterns.

As skills are learned the child is able to increase his feeling for fine distinctions of meaning by extending his vocabulary. Whatever method is used in the teaching of this reading process, it is of prime importance that the pupil should maintain his interest in learning. Figures have been offered from time to time that suggest that between ten and twenty per cent of the adult population of Great Britain do not read well enough to read *for pleasure*. The British Army has a School of Preliminary Education where young men whose reading age is so low as to be a bar to their effective use in the Army are taught to read. The results from this school are very good indeed, although the time allocated to the course is a brief ten weeks. One important reason why this complex skill can be taught so quickly is that the young soldiers have recognized the value of reading, seen their need of it and have been motivated to learn.

In the junior schools, creative writing, drama, and other pursuits are all used more or less efficiently to support reading. It has become increasingly recognized that to separate reading into an isolated compartment of the curriculum is to create an unnatural situation. If a child can communicate with others by talking, he frequently fails to see the point of learning to read better than he currently can, and if reading is considered to be a "subject" then it automatically takes on the appearance of artificiality and has an aspect of the mechanical. It is little consolation for the child to be told that he will need—and want—to read later on; the learning process needs immediate appeal. Thus reading should be relative to the child's present wants; encouragement to read is given by drawing the child's attention to books that have a relevance to topics that interest him at the moment.

Of course, when all the things that have to be said about the enjoyment of reading instruction and its purposefulness have been said, it must be borne in mind that reading is a skill. To attain competence in a skill, and especially in a complex skill, some educationists have reckoned it necessary to decide on the basic factors involved and then to practice these elemental skills repeatedly. Others believe that these factors which are the results of analysis have only limited use in the teaching situation, which is a synthesizing one.

Surely maximum reading attainment will come only if close attention is paid to those aspects of reading that could be described as formalistic. A child must be taught to recognize similarities and differences in the sounds, shapes, sizes, and—in some schemes—colors of images. He must have a knowledge of the sound values of letters and the techniques whereby this knowledge is used in the recognition of words. Also he must know that we write from left to right and down the page and that if he is to read effectively, then that is the way that he also will have to do it. With these skills it is hoped that the child will become able to break down new, unknown words into syllables for easier recognition and learn to read phrases instead of mere words. The teaching need not be a drudgery, and good teachers in our junior schools have found many and varied ways of making the learning interesting. Many tests of mechanical reading attainment are used in English junior schools, and some of these are dealt with in the section of this chapter that deals with testing.

So far there has been discussion about those who come to the junior school from the infant school already able to read. For some twenty per cent of the children who come to the junior schools the picture is not nearly so rosy. These are the children who are badly retarded in reading ability, some of whom are inevitably doomed to crippling illiteracy, and it is doubtful that the position can ever be completely cured by increasing the time or the level of instruction in the infant schools.

The causes of backwardness in reading are of many kinds and of great complexity. Some children are backward in reading for such reasons as physical illness, which has resulted in prolonged absences from school. Others suffer from poor home backgrounds where reading is not valued, for the school in England has embraced middle-class values, and cultural disadvantage is a serious factor in the poorer areas of both the large industrial cities and the pastoral and agricultural areas. Additionally, some children in our industrial areas have had poor teaching in their infant schools for a variety of reasons. Some areas are so unpleasant that good teachers will not stay, and infant schools have almost permanent vacancies and large classes. In other schools there is a high percentage of non-English-speaking immigrants making exceptionally heavy demands on the teacher's time. For all of these children, the junior school can diagnose areas of weakness and then apply remedial methods or forms of intensive coaching, which will bring the child up to a much improved level of literacy. Where staff is available and space can be found there is hope for such children.

Further, there is a group of children whose background weakness in reading does not stem from these artificially induced causes. These are the children whose inability to succeed is due to causes that originate in nature. There can be little doubt after the work of F. J. Schonell (1942) that there is a high positive correlation between intelligence and reading ability, although Houghton and Daniels (1966) have shown that it is possible to teach children to read even though their intelligence quotient suggested that they were ineducable. There are children with possible brain damage who have difficulty in the recognition of words, and some of these have the added disadvantage of poor articulation. It is uncertain how many such children there are in the United Kingdom, for although one survey found that they represented 1.5 per cent of all of the children in a limited area in the South of England, another leading authority found no positive evidence at all of such children in the South East of the country in 1966. For these children, few though they may be, it is probable that illiteracy is inevitable. It is not suggested that they cannot (with sympathetic care and skilled instruction) be taught to read. What is suggested is that in the British classroom of today with forty or more children and probably lack of equipment, space, and help it is almost impossible for the good, caring teacher to devote enough time to these children to enable improvement to be sustained or significant.

At a lecture to the International Reading Association, in London in 1963, Professor M. D. Vernon said:

Recent surveys have shown a decrease in the frequency of reading backwardness, but at eleven years about one per cent are almost totally illiterate and about twenty per cent considerably retarded. About nineteen per cent of entrants to junior schools are virtually nonreaders.

Reading Tests Used in Junior Schools

Reading is a multifaceted process, and as such it is necessary that progress in its attainment and diagnosis of areas of weakness should be measured. Teachers in English junior schools are largely aware of these needs, and a variety of tests are available for their use. A book of tests that is very widely used is that by Daniels and Diack (1958), and another, an excellent all-round book on reading by Moyle (1968) designed for preservice teachers, has a chapter on tests.

It is possible to separate these tests into three categories: tests available to measure *reading attainment, comprehension,* and *to diagnose.* Those dealing with reading attainment furnish the user with a reading age for the subject of the test. At the present time, in a number of English schools "reading age" is considered to be the end product of testing. It is not realized that this one piece of information in isolation is of very limited value. But if it is used to measure progress in the individual over a period of time, to compare the child with his peers, or to find areas of weakness in reading, the reading attainment test is of far more value than when its end result is just seen as an isolated reading age.

READING ATTAINMENT TESTS

Graded word-reading tests are the most commonly used tests of attainment. These measure the ability of a child to recognise words without the assistance of context. The words are arranged in groups of ten, and the procedure for finding the reading age of a child using these tests is to count the number of words that the child has recognised, divide this score by ten and add five years onto the total, which is then given in years and a decimal fraction of a year. Three tests are in common use: those by Burt, by Schonell, and by Vernon. These were standardized by Vernon and now may be used interchangeably if *Reading Ability,* the pamphlet No. 18 issued by the Ministry of Education, is used to compare their levels of difficulty.

COMPREHENSION TEST

For children of junior-school age a comprehension test that is often used is the *Silent Reading Test* by Schonell. There are two forms of this test, A and B; the test is designed for children within an age-range extending from below seven to over thirteen years and so covering the large majority of the children in the junior school, except for the retarded and the very able. The test consists of a series of short paragraphs with a question at the end. Before the child can answer the question he has to have read and understood the content of the paragraph. Moyle (1968) states that he has found that children gain a slightly higher score on Form A than on Form B. In all probability this does not matter with two provisos: that the individual teacher consistently uses the same form and that it is recognized that the test result is not an absolute thing but is merely to be used comparatively, as already stated.

GROUP TESTING

Time taken in testing individuals is time lost to other work, and because teachers are faced with large classes making constant demands on their time, individual testing is often replaced by group testing. Teachers are well aware that these tests are not as useful as individual tests, but they are often used as indicators of progress of the group as a whole. Individual tests are then used for those children who are felt to be in need of more detailed study. In general, group tests deal with a more limited ability-range than individual tests and thus may prove frustrating for a child whose ability does not lie within this range, especially if the test content is too difficult for him to manage.

DIAGNOSTIC TESTING OF READING SKILLS

Diagnosis of gross inability to read is in the province of the remedial teacher, of whom there is not a high proportion in junior schools, because of the comparative smallness of most junior schools and the fact that in-service training of these teachers has been neglected in the past. Diagnosis is also the responsibility of the educational psychologist who is employed by the Local Education Authority to be available for consultation as required by individual schools. He performs this function when made aware of the need in particular instances, and it is the duty of the class teacher to notify him about the cases, in the first place. A number of diagnostic tests are available; for example see Daniels and Diack (1958). Although class teachers should be familiar with numbers of these tests, the experienced teacher often depends on past experience for awareness of weakness, and the diagnostic testing of reading skills is not very widely practiced in junior schools.

In her survey of reading in the county of Kent (1953), Dr. Joyce Morris asked sixty head teachers to list the causes that resulted in poor and nonreaders at the end of their junior school courses, that is, at the age of eleven. These causes were then classified into those centered *on the child, on the home,* and *on the school.* Of 218 causes, 114 were child centered, 62 were home centered, and 42 were school centered. At that time the child-centered causes were broken down:

Number	Causes
52	mental disabilities
25	physical disabilities
24	personality problems
9	attendance
4	migration

In the ensuing years the latter cause, migration, has assumed much more significance.

Of the causes centered on the home, lack of encouragement accounted for 32 cases, poor cultural background for 9, mother at work and consequent poor language development for four, with the other 17 cases divided between ten causes. It is significant that television was held responsible for only two cases of reading backwardness. There are many head teachers who would dispute this view now, which shows the advances that television has made in the last fifteen years.

Of the school-centered causes, both methods and teachers were blamed as causes in 16 cases. The method most often criticized was that of beginning formal instruction too early. The teacher fault most often noted was lack of interest in the children. Both of these were blamed six times. Organization was held to be at fault seven times and wrong materials three times.

This survey presents a highly subjective view of the problem, but it has a value in that it does show the beliefs of those actually involved in the teaching, and, if the faults held to be school based are (or appear to be) underrepresented, this is understandable. A later paper by Dr. Morris published in Downing (1964) states:

Additionally, comparisons of poor and good readers left no doubt that, in general, juniors who are backward in reading are as under-privileged with their teachers as they are in respect of the age and ability range of their classes, their material classroom conditions and reading environment.

The writer concludes that late beginners who need the most encouragement in later schooling to become effective readers get the least, and so she blames a good deal of reading backwardness on the schools.

Methods of Teaching Reading

It is certain that no single method of teaching reading is used exclusively in any junior school in England. There is widespread feeling that no clearly superior method of reading instruction exists, and the wise teacher uses a variety of methods at what are thought to be appropriate times. The danger in using such an eclectic approach is that common to all eclecticism. The risk is that what is selected may not be fully understood and the teaching may disintegrate into a "hotch-potch" ("mish-mash") that serves only to confuse the children. Rule-governed operations are always easiest to assess, and in such a complex process as reading instruction the indiscriminate use of a wide variety of methods may serve to make the task of diagnosis of reading difficulty even more difficult.

Broadly speaking, there are two common methods of teaching a child to read, each with its eager advocates: the *whole methods,* such as "look-and-say," and the *part methods* typified by "phonics." The child of seven coming into the junior school has had little phonic training, and much of the previous emphasis in reading may have been on memorizing the shapes of words. Let us now look at some of the approaches most generally used in the junior schools, beginning first with "look-and-say."

WHOLE METHODS OF READING INSTRUCTION

Gates (1927) emphasized the importance of intrinsic methods of teaching reading rather than the phonic methods commonly in use at that time. This, together with the emphasis on silent reading in the late 1920's caused phonics to languish as a teaching method. It is claimed by some British experts that the **look-and-say method** (i.e., word-picture associations) has particular applicability for the duller section of a class, in that concrete words that can be illustrated help in vocabulary building. This method is certainly by far the most widely used of all methods in the infant schools where the child sees a word as a shape and not as a composite of individual letters. The child might first have his own name printed on a card; later he would learn the names of other children and common things in the room; finally, he would be able to obey instructions written on cards without ever having been made aware of the significance of the letters. However, mistakes that are made suggest that children (especially young children) have a limited span of attention; they do not see the whole word as a shape but pick out certain identifying indexes, which they use in word recognition. Look-and-say does in fact represent a change in emphasis from sound to the visual aspects of word recognition, and as a consequence of the introduction of this method publication standards have gone up; reading books have become much better illustrated. Efforts have also been made to build a certain vocabulary into books depending on this method—a vocabulary in which the liability to confuse word shapes is reduced as far as possible.

The **sentence method** is another whole method used widely in English schools, frequently in conjunction with the look-and-say method. In this, the whole is considered to be the sentence. The method has certain advantages because the sentences may evolve from centers of the children's interest. It is easy to integrate the reading scheme with other schemes when this method is used, and it has a motivational advantage. Typically, the lesson might begin with, say, a walk in the school grounds with the children free to observe. In the subsequent discussion their observations would be written down on the blackboard and later onto cards. The sentences would be discussed and pictorially represented, or they might be arranged into a "poem" which would then become the class poem. If a picture is used, the child would be asked to match the sentence below the picture with an identical picture. If a poem was made, the child might rearrange the jumbled sentences into the order of those in the poem. The method has value in so far as it is very child centered, and has meaning for the child.

Alongside the sentence method, the **kinesthetic method** is sometimes used. Initially, this method involved the tracing out of a word that was written on a card. The child says the word out loud as he does his tracing, and the tracing is continued until he has the ability to recognize the word instantly. It has since been extended to the tracing out of sentences that have been used in the sentence method and the subsequent reading of these sentences to the teacher. A further extension of the term *kinesthetic* permits the use of touch in virtually any form as an assistance to the learning of reading. Where drama plays a part, or movement, or drawing, or touch in any other guise, the method can be described as kinesthetic.

While not strictly a *method* of teaching reading, the **use of comics** is sometimes encouraged in British junior schools, and might be more common were it not that we are a traditional and conservative nation for whom the coupling of work and pleasure or school and fun is a concept not always readily accepted. The comic magazine serves a very useful purpose: for the child from a culturally deprived home, it represents his only contact with literature. If he can be shown that his enjoyment of this means of communication can be both intensified and lengthened by learning to read, then he will be motivated to try. It will then be possible to wean him to other literature. Schools in the more depressed areas of our cities use the comic, much more extensively than those in middle class suburbia.

Critics of the comic complain that the vocabulary is not graded. They say that the difficult words that require to be broken down and analyzed obscure the sense of the story for the slow reader, and hinder rapid reading. On the other hand the young reader becomes increasingly independent as his word store increases, and it has even been suggested that spelling is improved later on, because close attention has to be paid to words and parts. This however is no more than a tenuous theory.

PART METHODS OF READING INSTRUCTION

Clearly, at some stage of progress in reading, children have to learn the sounds of letters and use this knowledge to build up the sound of an unfamiliar word. **The phonic method** is not widely used in the early stages of reading because of the belief of teachers that children do see whole word patterns and that look-and-say offers unique advantages. Daniels postulated a theory in Downing's symposium (1966) that "children are part-seeing and whole-saying." The method advocated by Daniels and his associates for the teaching of reading by phonics is not the old one of sounding out each letter but consists, rather, of a very carefully graded set of readers and auxiliary

materials that pay close attention to the phonetic structure of the
English language. This method seems to answer the most common
criticism of phonics, namely that it is concerned with an attention
to form rather than meaning and so results in a deterioration of interest. It is significant that the phonic method tends to be used as a
last resort technique in our junior schools, often with good results.
If it works for those who have resisted other methods, it must be
worth using at an earlier stage.

The work of Daniels and Diack in the early 1950's has, in fact,
attracted attention to the value of phonics in the junior school schemes
of reading. These authors claim a clear advantage for their phonic-
word method in a number of experiments using the *Royal Road Readers* (Daniels and Diack, 1954), which they devised. But it is not
their work alone that has been responsible for the revived interest
in phonic methods over the whole range of primary education. The
initial teaching alphabet (i.t.a.) introduced by Sir James Pitman
(1961) which secured official approval and special grants for equipment in many areas created its Hawthorne effect of induced enthusiasm for phonics. A later method developed by Gattengo (1963),
"words in color," introduced another diacritical method and is receiving a measure of support.

In a way, if one wishes to make a very fine point, the initial teaching alphabet is not a system for the teaching of reading. Its inventor
and many of its most enthusiastic supporters maintain that it is merely
a method of writing down the English language and that it can be
equally well used with any reading system—whole, part, or eclectic.
Its value as an educational aid for teachers in this country is that it
has a simpler form than the conventional English as each symbol
has only one meaning. [In fact, this is not strictly the case.] It seems
to have had a rapid upsurge of popularity in this country but is now
declining in popularity. Teachers criticise i.t.a. on several grounds:
many of them can cite reversions to first learning patterns in their
children. For instance, children who have been taught Marion Richardson script and then cursive script later may revert to Marion
Richardson when they need to write quickly. Teachers have observed
this in children and some are afraid that i.t.a. methods may cause
confusion and difficulties with spelling in later school life. There can
hardly be another area of pedagogy which has attracted the research
attention concentrated on i.t.a., and yet no clear pattern has emerged.

The variables of novelty and of teacher enthusiasm and so forth soon contaminate the most rigorous experiments.

Although it may be said that the original intention of i.t.a. was to prevent reading failure, it has been adapted, in some junior schools, with a view to curing backwardness in reading. Such schemes frequently use infant i.t.a. materials. Much success has been reported from experiments in this direction, both in acquiring reading skills in i.t.a. and—a vital point—subsequently in traditional orthography.

Gattengo's **words in color scheme** which was introduced in 1962 has been used in junior schools to help in the teaching of backward readers. It is an attempt to reduce the effect of irregular spelling and pronunciation while at the same time leaving the orthography unaltered. This scheme is achieved by having a color code for each of the sounds represented in English. For instance, the letter *a* as it is used in the word *happy* is colored white. When the sound of the *a* is that of *blade* the color on the chart is blue-green, and that is true of all the combinations of letters that make this sound. The *ai* in *paid,* the *ea* in *great,* the *ei* in *Seine* will all have this blue-green color. One of the objections to the scheme from the infant's point of view—the requirement that all other reading material should be kept from the children—does not apply to the really retarded reader or to the non-reader in the junior school. He is certainly not motivated to read, and this presents no hardship to him. The scheme makes no concessions to whole methods such as word-picture associations and is a singularly phonic approach.

In the beginning of the words in color scheme the first sounds to be introduced are the five vowel sounds as in *sat, set, sin, sop,* and *sup.* Every sound has a color, and every color has its own sound. The consonants are then introduced one at a time. From the beginning, children are asked to write down the sound they hear; thus the elements of writing are dealt with at the same time as those of reading. It is claimed by enthusiasts that remarkable results are achieved with backward readers using this method. The books are rather different from those we have come to expect as they carry no illustrations; it is a *programed* course in so far as each step is simple, is a measured progression, and carries with it some measure of success and achievement. Gattengo believes that there is sufficient stimulus in his work and is not in favour of any motivation that is based on a desire to please the teacher. For backward readers, then, the business of providing motivation through the content of the scheme is of vital importance, and as wider areas of interest catering for wide age and interest groups become available this scheme may very well become more widely used for backward readers in junior schools.

The New Media in Reading

Education in the United Kingdom does not get the kind of financial support that it needs. It is accepted that the junior teacher who has to work with a class of forty children has little opportunity to do much remedial work nor the time to determine accurately where remedial work is necessary. The average junior teacher is hard pressed to get the books and supplementary readers that are necessary and is rarely in the position of being able to avail himself of the new technology, no matter what his personal predilection may be. However, modern media are gradually coming into use and can be expected to increase steadily in importance.

Programed reading courses have been published, and some teachers have experimented with them; but the sheer cost has proved a serious drawback when reading has to be taught "economically." Some **teaching machines** have been tried, and of these the Bell and Howell *Language Master* has probably proved the most effective. It would seem that there are wide ranges of use open for this machine in the schools and the Bell and Howell Company has been encouraging experimentation with the *Language Master* as an aid in the teaching of reading in such fields as backwardness and for non-English-speaking immigrants.

The **tape recording** principle has many obvious attractions for the reading teacher, and many types of usage are being practiced. Reading and speech are complementary activities, and it is valuable to have children make their own recordings. These recordings may range from the very simple right through to drama and school "radio." Quite apart from the direct benefits to the children's speech, the writing and reading of scripts, scenarios, and so on, are of inestimable benefit.

Another use of tape is for the recorder to play the role of notebook or to act as a stimulus for drawing, painting, or writing. Children can take portable instruments when out on a nature walk and record their impressions and observations as they go along. On return the tape can act as stimulus both for the same children and for others. There are innumerable ways in which the capturing of sound and subsequent replay can act as a potent force for freeing the child's imagination, thus leading directly and indirectly to improved reading—and equally important—to an enhanced motivation towards reading.

On the more mechanical side, tape recording can be used to build vocabulary. The *Language Master* offers a special convenience here in that a **talking dictionary** can be built up to accompany any scheme or reader. Rather than inquire from the teacher or from another child, the young reader can match an unknown word to a pre-recorded *Language Master* card and play the card as often as he wishes. Various **games and puzzles** can be devised using these cards, including forms of "Snap," matching sets of word-cards to pictures, and so on. Some teachers have successfully used tape to give instructions, or to deliver a running commentary, e.g. to a child looking through a basic reader. In essence, machines allowing the spoken word to be reproduced at will introduce an entirely new dimension into the teaching of reading and permit a very rich range of activities to be undertaken. One final point in this connection: all reports seem to indicate that even very young children are able to readily manipulate the devices of modern technology; and slow learners are no exception here.

Where new **audio-visual media** have been used in English schools to any great extent, their use has been due to the good offices of commercial firms coupled with the sincerity and persuasiveness of the head teachers of the schools concerned. The authors had the opportunity to see such a junior school just north of London. Here, Rank Audio-Visual, Ltd. had cooperated with the headmaster and had agreed to supply a wide variety of both hardware and software for a period of five years. This equipment is used by the children themselves under the structured guidance of their teachers and forms the basis not only of their reading schemes but of school days, which are integrated around the use of these aids. Although the school is situated on a working-class estate where there is only a very little cultural background, the children are extremely confident, advanced for their years, and self-sufficient. It is not claimed at this school that no pupil leaves unable to read; but the vast majority can and do read well. The machines have supplied them with a motivation and a wide range of experiences, the full enjoyment of which depends on their ability to read well; and all but a very few have responded to the challenge. Such intensive use of hardware seems to go beyond the scope of most of the junior schools in England at the moment. Many of these have to depend on the good offices of Parent/Teacher Associations to supply them with such technological devices as tape recorders and **film strip projectors.** Numbers of Local Education Authorities do, however, supply **television sets** to schools, and wide use is made of them for various educational programs, which are often well presented. Some broadcast television material has been aimed at backward readers, and this field is likely to expand.

Reading Failure and Its Treatment

In a paper entitled *The Aetiology of Reading Failure* read at the First International Reading Symposium at Oxford (1964), K. Lovell discussed the causes leading to reading failure in developed countries. Several of his conclusions are worthy of mention in the context of this chapter. He found that the child who is backward at reading at the age of eight-and-a-half or nine years makes only limited progress thereafter, in the majority of cases. He states that reading backwardness occurs in boys more frequently than in girls, that intelligence is normally distributed for backward readers. He does not see maladjustment as a major cause of reading failure—although a child may be maladjusted as a *consequence* of reading failure. Most significantly, he says that "what it is that backward readers cannot do remains a mystery at present." [1]

Certainly some children—some would say about half of all children—come into the junior schools needing the kind of teaching that they had been having in the infant schools. These are the boys and girls who will become that large proportion of adults who do not read well enough to do it for pleasure. As already shown, backward readers in the junior school tend to be underprivileged with regard to their teachers. Let us now look at ways that good teachers attempt to help those children who are backward. Any good readiness scheme for juniors who cannot read contains certain elements: it attempts,

[1] J. Downing, *The First International Reading Symposium* (London: Cassell, 1966, p. 145).

first of all, to improve the child's visual discrimination; this is done by using associations that exhibit both similarities and differences. Such questions as "What is the odd one?" "What is missing?" "What is out of place?" can be asked, and arrangements can be across the page or in a column, depending whether the child is being involved with lateral flow or with downward progression.

Rhythm and flow patterns in words need to be stressed to improve auditory discrimination and to show that meaning which can be changed by inflexion can be changed by accentuation. Although the average English junior classroom is short of the devices of the new technology of education, good teachers make use of what they have. In order to improve auditory discrimination, piano, recorder, cymbals, and other sources of sound are called into play. Tape recorders, *Language Masters,* and earphones are all used, and the Army School of Preliminary Education has (and uses) its own language laboratory. Concurrently with all other activities both vocabulary and speech are constantly practiced and improved by the use of tape recorders, games, drama, and music.

The basis of remedial reading is an awareness on the part of the teacher of several factors, each of which is significantly dependent on the personal relationship between teacher and child. In particular, the teacher needs to be sympathetic to the child's needs and difficulties and to recognize that reading is to many children an arduous and difficult task offering small hope of pleasure or reward. Considerable importance is attached to building up self-confidence, often basing it on success in other subject areas and from this success and self-confidence (hopefully) will come the child's motivation to read.

It should be obvious, but unfortunately it frequently is not, that a child who is backward in reading is not likely suddenly to spring ahead with the same old material. If he has failed with it previously, then the chances are that he will continue to do so. A number of remedial schemes are really based on little more than novelty, and this not infrequently proves to be sufficient.

Conclusion

Nobody in the British junior schools feels complacent about the teaching of reading. The schools have too many deficiencies for that: they lack adequate facilities, and the teachers face the difficulty of facing large numbers of pupils with minimal resources. To some extent this is the teachers' own fault as well as being the fault of the authorities. Teachers are so jealous of their status as a profession that they are reluctant to permit unqualified persons to come in contact with the children within the classroom. If such auxiliaries, after suitable training, were recruited to take some of the unskilled routine out of the teaching task, the teacher would then be free to exercise his professional skills more efficiently and systematically.

Reading backwardness is a major worry and problem in this country. It is a problem that has not been solved, nor is the method of its solution in sight yet. The teachers are aware of it, however, and reading research units are being set up in various parts of the country. It is a pity that research is so often considered to be the province of higher education—and in higher education, to be the province of the universities. It is still too difficult for the serving teacher (especially the junior teacher who has no academic qualification) to originate research that is then controlled and directed by competent people whose prime qualification is experience and ability in teaching. Education in Great Britain is dominated from above in both the administrative and the academic sense. It is as difficult for the nongraduate serving teacher in this country to obtain a first degree as it might have been for the proverbial camel to pass through the eye of a needle. When this is changed, and when the good junior teacher is recognized for what he or she is, many of the problems that currently beset us in education will be behind us.

Further References

Butler, Kathy. Some Thoughts on the Teaching of Reading. *Reading*, Vol. 2, No. 2, 1968, pp. 2–7.

Daniels, J. C., and Diack, H. *The Royal Road Readers, Teachers' Book.* London: Chatto and Windus, 1954.

——, and ——. *The Standard Reading Tests.* London: Chatto and Windus, 1958.

Downing, J. *The First International Reading Symposium.* London: Cassell, 1966.

Gates, A. I. Studies of Phonetic Training in Beginning Reading. *Journal of Educational Psychology*, 18, 1927, pp. 217–226.

Gattengo, C. *Words in Colour*. Reading, England: Educational Explorers Limited, 1963.

Houghton, V., and Daniels, J. C., noted in *Bulletin of the United Kingdom Reading Association*, July, 1966.

Morris, J. M. *Reading in the Primary School*. London: National Foundation for Educational Research, 1959.

――. *Standards and Progress in Reading*. London: National Foundation for Educational Research, 1966.

Moyle, D. *The Teaching of Reading*. London: Ward Lock, 1968.

Pitman, I. J. Learning to Read: An Experiment. *Journal of the Royal Society of Arts*, No. 109, 1961, pp. 149–180.

Sanderson, A. E. The Idea of Reading Readiness: a Re-examination. *Educational Research*, Vol. 6, January 1963, pp. 3–9.

Schonell, F. J. *Backwardness in the Basic Subjects*. Edinburgh: Oliver and Boyd, 1942.

――. *The Psychology and Teaching of Reading*. Edinburgh: Oliver and Boyd, 1945.

7. Teaching Children to Write Creatively

VERNON HALE

VERNON HALE is Headmaster at the John Hampden Junior School, Thame, Oxfordshire. He has previously been Head of English Departments in two Worcestershire secondary schools and was Deputy Head of West Kidlington County Primary School, Oxfordshire. He was educated at Ruskin College, Oxford, and the City of Worcester College of Education after a period in industry.

I was watching an infant boy of six taking part in a movement lesson. He was sitting so still that I almost forgot the other children around him; they were sliding and undulating and making a cacaphony of sounds impossible to isolate from the situation. He stayed like this for two or three minutes until he lifted himself up and balanced on one leg with a total control over his body. It seemed to me that the boy was floating. Quite soon he sat down and waited for his colleagues to finish; he was content with two simple movements and was unconcerned that the others were still active.

The next day I happened to go into the boy's classroom and he came straight to me to show me a swan he had made from a fallen twig, on which he had glued two feathers of a dove. He told me that he could "blow it along the water like the wind does." I asked him whether it would float, and although he did not answer the question directly he was interested in what else could be done with the feathers other than using them in the simple artifact. However, I was impressed so much by our dialogue that it seemed relevant to relate the two incidents that I had observed.

In the English primary school the children begin their explorations with simple experiences that involve the senses: listening to the plop of bricks in the water tray, touching the roughness of bark, or tasting the saltiness of a shell. They feel the rhythms of life around them and become aware that their own bodies can respond sympathetically. Using words to communicate these rhythms becomes an inherent need, and where a skilled teacher creates an environment delicious to the senses a child's speech and writing patterns can change radically. This becomes especially true when the philosophy of the school is based on integrated learning.

The content of school experience changes for the growing child, but imaginative potential is constantly being nurtured whether the activity is movement, music, mathematics, or science. Language therefore grows organically as I will try to illustrate by bringing to life a group of older juniors I had the pleasure of observing.

These children were enacting the feeling in their fingers of the sharpness of thorns; they were stretching their arms like a tree growing and shaping their bodies in a tangle. Groups of three and four came together to make the thickness of an old hawthorn and moved with the heaviness of leaf; they made the light scratch of birds with their nails and swayed to the wind turning across the fields.

We had been listening to Stravinsky's *The Rite of Spring (Le sacre du printemps)* and through a series of movement sequences we were trying to understand the rhythms and undercurrents of music that vibrated and celebrated the mystery of life. There was so much of spring in the wild patch outside the classroom: the busy rooks high in the elms; the alders shivering with leaf—ginger-colored in the sun; spawn slobbering on the edge of the pond; the scrabbling of shrews through grass tunnels. The children were free to wander in this environment collecting and identifying specimens or simply waiting and watching for a revelation. There was much to observe and record, yet the children were ready to experience what D. H. Lawrence called "plant consciousness, insect consciousness, fish consciousness, animal consciousness . . . the natural religious sense." They were ready to make imaginative use of their bodies to explore the sources of growth, of order, of burgeoning in nature. They felt a need, too, to reinterpret their discoveries with painting, printing, and drawing—but particularly through imaginative language.

Two girls who had responded especially well to the Stravinsky music wrote for about one quarter of an hour, standing on the step of the classroom and watching the change of light and color under swiftly moving clouds. They wrote:

> *Sun shining on ginger alders,*
> *Water lifeless lies.*
> *Then wind whips,*
> *Howling*
> *Whirling whistles.*
> *Water shedding its skin,*
> *Snake skin of ripples.*
> *Reeds in beige light,*
> *Calm, to be disturbed*
> *By the scampering rat wind*
> *Which stops to gnaw.*
> *Gull inland*
> *Shines silver,*
> *Flashes.*
> *Is gone.*
> *Tangled growth withered*
> *As clouds hide the sun.*
>   **Jayne and Terry (10+)**

The first impression of the wild fields, humpy as far as the school fence, is one of complex, maze-like growth. In winter the dominating colors are brown and dun except for the black tracery of branches. Underfoot it is so wet that a darkness spreads over the grasses and sedges. This setting is a source of eerie wonder in the children, and frequently it has been a starting point for talking about strange landscapes and distant places. Often, we have sat quietly in the classroom at the end of a January afternoon and watched the sky empty of all but the cold dampness and the pools of water hardening into ice-moons. These occasions have been opportunities to read poetry and listen to music, thus extending the area of imagination and enriching the vocabulary of the children. The worlds created have been quite alien to the actual area. One boy wrote:

The sounds echo on the walls and bounce off in all directions. The wind twirls into a cone of music and plays round the old ruin. It makes its way across the distant desert and creates a blinding terrifying sandstorm. A camel train goes slow. Then the wind blows over the sea and lashes the water to a white foaming top and the ships dip between mountains. Finally the wind finds a deep valley and destroys all things that are weak and defenseless. People go low as the wind surges harder and harder, until it blows itself out.

Andrew (10+)

It was interesting that when this piece of writing was read aloud, it stimulated the rest of the class: two girls made a monochrome of curling abstract shapes like a wind of barbed wire; a boy made a brown-and-white collage from sample pieces of wallpaper, creating a picture of ice that seemed to be drawn by the moon along furrows of waves where birds floated like thrown sticks. Others sketched the grass tangles in a series of charcoal studies, which in turn gave rise to talking and writing about strange plant forms such as the giant hogweed, the exploding seed pods of impatiens roylei, or their own "death flowers." One child was inspired by this discussion and wrote a poem:

She turned back into the soil
And curled over the roots and buried things.
She felt her large brown leaves
And her stem which went deeper.
Her petals bore a crystal of snow.

Katherine (9+)

The dialogue was enhanced by bringing objects and pictures to the classroom and displaying them in a context of color, shape, and texture. I gathered together fabrics in browns, greys, and blacks and arranged dried grasses, roots, and branches as well as stone from local quarries, animal skulls, and bones. In the center of the display I placed a painting by Giuseppe Arcimboldi called *Winter,* which portrays a face made as a dead tree stump, with hair of entangled ivy and two grey fungi for lips. I allowed the display to grow and change as I was able to introduce the childrens' poems, their descriptions, their art. The experience became one in which the children were exercising all their senses and demanding a wide range of related media for communication.

In spring, summer, and autumn it was possible to be closer to the environment and to study it in detail. Many more particular references to fauna and flora were contained in the childrens' writing:

The willow is hollow. The bark is ridged and bumpy. Thin moss clings to the trunk. Underneath there is ripe brown wood. Down at the bottom are insects crawling in holes. The tree trunk makes winding and twisting shapes with spinning leaves hanging. The sun glitters through zigging twigs. Ledges step up in the hollows in which lie small pieces of broken wood, twigs, left leaves and wood dust. Black wood spirals around in the holes.

Diane (9+)

A blooded breast;
Eggs of rust and white
In a den of thorns,
Watched by a black bird.
Moss-padded walls,
Grass of bronze makes the nest.
Eyes looking for food.

Nigel (10+)

A weasel flashes by after a rabbit.
A flurry of fur and bone,
Bones of weak ivory.
Weasel and rabbit are gripped,
A clutching of throat
A squeezing.
The rabbit's jaw is separated from face,
Eyes torn, once looking like diamonds,
Now broken glass.
The weasel eats.
Again the survival of the fittest,
The weasel the fittest.

David (10+)

This quality of thought arises in an integrated situation where the children are involved in activities essentially interrelated and continuous. They need a flexible classroom structure where they are free to respond in many ways to stimuli offered by a spirited teacher. It would be limiting if a teacher merely encouraged the exploration of the environment with a set of reference books and a microscope and failed to understand that children have a natural inclination to be totally involved through the senses. At the same time, the imagination must be enriched by perception of detail and evaluation, which we can call "the scientific attitude." For example, the poetry of John Clare is full of precise observation that may be found in the notebooks of a meticulous naturalist. It reveals a patient waiting; he is the scientist

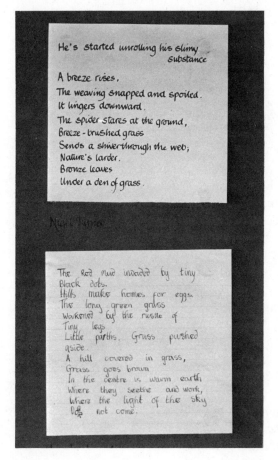

Creative writing from environmental work outside classroom.

in the field, yet with words Clare penetrates a mystery unrevealed by mere facts. So many children are artists in this sense and assimilate the complexities around them and make order.

It is interesting to see how children respond in an idiosyncratic way to the things they find around them. The teacher may intend the classroom display to be thematic, but pupils have a way of isolating an object, or plant, or flower arrangement and studying it for its own sake. Such an object frequently begins a train of thought that preoccupies a child for as long as a week. Perhaps it is dissected and examined under a microscope, or sketched in ink, or used as a lino-cut or woodcut design, or becomes the subject of a poem or prose piece. One arrangement of bulrushes, for example, elicited all these activities and after the velvety texture had been felt and the seeds magnified, and the designs had been cut Terry wrote:

Proudly the bulrushes hold their prizes which have burst from within them. They droop upon us, admit all their secrets. The leaves of the bulrushes twist and curl, just to remind us that they are part of the miracle as well. Seeds fly everywhere as though drawn towards the earth. Some escape through the open window and disappear into the sky.

The classroom displays are often supplemented by exhibits on loan from the local museum school service, including textiles, pottery, sculpture, embroidery, and stuffed animals and birds. For Jill, a William Morris design of golden flowers became "The Chrysanthemum Forest":

> *Fighting harder and harder,*
> *Stalks tangling around each other,*
> *Not letting my body through.*
> *Heads towering above,*
> *Swaying in the wind that makes it harder.*
> *Touching them and getting a shower of petals.*
> *Birds cheeping,*
> *Bees buzzing down to the nectar.*
> *Quiet,*
> *Then the disturbing wind whistles.*
> *Ants, slugs, snails creeping up the endless stalks.*
> *All the Jack the Giant Killers.*

> *Thicker, thicker, then thin,*
> *Then fades away.*
> *I look back at the chrysanthemum forest.*

For Alan, the heron displayed in tall sedges comes alive:

> *The high judge of the river*
> *Stands like a statue,*
> *Its slender neck folds bent.*
> *Its beak holds still,*
> *The eyes move slowly across the water*
> *Scanning its territory.*
> *Its legs are like burnt branches;*
> *Grey back and snow white,*
> *Elegant in its own way.*
> *Then it darts spearing the poor fish.*
> *The meal is quickly devoured*
> *And across the river in marshland*
> *The female sits on the blue eggs.*
> *Beyond, the curlew calls.*

During the year the class creative writing folder was filled with work written about foxes, Victorian ginger jars, sprigs of traveler's joy, a policeman's truncheon, a railwayman's cap, a waterboatman, a copper kettle, a ceramic cross, a fan, a piece of iron railing, and a giant pumpkin.

Primary children have the capacity to explore more fundamental themes, as well as responding to everyday experience. Many teachers still underestimate their pupils, but it is clear from traditional stories and nursery rhymes that from infancy the world is seen to be a serious place.

> *Barney Bodkin broke his nose,*
> *Without feet we can't have toes:*
> *Crazy folks are always mad.*
> *Want of money makes you sad.*

This rhyme might be about any number of things: the intolerable frailty of the body, the inconsistency of adults, the pressure of day-today family life. Young children do work out such problems as they mature, and it has been my experience in helping them to develop their language skills that their most profound achievements are made when they recognize personal anxieties and aspirations. In the later primary stages, the children show a considerable perception in dealing with things that will be with them for life: loneliness, sorrow and mutability, personal fulfillment and happiness, cruelty and compassion, violence and war, class and discrimination, and the ultimate meaning of life. If the relationship between the children and their teachers is a sincere one then frequently the creative writing is of deep personal significance.

Perhaps the most important new factor in English primary education is that children and adults have more common ground because discovery takes place at many levels, and although communication varies in sophistication, the intensity of experience is shared. In the classroom it is now generally felt that the teacher will be personally affected by the creative process that he sets in motion and will be extended by the insights and imagination of his children. The teacher has the resources—the "producible vocabulary"—to structure the environment; but like the artist, he releases a magic that works on everyone in the situation. In attempting creative work at his own level, the teacher inevitably reveals standards, beliefs, and inadequacies. His sympathies grow for the frustrations and joys that children feel in taking the devious routes to understanding. Teaching involves the faculty for appreciation, for discrimination which grows with our own pain and fulfillment in the creative process. I believe that we should expect a great deal from our teachers. Wordsworth might have been speaking of them when he said of the poet, "a man endured with more lively sensibility, more enthusiasm and tenderness, who has a greater knowledge of human nature and a more comprehensive soul. . . . a man pleased with his own passions and volitions, and who rejoices more than other men in the spirit of life that is within him; delighting to contemplate similar volitions and passions in the goings-on of the Universe. . . ." For children to live and work with such adults can do nothing but good during years when children are searching for life standards.

The interrelationship can best be illustrated by describing one of

Opposite: From an individual book on wood.

The Strange wood

Lines on a piece of wood which and curves making shapes like hats and faces. Dark and light brown makes patterns of the sea. The wood is damp rotten and smelly. In some places the wood is hollow. Jagged splinters spike out. Sometimes there are holes made by wood worm.

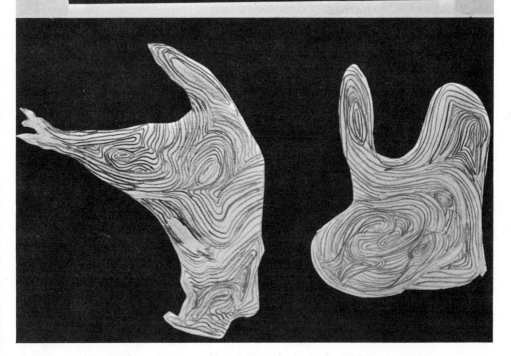

139

my first contacts with a class of ten-year-olds, after a long period of working with adolescents. We began by remembering the incidents of our earlier years, and I read the children a poem of my own about a legendary character, Wayland the Smith, who once lived for me on the distant chalk hill beyond my home. I described how I imagined the texture of his skin, the long hard nails, his groping in the hole under the ground, the ringing of his anvil across the downland, the frightened horses left in the dark. I told my class how the myth had receded as two years passed, during which time I bought a bicycle and cycled to the place where previously only my thoughts had flown. The children were beginning to understand the concept of passing time and how it can suddenly change awareness. I showed them how the Cornish poet, Charles Causley deals with this theme in his "Nursery Rhyme of Innocence and Experience" in which he describes three years in the life of a child who longs for the sailor to bring her toys from across the sea. Three summers later the sailor returns with the plum-colored fez and a drum once desired, but the child asks, "Why have you brought me children's toys?" I read this poem and it immediately evoked graphic reminiscences. One boy described his new birthday penknife and how he found himself whittling into the wood of a loved doll. Another told us about his waiting on the wall looking at the base of a horse chestnut tree and seeing a thrush fly down. He described how he took a catapult from his pocket and shot a stone, which thudded into the bird's speckled breast. My pupil said, "A drop of blood came from its beak and I cried. I hid my catapult in my dad's garage." For these children the dialogue was a profound oral release and therefore complete. Others wanted to write about it, but it would have been artificial to ask all the class to do so. If we accept that our work must be child centered, then they must have the freedom to assimilate ideas in their own way and if necessary reject them. Creative writing is a natural means of communication for many children but the primary way is speech. Therefore to suggest that written work could always follow experience would result in frustration and superficiality. This view is substantiated by the compositions of children being educated in formal subject situations where style is cultivated and overgrown. Then it becomes difficult for the teacher to deal with the basic skills that ought to be acquired in a context of need. Here are a few pieces, the economy of which resulted from ordering real responses, which were deeply felt and unimpaired by teacher-centered discipline:

My old bear had no legs and I had to tie up his back with a stick. He didn't say much from his mouth that used to be a line of stitches. I hung him up from my bed on a piece of string and every night I kissed him and twisted him around to make him twirl. One morning he had fallen on the floor and I forgot to pick him up before going down to breakfast. The dog tore him to shreds but I didn't seem to care.

John (10+)

A pair of eyes came out of the dark at me. It was an owl sitting in the fir tree at the end of the garden. One day I drew a picture of an owl on a big piece of paper and the yellow eye I put in made me tremble from head to toe. So I fetched a pair of scissors and cut it up and scratched the piece of paper right across. Then I found a piece of wood to make an owl but my knife wasn't sharp enough and the wood was hard. I went on to something else.

Susan (10+)

John stood by the clump of trees where some cows had left turds and he looked into the water. He thought of all the fish that Henry had described on their trips to the Oxford canal. He remembered the spiny-finned perch with the stripes you could see under the water, especially when it was sunny. That upset Henry when it struggled on the end of his own hook.

[J:] Bigger than what?
[H:] On your tackle he might be quieter.
[J:] He's on yours.
[H:] He wouldn't have torn and bled.
[J:] You are always ripping them. If you throw him back now the bacteria won't eat him away.

Martin (10+)

When the children's themes begin to take shape and truths emerge, there are many opportunities to introduce literature which can enrich their learning and take the children on other journeys of discovery. Unquestionably the teacher must use prose and poetry that he has enjoyed and evaluated as an adult. Sometimes, it is superficial to search for appropriate "Children's books" and debilitating to search through school anthologies of mediocre verse. There is a wealth of material in the English language—both traditional and modern—and translated from world literature. In recent years, however, the quality of children's literature has improved enormously.

For the winter theme I chose *Elidor* by Alan Garner—a book full of strange and wonderful magic, pervaded by the symbols and myths common to men. It is an exciting contemporary story with some of the qualities of science fiction, yet powerfully affected by English history and landscape. The total impact of the novel is one of continuity and permanency. In it there are the ancient monuments of our civilization, such as standing stones and castles; caves go deep into the earth; morality is polarized, and men stand shining in light or live in darkness; the silver unicorn snorts and thunders and finally lays its head in the lap of a girl. The children in the story find a ruined church in a city redevelopment area and are called by Malabron into Elidor, the Green Isle of the Shadow of the Stars. There, they are entrusted with four treasures that are the symbols of enlightenment. Roland, Helen, Nicholas, and David bring these back into their own world, yet are pursued by the forces of darkness even into the safe world of suburbia. This book was especially significant for the children in my class because we were able to relate the wild uncultivated land around the classroom to the desolation of Elidor. Consider this fragment:

Roland looked back: but he had nowhere else to go, and at that distance the castle was a tortured crag. He clutched a handful of gravel and rubbed it against his cheek. It hurt. It was real. He was there. He had only himself.

Within the forest the road dwindled to a line of mud that strayed wherever there was ground to take it: fungus glowed in the twilight, and moss trailed like hair from the branches. There was the silence of death over everything: a silence that was more powerful for the noises it contained—the far-off crash of trees, and the voices of cold things hidden in the fog that moved in ribbons where there was no wind. Oaks became black water at a touch.[1]

This kind of writing has an immediate effect upon the children's shaping of experience. It is as though they have been given a key to unlock the store of language patterns and vocabulary that have been accumulating since infancy. The physical actuality of light and shade,

[1] Alan Garner, *Elidor* (London: Collins, 1965), pp. 28–29.

of softness and hardness, of growth and decay, of hills, trees, distant towers, they can take within their imaginative grasp and set in order. The words they find, or the materials that are to hand set in motion a questing, which the teacher must encourage with further infusions of ideas, by introducing the other arts, by aiming for "an exquisite sensation of wholeness."

At one point in *Elidor* Roland passes through a door in a mound of earth, into an underground passage. When I read this episode, the children's faces were a mixture of excitement, curiosity, and fear as though they were being drawn under the ground to an experience quite overwhelming. This observation was borne out by their intense interest in the subject of caves and mines; many of them found reference books on physical geography and recorded many facts, but again the research was valuable in helping them to be precise in their speaking and creative writing. Further, this discovery work also formed the basis for a series of movement sequences when we concentrated upon the contrasts of space and confinement; we listened to Bartok's *Music for Strings, Percussion and Celeste,* the third movement of which begins with sounds like the slow drip of water echoing in deep galleries. The children also made their own sound effects on a range of Carl Orff instruments, taping their compositions at one speed and replaying them at a slower one. They pinpointed each sound: the liquid flow of darkness, the tap of picks at the coal face, the sudden rush of sea against cave walls, the creak of pit props, the abrasion of sand and shells.

Drip, drip, drip. The water drops into the dark pool and ripples run across it. I stand silently watching. The walls are jagged and roughly cut around me. It is frightening, yet wonderful like a new world without light, an underground world. I move on slowly over the rough floor. The cave is damp and water trickles in little streams over the floor and over my wet feet. I carry on walking and wonder what else will come before my thrilled eyes.

Michael (9+)

> *Rushing water*
> *Beating the rocks*
> *Forming over centuries*
> *A cave now complete.*
> *Calm water goes in and out as it pleases.*

Shadows of rock make queer shapes,
The shape of a needle
Formed on the water by a great stalagmite,
Ages to grow, ages.
The sun shines through the entrance
And I see a lizard-like creature.
The jutting rock like whales' teeth,
Rugged rock.

Alan (9+)

The underground is a world of its own. The blackness is at full strength and God is only just with me and my sense of feeling is floating through the tips of my fingers. This low dark tunnel of seeping limestone echoes every move I make. A strange power has overcome me and I seem to be led through row on row of dismal tunnels. This in my mind will go on for ever, for ever, for ever.

Andrew (11+)

I was able to gather this small group of boys together and follow up their work by reading them selections from writers who I felt had explored similar themes both factually and imaginatively, including George Orwell and Franz Kafka, Coleridge and Mark Twain.

Alan Garner's novel finishes with a reinterpretation of the unicorn legend. Findhorn—"silver and dark with wounds"—is being pursued relentlessly by the men of darkness carrying spears. The great animal rests finally in the lap of Helen who is holding one of the treasures. The children know that Findhorn must sing to save Elidor and in a magnificent climax, when the last spear pierces the beast's heart, "a brightness grew on the windows of the terrace and in the brightness was Elidor, and the four golden castles. Behind Gorias a sunburst swept the land with colour. Streams danced and rivers were set free and all the shining air was new. . . ." [2] Some of the children were moved to tears by this ancient story and wanted to know more about the myth. I obtained pictures of the Flemish "Hunt of the Unicorn" tapestries, now in the Metropolitan Museum, New York. These intricately woven pictures are filled with animals and hunters; the unicorn

[2] Garner, op. cit., p. 159.

Opposite:
Ink drawing of classroom display used in a class book of children's poetry.

The river ripples
Swirls,
And lives

Far away
The sun departs
And Leaves the sky

Emptiness and darkness
Hollow
Is the cave.

The Moon reflecting on Earth
Gone
Morning.

Amen.
Death.
And bones.

Snow flakes
corn flakes
sugar puffs.

is milk-white against dark greens and blues and is pursued through a maze of leaf and flowers, until he is finally secured to a pomegranate tree. One girl decided to make her own fabric collage of the story and found as many scrap materials, sequins, and buttons as she could and created a beautiful yellow unicorn leaping into the sky, which seemed to be filled with glittering spears and tattered clouds.

For a number of weeks groups of children discovered similar myths from many cultures and made their own miscellanies. One miscellany even contained the Greek legend about the imprisonment of the Minotaur and the flight of Daedalus and Icarus. The children included in their collection Breugel's painting of the fall of Icarus together with W. H. Auden's poem on the same subject. I read a selection from a contemporary treatment of the maze myth by Michael Ayrton, a British artist. We also devised our own version of Demeter's dancing floor and danced through the whirling, serpentine shapes that we drew on the school playground.

It becomes clear that literature should not merely be seen as an initial stimulus for writing; its value is in its centrality. Literature imbues the child with the communicated and eternal perceptions of mankind. Therefore the committed teacher in the English primary school feels a profound responsibility to the children in valuing the word and views with suspicion those educational technologies and methods that undervalue books. A gross example has been the recent production of creative writing kits and film loops which aim to supplement the teacher's own resources. There are of course no substitutes for the teacher's vision and his capacity to live a full life.

During the summer months many children learn to swim in the school pool. Swimming is a physical achievement comparable with balancing on a bicycle, or climbing a tall tree, or breaking through a seemingly impenetrable wood. It is a personal triumph over an element, a natural hazard hitherto powerful and alien; the attempt to succeed can cause pain and disappointment, yet with success comes a general growth in confidence often favourably affecting a child's social attitudes. Achievements of this kind are so important that children readily draw upon them when writing:

My toes dangled into the cool water, forming ripples on the surface and making the blue bottom of the pool disappear. Somehow I felt strangely frightened and yet I was excited by the thought that

I might succeed in reaching the opposite side. I pulled my bathing cap further over my ears. My head hurt under the pressure of it. My hair was being strangled. I jumped and water whirled around my body taking my breath away for a few seconds. A splash of water surged down my body, making me see my friends around me. . . .

During our discussion of this piece of child's writing, a boy made a comment that crossing a width of the pool was like taking a long journey; he tried to articulate that distance was relative to the state of mind of the traveler and the hazards that beset him. We tried to compare a flight across a large continent such as South America with a trek of a few miles in the same area, on foot and without the aids of civilization. The children understood that to contemplate the unknown gives rise to irrational fears and exaggeration. I told them of the 16th-century Oxfordshire geographer, Peter Heylyn of Burford, who described Australia as "Terra Australis Incognita or the Southern Continent, Utopia, New Atlantis, Fairy Land, the Lands of Chivalry and the New World in the Moon." We looked at old charts of seas full of strange monsters, whirlpools, and fogs and talked of the myths that Homer chronicled of the wandering Odysseus.

However, in the June of the term we were hearing journalists' dispatches from the Arab-Israeli war front, and I read aloud an account of how Egyptian soldiers were retreating across the Sinai desert, caught in sandstorms, without water, and suffering from wounds. The exchange of ideas that resulted was revealing for I had not expected such a divergence of opinion on war. For most children war was conceived in fantasy terms, and the destruction of a town with bombs was no more real than throwing beanbags at bricks. I decided to confront the children with the meaning of war as experienced by soldiers, civilians, artists, and writers through the ages. I mounted an exhibition of photographs, comic strips, and souvenirs loaned by parents; there were shells, helmets, regalia, service pay books, scrapbooks, and letters written from the front. We spent time looking at Goya's drawings and read from the Anglo-Saxon epic poem *Battle of Maldon,* parts of Froissart's Chronicles, from Ernest Hemingway's Spanish Civil War dispatches, and Bertolt Brecht's narrative ballad, *Children's Crusade* 1939.

I suggested that the children might like to interpret war pictorially and gave them chalks and charcoal, limiting colors to black, white, brown, and grey. Once again we explored the immediate environment for inspiration and found a hedge blackened by chemical spray and two trees whitened by lightning burns. We also looked at a partly demolished building, with splitting beams and sharp masonry. One abstract charcoal study was of remarkable quality: a grey storm of ash seemed to spiral into a blackening sky, taking with it jagged slabs of concrete and white match-like figures with broken triangular limbs.

One photograph of the German occupation of Paris (confiscated from a prisoner of war) evoked a lengthy discussion on the morality of this kind of act, on how personal relationships can break down and how decent people can be debased by organized and socially approved violence. The children understood this type of breakdown in social mores when I described the experience of the boys on the island in *Lord of the Flies*. This is not a book that can be read to young children in its entirety, but I was able to read them one small part that I felt might be a clue to some who may have been thinking deeply about behavior:

They scrambled down a rock slope, dropped among the flowers and made their way under the trees. Here they paused and examined the bushes around them curiously.

Simon spoke first. "Like candles, candle bushes, candle buds."

The bushes were dark evergreen and aromatic and the many buds were waxen green and folded up against the light. Jack slashed at one with his knife and the scent spilled over them.

"Candle buds," "You couldn't light them," said Ralph. "They just look like candles." "Green candles," said Jack contemptuously, "We can't eat candles, come on." [3]

The manner in which the theme was developing needed careful control to avoid pushing the children into an area of experience beyond their mental maturity. The extract from *Lord of the Flies* was a breaking-off point. It brought us back to talking about ourselves, how we differ from each other, how we experience the same things in personal ways, how our imaginations sometimes work, or fail to respond. Much of the writing that we finally collected into a book

[3] William Golding, *Lord of the Flies* (New York: Penguin Modern Classics, 1954), p. 30.

called *The Landscape of War* was a vindication of Coleridge's comment that "Children are much less removed from men and women than generally imagined; they have less power to express their meaning than men, but their opinion of justice is nearly the same. This we may prove by referring to our own experience." In the English primary school it has become possible to accept this general observation and at the same time teach the language skills required to articulate meaning. Consider these pieces:

It is quiet, but I can hear a child crying beside his mother. He is lucky or is he? He has lost his leg. It's like a ruined world. A chain holds man down to war. Why is there no peace? We are all people. What has happened to the world?

Robert (10+)

> *Listen to the warning*
> *Find me out*
> *From death and darkness,*
> *And flying dragons*
> *That pierce the sky with smoke.*
> *Flames fight with the earth,*
> *Flames that fall from the sky.*
> *Ruins and shattered glass,*
> *Ashes smouldering*
> *And bodies deadened by fire.*
> *Clouds that sail in the shape of war.*

Lesley (11+)

Burning sand and hot dried up mud. The mud is shrinking. There are the ashes of a plane that has crashed. A great war devil crosses the land, taking the people, telling them to come into the desert to have a better land. They go, leaving behind a happy place. But now it is dark ashes and ruins. The land they seek cannot be found, for there is no such place. But the devil draws them on. Their skin shrinks like the burning mud.

Susan (10+)

Although primary children have this sense of justice and natural sympathy, often manifesting itself in a chivalrous, romantic commitment, their grasp of abstract moral concepts is often transitory, and may not survive the immediate context. Children of this age are readily diverted from ideas about the reverence for life or social responsibility to discovering how the natural world functions. Yet they are engrossed by origins (first causes), and it has been gratifying to observe them following the course of a thunderstorm, or finding out how waves begin their journeys across the ocean, or waiting for young chicks to break from the eggs warming in the classroom incubator. They show extraordinary patience in tapping away at rock to find fossils and intense absorption in the lives of primitive people.

This type of concentration was made clear to me during two out-of-school activities, a weekend camp and a visit to an Oxford Museum and Art Gallery, which happened to take place during the same time, and gave rise to one of our most rewarding themes: The Creation of the Earth and the Evolution of Life. We had pitched our camp on a piece of common land in the Oxfordshire Cotswolds, close to some old stone mines where centuries before raw fissile limestone had been brought to the surface and exposed to hard frost, split with hammers, and used as building slates for country homes, farm buildings, and Oxford colleges. Within the stone were treasures; rich evidence of fauna and flora existing millions of years past such as ammonites, belemnites, sea-urchins, fenestella, and cycads. Much of the stone still remains in grass-covered mounds and on chipping banks, and during camp we lifted the turf and dug into the ground where we found many samples to take back for identification. The site was also ideal for other researches, particularly about the Roman world. We were tracking through a wood when suddenly a boy found a large white shell which we were able to identify as a species of edible snail first introduced into Britain by the Roman settlers. This discovery led us on a search for other evidence that would enable us to construct a realistic picture of life in the Roman centuries. From the hillside we realized that below us a turf-covered road "petered out" in the water meadow and was shown as Ackerman Street on the Ordnance Survey map. Across two fields were the excavated ruins of a Roman villa with a fine example of mosaic and a well-preserved hypocaust (heating system). Here, the children discovered a mound of brick and tile left by the archeologists, in which they found many discarded examples of Roman materials and returned to school with a valuable collection.

In the neighboring village stood a simple 13th-century church with one remaining stained-glass panel—a green saint filtering pale light into the chancel. There were tombstones dating from the 17th and 18th centuries, and on the other side of the church wall was a 17th-century lockup where in days gone by the village malcontents were held for all to deride.

The day of our visit was hot, and as we looked down upon the village we saw the cottages behind nets of sunlight; they were like great fish from ancient seas, scaled in stone. The snails under the walls were drying and falling, the shells showing hollow gapes to the light. The brass cock on a tower rippled in the summer air and seemed to wait for slow and distant winds. The whole atmosphere was such that the children felt themselves in touch with the past; everything they had found demonstrated the continuity of things and people, while the village seemed to suggest permanency.

At the Oxford Museum and Art Gallery we saw the painting "A Forest Fire" by the Florentine painter, Piero Cosino. The work represents his vision of the evolution of man and depicts the struggle for survival during the Old Stone Age. It is full of strange beasts fleeing from a fire, yet beyond its narrative content it evokes the primeval distance and the simplicity common to all creatures, including man. I also showed the children the sepia and pen drawings of Samuel Palmer, the 19th-century English mystic, whose work is a vision of paradise, the Garden of Eden.

After we returned to the classroom, I read *The Dream Time* by Henry Treece, a writer of children's historical novels. His book is about a young boy, Twilight, who discovers within himself the power to use natural materials to represent his world. He rejects the uninhibited violence of his own tribe and comes to terms with life through his art. Not only is the book meticulous in recording the stages by which primitive man ordered his environment and developed an early technology, but it also involves the young reader in the life and imagination of a boy whose aspirations they immediately recognize as their own.

We also made use of a drama series broadcast by the BBC School Service, which helped the children to explore through movement and music the evolution of life from single-cellular squirming to upright man and on to the invention of tools and machinery. The latter presented us with opportunities in mathematics, to experiment with pulleys and levers, with weight. With marbling inks that spread on water the children took prints of swirling shapes and gaseous explosions of color. Finally, many of them wrote about evolution:

Nothing but space, all nothing, endless. Gas whirling around trying to make something out of nothing. Weird shapes and colours arc. All is careening around. Then it cools, hardening, beginning to be something, to take form. Small life-shapes move. Water. Then on land vegetation gets thick. Screams and cries echo across the volcanic islands. Then eruption. Red lava oozes out and pours down the side like a fire-tide. Smoky pieces of rock hurtle through the air. Life-shapes screech and burn to death in distress. Spitting and spurting the volcano kills. It burns itself out and it is dead. Murky lava bubbles. The last convulsions of the life-shapes in a changed substance.

    The eruption of the volcano expands the island, but in the ground are small creatures which can only crawl across it. Vegetation begins to grow again. But sticky bogs are hidden by the undergrowth. Tempted by the green the larger creatures come to feed, but some disappear into the bogs never to be seen. There is another change. New upright forms have come. They kill animals with sharp tools. They bring fear.

Philip (11+)

The children involved in these many experiences were from a variety of backgrounds where it would still be generally true that their parents place less significance on cultural inheritance than on ultimate material success in a competitive society. Because of this attitude there is always a temptation for teachers to prepare children for the next stage in their education and to forget the immediacy of response that is always manifest. So often there is a gulf between the potential of young children and what teachers expect from them. There develops a separation of school from living, as learning becomes a preparation for social status rather than a continuing part of the life process. Then it becomes necessary for children to use language for social conformity instead of for exploration: the clichés overwhelm their imagination. It is true in children's writing (as it is with literature) that the metaphor and image become the creative factors. These forces are conceived emotionally and intellectually and then exist "out there" for the group; they are powerful enough to reveal truths otherwise unattainable; they are subversive and erode superficial modes of thought. Most children are capable of using language in this way, given that the sources of experience are not confined.

Hitherto, in English education, school has offered pupils fragments of knowledge, only a little wisdom, and strictures about passing examinations. Under this system succeeding generations of the young have withered and become joyless adults, as the teacher and poet, Charles Causley understands in "School at Four-O'Clock":

> *Though men may blow this building up with powder,*
> *Drag its stone guts to knacker's yard, or tip,*
> *Smash its huge heart to dust, and spread the shingle*
> *By the strong sea, or sink it like a ship—*
> *Listen. Through the clear shell of air the voices*
> *Still strike like water from the mountain bed;*
> *The cry of those who to a certain valley*
> *Hungry and innocent came. And were not fed.*[4]

Teaching children to write creatively is therefore understanding how they live and how they grow; and ultimately valuing the integrity of each personality searching for fulfillment. In this there is more love than pedantry.

[4] Charles Causley, "School at Four-O'Clock," *Underneath the Water* (London: Macmillan, 1968), p. 8.

8. The New Mathematics

JAMES BOUCHER

JAMES BOUCHER *is a Research Fellow of the Nuffield Foundation for Educational Research and Headmaster of Thames Primary School, Blackpool. He is probably more widely known as a television teacher for the BBC Schools T.V. Service and the film,* I Do *and* I Understand. *He was lecturer abroad for the British Council and was in Central America and the Bahamas (1968). He has worked for the last five years with the Nuffield Primary Mathematics Project and the Schools Council on the development of Primary School Mathematics as author of the Computation and Structure Guides for the Nuffield Project.*

New Math and Old Math Compared

Much is heard about "new math," "modern math," or "Nuffield math" —but none of these really define what is actually happening in British primary schools. There is not very much *new* material; *modern* conveys the same uncertain meaning; and surely there is no such thing as *Nuffield* mathematics, any more than there is a *Woolworth's* math. There has certainly been some new thinking towards modern requirements, and it is true that the Nuffield Primary Math Project has been experimenting and producing Guides for teachers, but mainly there has been a call for a change in attitude towards mathematics in the primary school and on into the secondary stage—from five to thirteen years of age.

For at least a century, mathematics in the primary school was largely arithmetic or, to be even more honest, "doing sums." Math period came between scripture and playtime, and from the early age of five years, children were taught by rote to learn, parrot fashion, the so-called skills of: counting, number bonds, the four rules of number, weights and measures; fractions, decimals and percentages. The approach to this was mainly through mental and mechanical arithmetic and problems on one day per week. Children were taught tricks—an awful example of which was the method taught for division of vulgar fractions: "Turn it upside down and multiply!" Most children found this diet of memory work and getting the answer right as quickly as possible quite indigestible, and only a very few found the math lesson a pleasant experience.

In the past we have tended to fit children to *our* mathematics, but a sincere attempt is now being made to fit mathematics to the children. The all-round development of the child is the concern of

A sincere attempt is now being made to fit mathematics to the children.

every school and its teachers. It is our job to teach mathematics to all children regardless of what we think is their innate ability; and although some may be limited in the depth of their understanding, we cannot place a limit on the breadth of their experience. Within the bounds of their ability there is no reason why all normal children should not receive a full mathematical education.

Before proceeding further it would be well to say that "new mathematics" does not imply that the old or traditional is being discarded completely. Much old math is still being taught, and will continue to be taught, but perhaps the main difference is that instead of teaching what we are to examine, we are now examining what we are to teach. A critical appraisal is being made as to what we can safely do without. How much of what we previously taught is really relevant to our needs? For example: Do young children really understand long division? Do we need to do masses of sums in weights and measures? What about operations on fractions and the resultant "tricks?" And, more important, how much of what we previously taught has really been understood by the child and has remained with him? The present aim of teaching math in the primary school is to provide the child with every opportunity to discover, experiment and become involved in a wealth of mathematical experience, using concrete aids as much as possible, with computational arithmetic as a means to an end, not an end in itself.

TERMINOLOGY

Many people have heard vague references toward *sets* and *structural apparatus, number bases* and *modular arithmetic.* The Binary scale has suggested computers, whereas trundle wheels and metal chains infer either the beginnings of surveying or simply wasteful activity. Now, these are included in the new approach with no apologies required, but nothing has been overemphasized; and there is certainly no such thing as "instant math" any more than there is once-and-for-all learning at any stage of education. There is an endeavor at all times to bring out the pattern and order to be found in mathematics, and the idea of *set, sub-set,* and *elements of a set* is fundamental to mathematical thinking. These ideas are emphasized whenever the opportunity occurs, during any particular lesson or activity, so that it becomes an established part of a child's thinking, providing a language suitable for logical expression. *Number* is obviously still important, and children are encouraged to look upon this as an ordered structure, working from the set of counting numbers toward the *integers* and the set of *rational numbers*. This is being done in a slow but much more thorough way.

EXPERIENTIAL APPROACH

Through practical work, the children become conversant with British units of measure, understanding their relationships and uses. Lately, of course, because of the almost imminent change, the metric system is being used more and, soon perhaps, the British units of measure will have merely an historic value!

Since about 1955 there has been a growing acceptance of the view that the learning of mathematics should be as active, individual, interesting, and important in the eyes of the children as other subjects of the curriculum are expected to be. This view has created an excellent situation, for children's learning is usually intended now to ensure that they understand what they are doing and why things happen as they do. To echo the maxim of H.M.I. (Her Majesty's Inspector) Miss Edith Biggs who has done so much for primary math, "children learn by doing."

Through a wide experience of shape and size, both plane and solid, the fundamental ideas of geometry are learned, again in a practical way. Instead of the usual constructions made with pencil and compasses, set-square, and protractor, young children are encouraged to cut and fold, make and mend, fit together, pull apart, turn and move, leading them toward the more abstract notions of *bilateral* and *rotational symmetry, translations, properties,* and *proofs.*

Many of the new ideas on methods of teaching have been derived from the best of our infant schools. Here, dedicated teachers have for years realized the value of the practical approach in the young child's learning—Piaget has confirmed this approach and, thankfully, British teachers are now continuing to follow it long after the infant stage, in fact, right through the junior age-range (7–11) and into the secondary stage.

METHODOLOGY

Pictorial representation is now a well-established and popular ingredient of the primary math syllabus. Graphs, mappings, and Venn

Diagrams adorn classroom walls. From these is derived as much computation as possible, and most teachers agree on one common discovery: this work fosters and improves the use of English, both spoken and written.

The recent addition of such topics as *sets, working in bases other than 10, finite arithmetic* and so on, have made teachers more aware of the importance of **computation and structure** and relations in comparison with memorized techniques of computation. This has come about, in part, through the use of structural apparatus, the most useful type of which is based on cubes and rods that represent the numbers 1 to 10 by their respective lengths. This representation of the Denary (base 10) system by lengths (and later by areas and volumes) affords possibilities for extension to measurement, powers of number, and spatial ideas, as well as its obvious and more common use.

Nothing has been abandoned completely; only a wider variety of methods are being used. Consequently, there is more **discussion** between teacher and child and among the children themselves; more attention is being paid to the value of vocabulary and English, because it is well known that lack of understanding in mathematics is often due to an inability to comprehend the written or spoken word: math is now being talked about much more. A recent investigation showed that for most math text-books written for 7–8-year-olds, a reading age of 12+ is required!

Briefly, the new mathematics in British primary schools now caters for the subject as a whole, it is not just arithmetic. The mental, mechanical, and problems-solving approach has given way to considerations, such as: Computation and Structure, Pictorial Representation, and Shape and Size. These methods are derived from practical and concrete experiences that are used as forces of motivation and interest, so that the child finds math a pleasant subject, interesting and sometimes exciting. Most young children cannot cope with the abstractions of mathematics until a platform of experiences has been well and truly laid. As much work as possible is carried out from the environment, and children are encouraged to observe and take an interest in the math around them arising from everyday situations. At the commencement of the Nuffield Project in Primary Math. the Organizer, Dr. Geoffrey Matthews told his team, "When you are writing materials for the primary school children, remember the four 'P's': Keep it Practical, Pleasurable, Purposeful, but Pure."

At the infant stage one finds very young children sorting and classifying sets of objects according to **color, shape and size,** or some other property. The usual conkers (horse chestnuts), shells, buttons, and sticks, and so forth are still being used, perhaps more than before, in spite of the newly acquired "rods" which have added to the variety of materials used in providing boys and girls with beginnings in mathematical thinking. Sand, water, rice, beans, and lentils are fillers for different containers of various shapes and sizes. They are weighed and measured, poured—and spilled—as always. Young infants use arbitrary measures of their own to do their measuring: cupfuls, tinfuls, feet, spoons, sticks, string, and ribbon—all contributing to their general understanding, before standards of measurement are even mentioned.

New to the infant classroom is probably the introduction of graphs (pictorial representation). One sees Venn Diagrams, block charts, and mappings on almost every wall, revealing the simple statistics of the particular class of children: color of eyes, the pets we keep, our birthdays, our favourite color, even length of socks.

A mathematical climate is being created amidst shops and milk-bars, post offices and savings banks. Working in this climate the skilled teacher is gradually asking revealing questions about, for instance, the concepts of inequalities, as well as equalities; the need for standard units of measurement; thinking processes required for sorting and classifying, followed by "how many?" or "how much?" This line of questioning then reveals the need for efficient counting and an understanding of the composition and conservation of numbers. **Set language** is used where appropriate. Children are encouraged to talk about sets of objects and data—they can "see" the empty set on their graph—probably for the column labeled "Elephants" under the heading "Our Pets." They partition sets and make sub-sets when discovering that, for example, 9 can be written $3 + 3 + 3$ or $8 + 1$ or $5 + 3 + 1$, and so on.

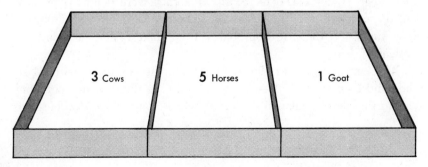

3 Cows   5 Horses   1 Goat

Often, the set of objects under consideration are farmyard animals with fences used to partition them into various sub-sets.

Counting is as important as ever, but not memorized chants. The child is taught *cardinality* and *ordinality* and is given much experience in counting and writing, say, the story of 6; and teachers make certain that the child knows that 6 is less than 7 or 1 more than 5 so that, later on, $9 + 7$ will probably be thought of as $9 + 1 + 6 = 10 + 6 = 16$—a considerable help in simple addition and number bonds. A thorough understanding of numbers up to 20 is as far as most children up to seven years of age are expected to achieve, but they now have a greater variety of experiences in shape and size, pictorial representation, and the **understanding of number.**

Because it was felt that too early an introduction to the signs and symbolism of arithmetic stifled understanding, an attempt has been made to simplify the shorthand to something more likely to have an intelligible meaning to very young children. One cannot emphasize too much the need for more talking about mathematics and for infants to make a fully written account of what they are actually doing; for example: "I had 4 conkers and then got another 5 conkers, so altogether I now have 9 conkers." But, of course, most infants cannot write that easily, if at all. This is a pity but it is worth the effort to try and obtain as full an account as possible, probably written by the teacher in many cases.

Here is an introduction to **simple illustrative recording** as suggested in the early Nuffield Teachers' Guides:

$$5, 4 \quad \rightarrow 9$$
$$\text{later} \quad 5 + 4 \rightarrow 9$$
$$\text{then,} \quad 5 + 4 = 9$$

The idea here was more or less obtained from young children themselves. When asked to record what they were doing when adding the numbers they had counted from two disjoint sets of objects they suggested the arrow, probably from their earlier mapping experiences.

The comma was introduced to obviate the confusion with 54 so the child then wrote $5, 4 \rightarrow 9$. It is easy to see the development from this to the more familiar $5 + 4 = 9$, which comes when teachers are

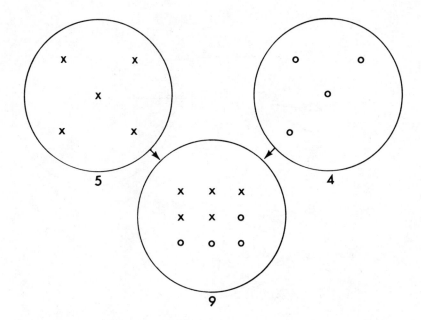

satisfied that children understand + and =; although, long before this, children are encouraged to use the signs of inequalities, i.e.:

$$9 > 5$$
$$5 < 6$$

From simple illustrative recording it is usual to find children interested and more aware of numbers. Gradually, they are able to abstract from the patterns and simple relations to which they are exposed. However, most of the time children are concerned with using apparatus, doing things, and talking about their experiences, much more than recording "sums."

It is not difficult to imagine the mathematical activity in an infant classroom when one considers their typical materials and activities: building blocks that give rise to construction of bridges, houses, cars, and rockets; the cutting of colored paper into various shapes; graphs and charts; weighing and measuring; talking and playing—all part of the necessary experiences that go toward a foundation in thinking for themselves and enjoyment of the learning process. [Perhaps with good reason, many teachers cry, "Too much!"]

It has already been stated that good infant schools have for many years used **activity methods** and **the discovery approach** in almost

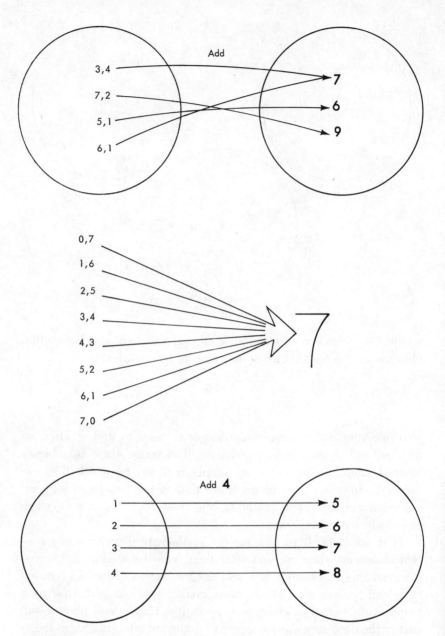

A few examples of the newer representatives in infant mathematics.

everything they do. It was always something of a tragedy when 7-year-old children, used to this lively and interesting way of learning, were suddenly pitchforked into the formal ways of the traditional junior

1	2	3	4	5
6	7	8	9	10
11	12	13	14	15
16	17	18	19	20

Training in *spotting patterns* is obtained through number squares and tables. The children are asked to color every other number, starting at 2, then to write these numbers down—with many variations of this.

1	9
2	8
3	7
4	6
5	5
•	•
•	•
•	•

Children are encouraged to discover the pattern here. Other *number bonds* are learned.

school. Happily, this has now been amended and junior-school teachers are continuing with the practical approach, using the child's natural curiosity and spontaneity to progress towards more abstract ideas.

It is fairly evident that, using a practical approach, there are problems to be surmounted, especially with the oversize classes of 40+ which almost every British primary-school teacher is encountering. Faced with this situation of large classes and varying abilities, it is also evident that children have to be arranged in groups. Groups of four children seem to be useful units in junior schools and offer a certain flexibility. Usually the groups are composed of children of compatible abilities and some choose friendship groups, whereas many teachers prefer to have children of varied abilities in a group, assuming that a bright child can then lead the not-so-bright children—if only in the matter of reading an assignment card. However, it is my experience that children can be intolerant and will ask for "nonproductive" members of the groups to be transferred. There is also the danger that the more forward pupil will do all the discovering while the others will be content to let them.

In a large class—sometimes up to 12 groups of four each—purposeful work can only proceed if some of the groups are more-or-less in-

Mathematical activity in a good primary school includes much weighing and measuring.

dependent of the teacher. This arrangement necessitates well-varied and carefully prepared assignments by the teacher, but it is the only way if we believe in the basic principles of experience and discovery. However, it must not be thought that **learning in groups** is the only way, though it is now a vital part of the method.

Teaching in this way may seem to be inefficient at times compared with the more formal drill methods of traditional class teaching, but the big difference lies in the fact that children in the new discovery situation should at all times be involved in intellectual effort, **thinking for themselves.** The intellectual effort of a child who is placed in the position of having to find out for himself some way of computing approximately how many peas there are in the jar (without counting them in ones) or of finding the height of an inaccessible wall is of a far different order from that of a child "doing" long division sums to no real purpose. Instead of working from a formula we are now working towards it.

Many useful pieces of **commercially produced apparatus** have al-

The enterprising teacher often engages about a third of her class in outside activities.

most become standard equipment: geo-boards (nail boards), abaci, equalizers, clinometers, trundle-wheels, plastic shapes, map measurers, ranging rods, structural apparatus of all kinds, tools and instruments, scales and containers for weighing and measuring. These are all useful, and perhaps desirable, but what is commonly called "kitchen-sink" **apparatus** is even more valuable: cartons, boxes, tins, packets, bottles, straws, elastic, wire, cotton reels, matchboxes, string, paper, and cards. These easily available objects are better for children to use because they become involved in searching for other useful mediums—seeing possibilities for themselves in the world that is theirs, beyond the classroom. Jam jars and cheeseboxes have so much more significance! It is far more rewarding to make a clinometer from a postcard, with the outline of a protractor drawn and graduated complete with milk-straw sighting and a plumb-line of cotton with a plasticene weight—especially when it actually seems to work:

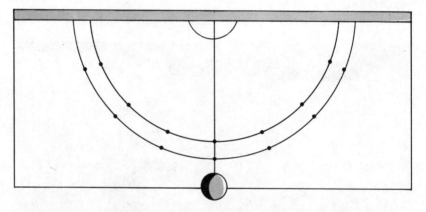

A most stimulating activity in the junior school, for both teacher and child, is experimental work, making use of the **school environment:** scale plans of buildings and playground, traffic counts, shapes around us, simple statistics of milk consumption, school meals, attendances, hobbies, pets, and numerous other collections of facts and figures. This type of activity makes for real and genuine interest. This side of the math program provides the enterprising teacher with an opportunity to engage about a third of the class in outside activities, while some groups inside the classroom are engaged on other experimental work, leaving the remainder more or less static, perhaps writing up the results of their discoveries or, yes, practicing arithmetical computation.

Obviously this description does not mean to convey a picture of groups of children surrounding tables of apparatus and junk materials, or pushing trundle-wheels—perhaps discovering little or nothing at all—and woefully lacking in necessary skills. Let me point out once again that essentials are not overlooked and all traditional teaching has not been discarded.

It is not true that multiplication tables are no longer learned, or vulgar fractions abolished! There is still room for a normal class lesson, individual tuition, and computational practice. Multiplication tables are learned, but not solely by chanting and remembering the "tune" rather than the facts. A gradual process building up towards memorization is employed through carefully prepared number work and practical applications. Then by about nine years of age many children are asked to memorize "tables," although brighter children achieve this naturally. Those children who cannot do this are allowed to use a "table-square." We do not stop the mathematics for the sake of **learning tables.**

Children's **use of vulgar fractions** comes naturally as they are a part of their daily vocabulary, e.g. ½ lb. sweets, ¼ lb. tea; halving doubling occurs in puzzles and real life situations. In short, parts of concrete wholes including whole numbers are still taught, but many British schools now shun the teaching of operations on vulgar fractions through the medium of tricks (e.g. "turn it upside down and multiply").

Class lessons often occur when discussion takes place concerning a particular concept, inquiry, or appraisal of some discovery or data collected. The whole class shares the experience.

Computational practice is still necessary but reduced to minimum requirements. The chief concern of the teacher is when to practice a skill or skills and how much time to spend doing it. Many teachers use duplicated sheets of examples so that laborious copying of sums is restricted; children only have to be concerned with working the problem and recording their solution, and in this way time is saved.

The Nuffield Teachers' Guides have stressed throughout not only computation but also structure of number. **Properties of operations** are **emphasised,** and although many British teachers were aghast at words like *Commutativity, Associativity,* and *Distributivity,* at least they have accepted the ideas as important. Without necessarily using these words, children are exposed to experiences where these properties do or—perhaps more important—do not hold, e.g.:

$$6 + 4 = 4 + 6$$
$$6 - 4 \neq 4 - 6$$
$$6 \times 4 = 4 \times 6$$
$$6 \div 4 \neq 4 \div 6$$

Order in everyday life is explored to discover relations and their properties so that varied experience is encountered which encourages a critical and appreciative mind. For example:

Does it matter whether one puts on shoes first then socks, or socks then shoes?

If John runs faster than Peter and Peter runs faster than Paul, do we know that John runs faster than Paul?

If Mary likes Susan, can we honestly say that we know Susan likes Mary?

These usually oral exchanges with children help to stimulate logical mathematical thinking.

Mention has already been made of the vocabulary and English that can be derived from the new approach to mathematics. A **clear exposition** of an investigation carried out is far more valuable than the hackneyed type of composition carried on in many schools of the past. Math can also be integrated with other subjects, even scripture—some very exciting math work has been observed, arising from the relative sizes of David and Goliath, measured in cubits and spans, and the building of Solomon's Temple! Geography and history, science and nature study all provide enrichment for the math education of junior children. Teachers are realizing (as good teachers always have) that math may arise at any time in any subject, and if the children are interested, then is the time to deal with the particular topic.

Almost every day it is possible also to find some **item of news** that lends itself to discussion and has a considerable math content. The Olympic games, elections, and facts and figures all serve their purpose in providing talking points for discussion about decimals, percentages, scoring methods, and the metric system. Perhaps more important is the fact that they furnish the opportunity to help children realize the usefulness and purpose of mathematics in relation to the world around them.

Some say that all mathematics is mental, all mathematics involves problem solving—I have never heard it said that all mathematics is mechanical. However, it must be said that mathematical problems often present a child with words and phraseology, much of which is irrelevant, and we owe it to our pupils to help them read with such understanding as to be able to sort and classify relevant data in order to reach an accurate solution. Class discussion of everyday problems from newspaper and T.V. provide opportunities for this. But, also important, is the problem produced by the child himself. It is not good enough just to produce our problems for children to solve in a passive way. A child is much more likely to think harder if asked to produce his own problems. An inquiry concerning an aircraft can produce involvement in speeds, altitudes, distances, fuel consumption and a host of other things which will widen a child's knowledge considerably. Math teachers feel that to answer a few questions may teach a child to use a timetable, but if a child is asked to construct a timetable he is well on his way to becoming a mathematician.

A most important part of the child's mathematical activities and investigations is the way he records his results and conclusions. Methods of recording can be of considerable help to the young child who may not be too articulate or even literate.

At the earliest stage, recording may be done by word of mouth, and the teacher may write for the child. But here are some other means of recording that are now open to the preliterate child:

A set of objects may be drawn and then partitioned, or a block graph may show the partition of a set into sub-sets.

When a child can read and write then he can also record in writing or in symbols. The child can now record by pictorial representation

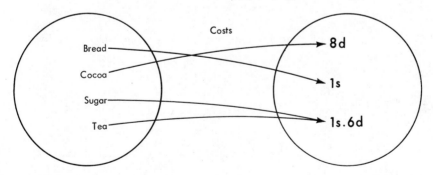

An arrow may be drawn between two pictures to show a relationship.

Name	Milk	Dinners
Jane	✓	✓
John	✓	
Caroline		✓
Susan	✓	✓
June	✓	
Peter		✓

Crosses or ticks may be entered in a table—a simple way of recording data.

or in his own words. Later, properly drawn tables can be used to record or store information neatly, or calculations can be set down in tabular form, e.g.:

longs	units
1	2
1	3
3	0

Linear forms of recording calculations are often more suitable for certain number work, e.g.:

$$167 + 132 + 18 = 200 + 67 + 32 + 18 = 100 + 60 + 7$$
$$200 + 100 + 17 \qquad\qquad 100 + 30 + 2$$
$$10 + 8$$
$$317$$

$$200 + 100 + 17$$
$$317$$

or:

$$28 \times 7 = (20 \times 7) + (8 \times 7)$$
$$140 + 56$$
$$196$$

The main thing is that a variety of methods are now being introduced, each appropriate in its own way, and children are encouraged to write factual information in clear English. It is better that one problem should be done three ways than three problems one way only.

Text Materials and Classroom Fittings

From the deluge of textbooks appearing on the educational market, one thing is now clear: few schools adopt a particular book and use this as their chosen syllabus, to be worked through, as in the past. Again, a variety of books are purchased and topics are chosen if considered suitable. Useful **mathematics books** are now an integral part of each class library and are gay and colorful as opposed to the austere pages of examples in black and white, the standard text not so long ago. It is interesting to compare the old traditional syllabus in arithmetic with the following range of ideas tried successfully with children between the ages of 5 and 13.

Sorting and classification: sets, sub-sets, intersection of sets.
Number relationships and notation (including different bases).
Quantity relationships: weights, measures, and money.
Decimal fractions.
The operations and properties of $+$, $-$, $\times$, and $\div$ within the set of natural numbers.
Modular or clock arithmetic.
The properties of common mathematical shapes within man-made and natural environments.
Dimensions: perimeter, volume, and area.
Symmetry: reflection, rotation, translation.
Similarity.
Graphical relationships. The graphical relationships covered include the family:

$$y = x^2 \; y = x^3, \; y = x$$
$$xy = 1, \text{ or, } y = \frac{1}{x}; \; y = x^2.$$

Positive and negative integers.
Simple probability.

It takes only a degree of understanding for one to realize that the modern methods and approach to the teaching of mathematics is very demanding on the teacher who has to relearn and constantly rethink attitudes and techniques. Teachers also must reorient their thinking concerning classroom furniture and fittings. The old ironclad dual desk is disappearing from the scene as quickly as four straight rows of children sitting obediently and passive.

Organization of the Changeover from Old to New Math

It may also be realized that the most important "piece of apparatus" is the teacher. Everything revolves around the teacher, and each teacher works out his own destiny within the requirements of the Head Teacher and the facilities available in his particular school.

Some schools have a math laboratory or workshop, the use of which is necessarily scheduled according to timetable. Others have tried this as an initial step but then found that teachers preferred to work within their own classroom. Whichever method is adopted, one thing needs to be emphasized most strongly: the advisability of starting slowly when making the changeover from traditional math teaching to the new approach. An old Creole motto encountered in British Honduras, "The hurrier I go, the behinder I get!" could well apply to this situation.

Teachers would be well advised to commence with one group of three or four children and to set them to work with a practical assignment while carrying on in the usual way with the remainder of the class. From observation of this first group and with additional assignments, perhaps two groups per day could be tried. On subsequent days, two different groups of children could be engaged on practical math. At least eight children per day would then have the benefit of doing mathematics in this way. During one week, each pupil in a class of 40 children would have one day's math lessons involved in practical work.

From this kind of beginning a teacher may then develop the approach to his own satisfaction, at his own pace. It is nearly always disastrous when a teacher tries an overnight change, trying to involve the whole class at once.

Here are a few suggestions helpful toward organization of the new method of teaching:

1. Make certain the children know what to do.
2. Appoint group leaders to obtain apparatus and, more important, put it back.
3. Keep apparatus in a set place, e.g. weight corner, map drawer, measuring corner (rulers, tapes).
4. Keep stopwatches, map measurers, and pocket compasses in the teacher's drawer. [These are attractive to children.]
5. Do not expect to record everything they do in mathematics.
6. Pose additional verbal questions concerning an assignment and get the children to make up additional questions of their own. [This can also help when you are harassed by more than one group of children.]

The timetable needs to be flexible enough to allow for math at any time of the day, or to allow children to complete an investigation or assignment. Nothing irritates interested children more than being compelled to stop and change lessons when they are deeply engrossed in an interesting experiment.

Children have to be trusted now and then to work without the constant supervision of a teacher, which requires training; but the golden rule seems to be that if children are sufficiently engrossed in their task, they can be trusted. This achievement is surely a worthwhile bonus to any teaching method. So long as children know what they are required to do and the instructions are plain and simple, then it usually follows that they can be allowed to work alone in small groups—perhaps in the playground.

Plain and simple instructions bring to mind the current trend of using assignment cards. These are taxing teachers' thoughts and energies to the full. Good assignment cards are thoughtfully prepared by the teacher with a vocabulary and degree of difficulty suitable for the particular class or groups of children, perhaps even an individual child. Not too much is explained but just enough to set children thinking, again depending on the children for whom the assignment is intended. Wherever possible the card is open-ended to allow children to carry on with their own ideas and thinking. A rather amusing incident occurred when I was teaching a class of 10-year-olds (3rd-year juniors). Their assignment card read:

M.10.

You will need the motorway of Gt. Britain, an O.S. map of Blackpool and the Fylde, and a map-measurer. From the map find the approximate length of the M.1., then the M.6, (to the nearest mile.)

How far is it from London to   a) Glasgow
                                       b) Edinburgh
                                       c) Dublin
                                       d) Manchester

You will have to discover the best route to take and the A.A. handbook will help you in the case of London to Dublin. Give, also, what you think will be the approximate time taken for these journeys.
Now, see if you can find a place or places roughly 1 mile from school.

The last instruction on the assignment card caused me some anguish. Three children in particular took the instruction quite literally and, with a yard trundle-wheel (wheelbarrow), escaped my notice and proceeded to trundle 1,760 yds. from the school gate. I can only say that I was relieved when they returned safely and beaming with the satisfaction that they had "found it."

In-service Training of Math Teachers

Teacher training is occupying the thoughts of all Local Education Authorities (L.E.A.) and Teachers' Centers following the lead of the Nuffield Math Project and the Schools Council are doing a most useful job in providing in-training courses and the opportunity to exchange views and ideas. Such "new" topics as Vectors, Graphs (leading to algebra), Statistics, Logic, and Motion geometry demand detailed explanation. It is gratifying to observe the coming together of secondary, junior, and infant teachers in a Teachers' Center. Each one helps the other in combined efforts to find ways of interesting children and improving the learning of modern mathematics.

British teachers were (and some perhaps still are) bewildered by the maze of new ideas and thinking. They were asked to do so much more than day-by-day, page-by-page arithmetic, and they needed help.

The Nuffield Math Project set up pilot areas throughout the length and breadth of Great Britain. The focal point of the pilot area was the Teachers' Center and almost every L.E.A. followed this lead. Teachers' Centers are becoming a very important part of the educational scene, some planned on a grand scale but most quite humble, with just a few being set up in old buildings previously condemned as unsuitable for schools. In the main, the Center is comprised of a fair-sized room or hall with flat-topped tables, display boards, and such equipment as duplicators, edge-binding machines, guillotines, and materials for producing mathematical assignment cards. Apparatus of all kinds is there for teachers to examine and use. Every Center has its teacher/leader who is engaged either full time or part time to provide and organize courses, lectures, demonstrations, and tuition for his colleagues. He or she also visits schools to encourage and help to link the schools with the Center and its program. Children's work is brought to the Center and examined—successes and failures in some particular field are discussed.

Usually, when teachers have had a year or so of the "practical approach" of finding out and discovering for themselves, they then become more interested in pure math and wish to learn more about certain topics—requesting lectures on Sets, Vectors, geometry, and algebra. It is not always easy to find suitable people to do this, but sometimes teachers emerge from among their own ranks, who can explain simply and sympathetically some topic of mathematics which is of interest and may never have been fully understood by many of their colleagues. Lectures in secondary math from a Training College often are a great help here.

In addition to the practical room or lecture-demonstration hall perhaps it should be mentioned that one all-important part of any Center is the lounge and kitchen. The proverbial English cup of tea together with a comfortable chair makes for discussion in a comforting atmosphere. A good library is also an integral part of any Center. Most Centers are administered by a committee of teachers who organize the program and make provision for this according to the grant allowed by their Authority. It can truthfully be said that if nothing else comes out of the New Math, the setting-up of Teachers' Centers alone has made it a worthwhile venture. Never before have teachers had such an opportunity to meet and discuss their problems or continue their training after student days. The value and importance of in-service training and the Teachers' Center is finally being realized.

Results of the Changeover to New Math

It seems appropriate to ask what has emerged from the ferment in primary-school mathematics over the past ten years. Without underestimating what has been achieved so far, it seems that we are only now on the threshold of a basis for major reform. There is most certainly wider content and a real concern on the part of everyone to help children learn and use mathematics. However, it seems that the emphasis is still on the end product: ideas understood, calculations performed, geometrical facts known, the different graphs that can be constructed, and the types of problems that can be solved. Attainment tests are being produced which attempt to measure all these factors. There could be a very real danger that, once more, we shall be teaching by testing. This would be a great pity inasmuch as the real thing for which we are aiming is the development of mathematical thought. We must train our children to think and face each new challenge with a certain amount of confidence. How many times have we heard from children, "We haven't had those yet" or "We don't do them that way"?

Some of the most outstanding developments in thinking and confidence have been in geometrical ideas introduced mainly through the provision of simple materials: paper for folding; sets of cardboard or plastic polygons which can either be tessellated or scotch-taped into solids; rubber bands and geo-boards; milk straws and pipe cleaners for frameworks; cardboard strips for rigidity; containers of all kinds; and pegboards for coordinates. It is indeed a pleasure to see the confidence and mastery of geometrical ideas possessed by some 11-year-old children who have had these experiences. Transformation geometry in the secondary school will surely have more meaning for children who have been involved in such activities in the primary school.

It seems hard to believe the paradox that for so many years children spent hours doing masses of calculation in measures of three or four units without any actual experience of measuring. We at least seem to have grasped the fact at last that you cannot learn to measure without measuring; and this truism applies to other topics. The main problems now seem to be organizing the use and storage of equipment plus the supervision of a reasonable progression in mathematical content. It is possible that we may still be trying to do too much too quickly.

A matter of current debate is the place and implications of modern mathematics in the primary school in the sense of "Sets and Relations," ideas of algebraic structure like *group, inverse, identity element,* and *closure.* It is not easy to strike a balance between what should be taught in the primary school for later purposes in the secondary stage and what needs to be taught, simply because it is significant at the primary stage. However, it does seem that where children have been brought up on a diet of interesting and meaningful practical work, they take to abstractions and are more ready to abstract, in the upper junior age-range (9–11).

The practical approach should not be regarded simply as "that which is useful" or "as used in everyday life." If it also means the use of apparatus and concrete materials involving physical actions and structure then we can distinguish between the different reasons for their use. Measurement and geometry at this stage are essentially practical; structural apparatus models number in various aspects, and it is through other simple apparatus and materials that children of primary-school age can be presented with situations that will engage them in thinking about real problems and in solving them. So much better than asking children to try to imagine situations from written problems. This last use of the practical approach needs to be emphasized more if we are to allay the fears of those who dismiss the use of concrete materials as "play" or simply as "visual aids," and do not recognize the value of this approach.

Many children will never discover very much at all if left completely alone with a problem. It requires a teacher's skill to deal individually with children and their individual problems. Understanding can be accepted as a useful idea if we realize that mathematical ideas have to be grasped individually and that concepts do not come as ready-made parcels. While some children are capable of abstracting and grasping mathematical concepts, other children need many more leading questions than others, and some need a great deal of help.

Conclusions

It should be mentioned that parents also are entitled to information and enlightenment regarding the new methods of learning mathematics. Understandably, they sometimes become anxious about their children's activities when they seem to be enjoying themselves—and the traditional standard measurement has always been, "How many sums were ticked right today?"

An obvious way of dealing with parents is to invite them to school for an evening to examine a display of children's work and to try their hand themselves at the mathematical assignments that confront their child. (A short talk on the aims of modern math teaching and reassurance that necessary skills are still acquired can precede or follow.) It is not easy to demonstrate that the much more important foundations of mathematical thinking and understanding are laid in children's experiences, but usually once the reassurances relating to formal skills have been given, parents will readily take on trust the value that comes from their own discoveries. The usual remarks from parents are, "I wish we had been taught mathematics this way"; or, "My child certainly likes doing it this way."

No one would be bold enough to claim to be in a position from which he could make definite claims concerning the outcome of all that is being tried in primary-school mathematics, but at least two positive outcomes seem clear: children *enjoy* math. today and there is now a widespread interest among mathematicians, psychologists, primary-school teachers, and parents in math teaching in the school. It also seems fairly obvious that against the background of a changing industrial society and an unpredictable future for a significant proportion of our working society, children must be given experiences and the kind of mathematics designed to encourage flexibility, adaptability, and creative thinking.

We have moved a long way from the days when a narrow arithmetic syllabus was followed mainly to provide competent clerks, civil servants, and shop assistants who could compute number and money speedily and accurately. Today we are concerned with teaching today's primary-school child to think logically and to approach each new problem with as much confidence as possible. Not all the benefits of the new approach can be seen in the primary school, but secondary-school teachers are already voicing their appreciation of the better attitude towards mathematics observed in new intakes from the junior school.

By now, most British primary-school teachers are quite familiar with the ancient proverb:

> *I hear, and I forget*
> *I see, and I remember*
> *I do, and I understand.*

9. | The New Science

LEONARD F. ENNEVER

LEONARD F. ENNEVER, *B.Sc., is Director of the Science 5/13 Project sponsored jointly by the Schools Council, the Nuffield Foundation, and the Scottish Education Department. He was formerly one of Her Majesty's Inspectors of Schools.*

(Miss Dean is discovered in her classroom. She is standing among the tables at which are working the forty or so ten-year-olds who make up her class. She is talking to two girls.)

GIRLS: But, Miss Dean, we couldn't count every single buttercup in the field because it's so big, and it would take so long that when we'd finish it would be all different.

MISS D.: Well, do you have to know exactly how many buttercups there are?

GIRLS: Not really. It was just that when John and David measured the area of the field they said there were thousands of buttercups, and Susan and I said there weren't, and they said, "How many, then?" so we thought we'd find out.

MISS D.: Isn't it like when you found out how many steps you took to the mile? You didn't walk a whole mile.

GIRLS: No, Miss Dean. We found out how many steps for twenty-two yards, and did it three times to be fair. I know! Couldn't we count the buttercups in a square yard or something, and then multiply up? David and John know how many square yards there are in the field.

MISS D.: Well you'd still have to be fair.

GIRLS: We could do it, say, in ten different places all over the field. Can we have a try and see what is comes out like? (The two girls go off to do it.)

180

(Miss Dean turns to George and Robert who are hammering at the workbench.)

MISS D.: What's this you're making?

BOYS: Well, we finished the Severn Bridge so we thought we'd make a model of a bowstring bridge and test it to see how much it would stand. You see they're both suspension bridges but they're different.

MISS D.: That's a good idea. I think that Mr. Thomas has a book with pictures of bowstring bridges in it. You might ask him to let you see it. (They go out to the library.)

(On the table by the window Frank and Julia are working with batteries and other apparatus.)

F. & J.: Please, miss, we can't make our electric bell work. What's wrong with it?

MISS D.: (Looking at it) I'm afraid I can't see at once. Suppose you ask Richard; he's the expert on these things.

(Miss Dean goes to the next table, and Agnes looks up from her writing.)

AGNES: Please, Miss Dean, we've nearly finished the work-card on pendulums you gave us; and it says, "Can you find a way to make a pendulum draw the path of its own swing on a sheet of paper?" Well miss, we think we can do it. Can we try?

MISS D.: Yes, if you think you can manage it. Do you want to tell me about it?

AGNES: We think we can do it with what we've got and what's in the junk box. We could bring what else we need from home. And, please miss, we'd rather just show you when we've done it.

MISS D.: Alright then, you go ahead and try.

(Miss Dean turns to Willie who has come up with a paper in his hand.)

WILLIE: Please, Miss Dean, I've finished that poem about the Barnacle Goose; you know, the one that started:

> *The Barnacle Goose*
> *Is out on the loose.*
> *No trouble has he,*
> *He's free.*

I did it at home. (He hands her the paper.)

MISS D.: (Reading it) that's fine. It's a jolly poem and I like it. I think the class will like it too. Will you make a copy for us, and put it up on the wall with the others about our visit to the Wildfowl Trust? We've got quite a collection now.

(Miss Dean stops beside Peter, who has his head down and his tongue out, writing with grim concentration.)

MISS D.: Why, Peter, that's a lot of writing for you! I've never seen you do so much before. What's it about?

PETER: It was that photograph of the sheep you let me take with your camera. I never took a photograph before. And I'm developing it and printing it. I didn't ever think I could do that, even if you helped me. I'm writing about how I did it. And if I put the photograph with it, could I put it on the wall?

MISS D.: Certainly you could. That's the first long piece of writing you've ever done. And it's good. (Peter glows diffidently.)

(Miss Dean moves on to the book-corner where she can see Kevin reading.)

MISS D.: Kevin, you said that you and the Weather Study Group were going to make some observations on different kinds of clouds. Have you finished doing it?

KEVIN: Yes, Miss Dean; and we wrote about it.

MISS D.: Can I see what you've written? (Kevin gets a paper from his locker and hands it to her.)

MISS D.: (Reading it thoughtfully) Are these all the kinds of clouds that you and the Weather Group have seen in the last week?

KEVIN: (Nods) Yes, miss.

MISS D.: Well I've seen a number of different ones as well. I think you must have forgotten to look sometimes. Yesterday, for instance, there were lots of mare's-tails. And there's something you've missed about those fine-weather clouds we were looking at. I think we'd better get the Weather Group together and discuss what you've done and what you might do next. You were going to talk to the rest of the class about clouds, remember?

This composite scene was made from actual incidents that happened as described and as near as memory serves. They did not all happen in the same classroom, nor all on the same day, with the same teacher—indeed, if they had, it would have been a very good day for that teacher. Nevertheless, the scene is none the less authentic for being intensified,

so we may profitably use it for analysis in order to uncover what makes
this kind of teaching possible; so that we may consider the part of
the iceberg that lies below water.

Concrete Observations and Questions About "Miss Dean's" Methods

When the scene started, Miss Dean was standing among the children's
tables: she was not at her own table; she rarely teaches from that position. Mostly she spends her time moving around the classroom helping
groups of pupils where they work, either inside the classroom or outside it. She discusses with them the work they are doing, suggests
possibilities, but rarely tells them what to do or how to do it. She works
a great deal by asking questions. Her methods are based more on encouraging the children for what they have done rather than on criticiz-
ing them for what they have not. There is a constant demand on her
by the pupils, which upset her at first, but now she can keep the needs
of individual pupils in mind and deal with them according to their
priorities. She can work in this way partly because there is mutual
confidence between her and her pupils; she is their helper not their
dictator. They work with her willingly and exercise independent judgment within an accepted framework, none the less aware—should ever
the point arise—that what she says goes.

Let us look at her classroom for a moment. It is small, about five-
hundred square feet in area, and it is the base for about forty children.
Everyone wishes it were bigger. It is furnished with light-weight stack-
able tables and chairs, some blocks of small lockers where pupils keep
their books, a few spare tables, a cupboard, and a small workbench.
She is very lucky in having a tiny storeroom—scarcely larger than a
cupboard—which adjoins the room. This furniture has no permanent
arrangement; sometimes the tables are in groups, sometimes in lines,
arranged according to the needs of the day. At other times part of the
furniture is arranged along the walls of a fairly wide corridor outside
the room, for displays, practical work, or even, reading and writing.
Often the lockers are turned end-on to the walls inside the room to
form bays that are devoted to special activities such as craft work,
science, reference work with books, or for the particular needs of one
group of pupils. Frequently there might not be a chair and a table-

space set out for every pupil in the class; indeed, if there were, there might not be a full class complement to fill them because some pupils would be working elsewhere—in the corridor, the auditorium, the playground, the field or sometimes even off the school premises.

The room became the way it is because the pattern of working in the school demanded it. The school is an oldish one, and when it was planned classrooms were arranged formally with desks in rows facing toward the teacher at the front. But gradually, as the way of working became flexible, the trickle of new furniture enabled a succession of teachers to plan the room itself in a more flexible way. Thus Miss Dean inherited her way of working and her room from her forebears on the staff, each of whom worked out her individual ideas yet contributed (under the headmaster's guidance) something unique to the general development of the school. Previously, in any particular class, there were only one or two groups of children working together, and that only at certain times in the week in certain specific subjects. Gradually, however, the numbers and the times increased, spread to more and more areas of the curriculum; until now when we looked in on Miss Dean, we were lucky to find so much science going on in the class at the same time. Indeed the science work itself developed with the freer way of working, and in its present form is not more than about ten years old. In the past it used to consist only of nature study which (inherited from the past and imprisoned in a restricted classroom) often consisted of copied pictures and a desultory display table. What a great pity, because nature study is one of the finest vehicles for education at the primary stage. Now, freed from the trammels that prevented investigation, nature study is coming into its own and forms part of the wider field of study we call science.

To continue our analysis of what we saw, we might well collect our observations into related groups and see what questions they stimulate us to ask. Here are some of the things we saw:

1. The whole class was in action at the same time; pupils were working individually or in groups of two or more, sometimes boys and girls mixed, and they were doing different jobs at the time we saw them. Not all were doing science work, indeed some on whom we did not remark about were doing work connected with other areas of study.

Do they always work this way? Do they never do the same kind of work at the same time? Does the teacher never give a lesson or talk to them as a whole class?

There is no fixed rule about the way of working, but because the emphasis is on individual development and personal interest most of the work in science and related studies is done in groups. Miss Dean often discusses work with the class as a whole, and this does throw up topics which sometimes she and they prefer treated as a general talk or lesson. The point is that she feels free to adopt whatever means appear best for coping with the situation.

2. Most of their tasks they had chosen themselves; some were set by work-cards.

What are these work-cards: what is on them? Do they never work from books? Does the teacher never just tell children what to do?

Miss Dean keeps a stock of work-cards that she has made herself and drawn from many sources. Some contain directions for performing an experiment (she emphasizes that they are experiments, not merely practical exercises), followed by questions about it that may lead to some sort of investigation or to reading from a book. Generally the questions are open-ended and permit a good deal of personal choice in the means that the child can adopt for answering them. Other work-cards consist of problems to be worked out or interesting passages cut from a journal that are followed by questions—again generally open-ended. Some cards may contain directions on how to do something or make something.

These work-cards are invaluable when several groups of children need to be started at the same time or when Miss Dean cannot give her attention to all of them at once. Sometimes they provide for a group work related to what they have been doing or give a group that has reached an impasse in their own investigation an activity likely to suggest the kind of lead they are seeking.

The children continually refer to books and often perform experiments to verify what they read. They acquire a taste for firsthand evidence, and some of them become quite critical about it. In these circumstances it is rarely necessary for Miss Dean to tell them what to do, unless it be a matter of class organization; rather, she sets the scene, provides a variety of opportunities, and asks questions that cause children to suggest their own activities.

3. A good deal of the work revolved around solving problems, many of which the children had set themselves generally from questions they had asked or observations they had made. Some of the problems

stemmed from suggestions made by the teacher, and some of them were on a work-card.

Do they ever do a straightforward piece of work that results in their gaining some item of knowledge that the teacher considers valuable?

Yes they do; frequently. They are always having to turn to books for information which they use in their investigations and in their written accounts of their work. Often they follow this up by reading on their own, or undertake a piece of work designed to inform the class about something, such as cloud formation for instance. A point worth bearing in mind is that some children need far more guidance than others.

4. Much of the work was of a practical nature and sometimes involved designing and constructing apparatus to help investigate some point, or making a model in illustration of something or other. Provision for doing this was made in the classroom.

Is all the work practical? Do they never just sit down and learn something from a book?

Much of their work is practical, but a good deal of what goes on is the reading and written work that results from their practical investigations. It is unlikely that Miss Dean would ever set them to learn facts by rote, although occasionally they choose to do it for themselves —one boy tried to learn the table of the elements, with some success, too.

5. Subjects were not segregated. Investigations in science seemed to involve work in English, art, craft, mathematics, geography, and could have involved other subjects as well.

Is the curriculum then one great "mush" of subjects all stirred in together? Is there nothing that can be identified as, say, science or mathematics or English?

What are referred to at the secondary stage as subjects are clearly identifiable in the primary-school curriculum, but they are not confined to set periods in a timetable. Where there are areas of overlap, subjects are allowed to merge freely with each other. Science is concerned with investigating the environment and thus gives rise to a good deal of overlap; and so it generates a lot of work in other subject areas. But there is still plenty of identifiable English, mathematics, art, and so on.

6. Children were encouraged to help each other and to use each other's expertise. Apparently it is customary to consult other teachers, and there seemed to be a suggestion that a given teacher was not to be considered an expert in everything.

What happens to a teacher's authority when she's continually saying she doesn't know?

The question doesn't arise. Miss Dean's authority does not depend on subject knowledge. It is founded on close personal relations with children whom she seeks to understand. The atmosphere is one of honest inquiry, not by the children alone, but by children and teacher together—she is seeking to find out just as much as they are. If she knew all the answers, the situation would be a false one; indeed, it is essential to the whole process that she should not know all the answers.

7. Although Miss Dean accepted what the children offered and gave them a good deal of encouragement for what they had done, this does not mean that she accepts their efforts entirely without criticism. She has clear standards as a teacher and doesn't remain content with work that she thinks is of a level lower than a particular child should be able to achieve. She varies her demands according to the capabilities of each child and the individual circumstances. The children seem to understand this, and they give her what she asks for. Her demands rarely come in the form of commands or recrimination, rather she lets them emerge through discussion and sometimes persuasion. An implicit appeal to a pupil's awareness of his own capability sometimes achieves her aim, for children are often their own sternest critics. But mostly they simply like to do good work for its own sake and to be praised for it: that is the situation she is striving for. If the work is good she says so, they believe her, because they know she wouldn't say it if it weren't so in the circumstances; and if after they've tried hard it still isn't good, they expect a sympathetic discussion on how it could be made better.

What does she do about children who are just plain lazy?

Children who are interested are not lazy; if they are not interested, Miss Dean will try to understand why and to remedy the situation. If they are never interested then something is wrong with them—it may have medical causes or it may be rooted in home circumstances. Whatever it was Miss Dean would probably discuss it with the headmaster and seek the cause: then perhaps with help from others, she might be able to do something towards putting matters right.

She may need tact and sometimes even firmness in helping children make a start; here their own sense of fairness is a help; but unless she has been unwise in her suggestions it will not be long before the children's own interests are stimulated and then supervene.

8. Display is an important feature of this classroom: it is the children's work that goes on the wall, not the teacher's. To see that everyone has something there at some time or the other is part of her policy of acceptance and encouragement. The children come to value themselves having produced something good enough for the others to look at. Miss Dean apparently spends quite a bit of her time mounting work for display so that it looks attractive. Undoubtedly, the children help her sometimes after school, because they enjoy working with her and they like their room to look attractive; after all, it is their room and they have a part in deciding how it shall be arranged.

She must get some stupid suggestions sometimes. Does she just accept them?

When she is discussing matters of this sort she doesn't just try to talk the children around to her way of thinking; if she did, they would very soon realize that their suggestions were not going to be accepted. Generally, they reach some sort of amicable compromise, but occasionally her reasons for accepting a suggestion from a child might outweigh the disadvantages of the suggestion itself. In cases like this she accepts the suggestion—if it is at all reasonable—even though she does not altogether approve of it.

9. Writing is an accepted part of the day's work. In general, children were observed to be enjoying the writing because it is part of something that interests them (and which they chose to do). They enjoy telling what they have done and what they think about it. Sometimes they express themselves by means of drawings or graphs or models, or some combination of all methods. A great deal of their work is done on paper so that it can be mounted and put on the wall: some is mounted in homemade folio books for others to read, some is kept in

a folder. They have exercise books that are used mostly for drill exercises. Communication is by whatever means seem best, and discussion
by the whole class or in small groups is an important part of it. The
discussion is not always formal; the greater part of it goes on with
each other and with Miss Dean while the work is being done. One
result of this is that children know what others are doing. This information spreads and interest develops and promotes comment, criticism, and mutual help.

*Do they ever have to re-do written work? What about marking? and
spelling mistakes? Don't children and groups ever interfere with each
other?*

If written work is not good enough, children certainly have to do it
again; if it is to go on the wall, they often volunteer to make a fair
copy. They like their work to look well if others are to see it; in recopy-
ing they put right any errors. As to the marking of mistakes in spelling
and punctuation, Miss Dean's policy of encouraging individual children
leads her to adopt flexible standards. She would never cover a piece of
work with red ink through marking every error if there were many;
she would feel that any benefit to the child from doing so would
be far outweighed by his discouragement at seeing his work treated
so savagely. She would adopt a selective method and draw attention
to the more important errors or to those that were relevant to the current undertaking.

She encourages communication between children and between
working groups, but she keeps an eye open for time-wasting and for
antisocial activities. These she nips in the bud, and the children know
full well that she will do it.

10. The class frequently goes on field trips and visits places of interest;
these are valued for the direct experience that children gain from
them. They give rise to work that continues, often for quite a time,
back in the classroom and are planned with this in mind. Trips are
also sources of chance occurrences, unpredictable ones for which Miss
Dean is always on the lookout and which often stimulate children to
produce work of high quality.

Does Miss Dean place any limitations on topics to be discussed?

These field trips, like some of the work in class, often give rise to
experience for the children that Miss Dean prefers to lie fallow. To

develop it at the time might well involve a maturity of outlook that children have not yet attained. Far better to leave it, she thinks, until they have this maturity. Then the impact of the later reference, linked to previous experience, is likely to be firmer and deeper.

11. Work that exposes the child to a variety of experiences and helps him to develop the experience that he selects as significant, often has unlooked-for results. No one could have predicted that the photograph that Peter was allowed to take would result in a turning point in his school career. He wrote at length for the first time—*con amore*. The praise he got was sweet, and the attention that he received when this surge forward was apparent helped his personal development. He climbed to a higher educational plateau.

What is the key to Miss Dean's success with the children?

It is worth noting that the outcome of the experiences to which Peter was subjected might have been considerably less had his teacher not been sensitive to his responses. Nothing replaces sensitivity in a teacher —although kindness helps.

Basic Questions About Teaching Science in Primary Schools

Let us stop this analysis of what we saw in order to deal with a few questions coming forward from the backs of our minds:

Does Miss Dean have a syllabus for her work in science?

No, she has not. She did a good deal of planning before the term started, so that when the children came into the room on the first day there was a collection of materials displayed to stimulate their interest and cause them to ask questions. She had a clear idea of some starting points that would be worth taking up and had made some general provision calculated to see her through the first week or so. By this time the pattern of the work should be clearer and further provision easier to make. She is certain about one point: good organizing beforehand avoids wasting the children's time and her own.

When children have started work on a particular topic—say, trees —Miss Dean often makes herself a flow-sheet indicating likely topics into which this study might move. This sheet serves a double purpose: it indicates profitable avenues into which children might be led if there is need for it, and it shows the kind of preparation she might have to make.

The very first time she allowed work to start in this way, i.e. without detailed planning of subject matter, she regarded it as an act of faith and was apprehensive about the consequences. No dire evils befell her, however, and now she regards it as the normal way of going about things: she knows the kind of way in which pupils will react and she has gained some confidence now in her powers of coping effectively with the situation. Regretfully, however, she wishes she knew more about science: she thinks it would make her work richer. Maybe so, but it would in no sense reduce the necessity for dealing sensitively with the children.

If other teachers work in the same way, how do they prevent work being repeated as the child goes up the school?

Firstly, all teachers in the school keep records of work going on in their classes; they make these notes during the course of the week and can refer to them to see what areas of work have been attempted and by which pupils. They also keep notes on each pupil—often just phrases in a notebook with the name of the pupil at the head of the page but, sometimes, a lengthy paragraph in special cases. These notes often prove invaluable especially when referred to after a long time has elapsed.

Teachers meet together and discuss their work and their pupils informally over a cup of tea in the staffroom, and more formally in staff meetings under the chairmanship of the headmaster. Here a good deal of planning goes on. Because work in science has not a sequential development, planning such as can be done at meetings of this sort can be very flexible yet effective; it is easy to ensure that children do work related to various aspects of the environment—unless there is good reason why they should return to some study, say, of dragonflies at the pond. If it should happen that they elect to tackle some problem that they have already worked on before, the chances are that their state of development is now sufficiently different to result in their approaching it in a different way with different outcomes.

An important question as yet unanswered is, *Do all schools teach science in this way?* The short answer is "No, but the number is rapidly increasing"; yet to leave the matter there would be to mislead you. It would be truer to say that schools are in different stages of transition, evolving from a formal teacher- and subject-centered curriculum to a child-centered one, and science follows the general pattern of the rest of the school curriculum. Thus there is a spectrum of practice in science: at some schools nature study has barely emerged from the restricted pattern already described—joined perhaps by physical sciences, but still teacher-dominated. In other schools there are varied degrees of pupil participation, but in the majority of them this tentative stage is disappearing, and in many schools it has gone altogether.

To a large extent the history of this changing pattern of science teaching has been that of the gentle revolution in primary education that started in the nursery and infant schools, spread to the juniors and is now just beginning in the secondary schools. Its philosophy was aptly stated by John Dewey: "Children are people. They grow into tomorrow only as they live today." Between the first and second world wars the revolution was slow and was unnoticed by many. After 1945 it gathered momentum, and in science—as in mathematics and French—it was consciously accelerated by planned effort in ways that we should now examine.

Background of the New Science in Primary Schools

After the war, many primary-school teachers and especially men who had returned from the services thought that physical sciences should be added to nature study. The attempt to introduce this change (and incidentally to bring the child more into the picture) was fostered by Her Majesty's Inspectors of Schools, by some Local Education Authority advisers, and by some tutors in a few colleges of education. The work also was aided by the Association for Science Education, the British Association for the Advancement of Science, the National Froebel Society, and the School Nature Study Union. Its greatest impetus, however, came in 1963 when the Nuffield Foundation decided to make a grant of money in order to set up a Junior Science Project that would (among other things) support the science projects that the Foundation had already set up for secondary schools. The project ran from January 1964 to December 1966, and the three years of its life were devoted to providing help for teachers who wanted to use science as a means for educating children aged between five and thirteen years.

The philosophy of the Nuffield Junior Science Project closely followed that of the child-centered primary school. The team propounded that:

1. Firsthand concrete experience was the basis of all understanding.
2. Problems of significance to children are their own problems, not those handed to them by someone else.
3. Children see the world as a whole, not in terms of subjects.
4. The thrill of discovery almost always leads to a desire to communicate.

The team concluded that science for children should be observational because children do not seek abstraction; it should be practical; in it children should raise their own problems, partly because isolating a problem is an important part of scientific thinking. They were interested chiefly in promoting an attitude of inquiry among children; to give them more experience of how inquiries might be pursued to whatever conclusion is possible. To this end they refrained from designing a course for teachers to follow but provided them instead with examples of work that they considered successful, work which had actually been done in schools. They thought that these examples might show teachers how to work out for themselves the principles that the project was propounding or—if they lacked the confidence to attempt this—might be copied as a first step in so doing.

The examples or "case histories" as they were called were supported by advice on how to start work of this kind, what apparatus to use, and how to keep and use plants and animals in class. These materials were published in 1967 in four volumes and three slim background readers for teachers.

The introduction of this work to schools and the testing of the materials that generated it is quite interesting. The grant from the Nuffield Foundation did not provide for teacher training; this aspect of the project was undertaken by the newly constituted Schools Council. They invited the 166 Local Education Authorities in England and Wales to volunteer to act as pilot areas for testing—of which they needed twelve. So many authorities wished to take part that a system of second-phase areas was set up for those undertaking test work a year after the pilot areas. (Of the twelve pilot areas, four acted also as pilot areas for the Nuffield Mathematics Project.)

In each pilot area the local authority selected a group of primary schools all contributing pupils to the same secondary school. The arrangement was that the Project would supply materials and advice by visiting team members *free* to these areas, and the Schools Council would provide free courses for teacher/leaders and administrators. The authorities agreed: to pay teachers' expenses in taking the courses; to provide each class taking part in the trials with £20-worth of apparatus and £20 to spend on materials for classwork, and—this was most important—to set up a Teachers' Center where work on the Project could be fostered. The plan worked out well; the project materials were tested, and work on science in primary schools received considerable impetus.

Outside the classroom the most significant advance that resulted was from the setting up of Teachers' Centers which have made a very valuable contribution to meeting that most intractable of problems— the in-service training of teachers. Their worth was soon perceived and their number grew rapidly. There are now about 250 of them, and their scope in some cases has extended beyond that of primary-school science and mathematics to include other subjects of the curriculum, secondary as well as primary. Teachers' Centers are of all kinds, from single rooms in school buildings with limited resources, to large buildings, well converted, with a full-time warden, a staff, and a wide range of facilities. So far, none is purpose built. In them local authorities hold courses; teachers meet to discuss their problems, display their work, and plan developments. Most centers have places where teachers can make apparatus; that is, give material expression to some educational idea—although some enjoy just making apparatus that could be bought. Some local authorities are most generous with the materials they provide for teachers to do work of this kind. Significant as this advance has been, however, it goes only a very small way as yet to meeting (with other influences) the massive problem of providing reinforcement for teachers in school faced with the task of understanding and taking advantage of present day developments in the school curriculum.

The Nuffield Junior Science Project helped to establish science firmly in the primary school as an area of study eminently suited to carrying out the accepted principles of educating children at the primary stage. The links with mathematics were not yet strong enough, which was a pity, and conscious of the weakness of their own backgrounds in science many teachers expressed their need for more support. This might have been given by an increased number of local courses, but authorities found it hard to staff them; this was a difficulty that the network of mutual assistance set up by the Schools Council went only part way toward meeting. Among those who might have staffed these courses were many with good knowledge of science but little understanding of how teachers work with children at the primary stage. Equally there were many well versed in primary education but not in science—the two together in the same person was rare. For such a course to be successful it must be directly relevant to what primary teachers see as their needs, and the results of it must be immediately applicable in the classroom; these are tough conditions. Courses in academic science do attract primary teachers but not for long—they are usually not sufficiently relevant to their needs—and courses in primary education rarely contain enough science. Quite certainly there are serious problems for all concerned not only with the in-service training of teachers but with their initial training as well.

It was abundantly clear that time limitations had prevented the Nuffield Junior Science Project team from addressing themselves to many problems that still needed to be solved; so a further project was established. This project, known as "Science 5/13" started in September 1967; it is sponsored by the Schools Council, the Nuffield Foundation, and the Scottish Education Department and is based on the University of Bristol Institute of Education. Science 5/13 is expected to run for at least three years, possibly more. It has a team of six, one of whom is charged with the special duty of liaison with Teachers' Centers, and another (part-time) acts as evaluator: both these special duties are new to projects in Britain. It is independent of the preceding Nuffield Junior Science Project but is expected to extend the lines of development begun by that project. Like the preceding project its purpose is to assist teachers of children between the ages of five and thirteen to apply discovery methods to help pupils gain experience and understanding of their environment and to develop their powers of thinking effectively about it. The terms under which Science 5/13 was established state its principal aim as "the identification and development at appropriate levels of topics or areas of science related to a framework of concepts appropriate to the ages of the pupils."

An examination of the literature failed to disclose such a framework, indeed it only succeeded in demonstrating our lack of knowledge about the concepts valuable to children studying science. These can be revealed only by long-term, fundamental research. The need for the team to formulate objectives to have in mind for children still remained, however; these they stated as a pattern of operational objectives and processes intended to be of value not only to themselves but also to the teachers they expected to help. Stating these objectives proved to be a mind-clearing exercise, but it revealed as many problems as it solved. Indeed, this whole matter of objectives is of central importance and must be discussed here.

The Objectives of the New Science

It is difficult to formulate objectives that are acceptable, clear, and useful; the process involves a lot of uncomfortable thinking and finally results in taking up a definite position, which at present is undoubtedly assailable. Whatever the result however, the process is a necessary one if the ground is to be cleared sufficiently to take a good look at it and to see what the way ahead may be. Broad aims to have in mind for children (such as "developing an inquiring mind and a scientific approach to problems") are easy enough to formulate and are valuable as statements of educational philosophy. But they give little guidance beyond that of general direction in helping to select experiences for children, through which the aims may be implemented. However, too specific a formulation of objectives results in writing a piece of programed learning. Thus, in the first instance there is no guidance and in the second no latitude. If teachers are to be responsible for thinking out and putting into practice the work of their own classes—as the team is convinced they must be if they are to retain the intellectual vigor present in primary education—then such objectives proposed for their perusal must be stated not only with sufficient precision to give guidance but also with enough generality to permit individual interpretation. Ideally, it would be best if teachers formulated their own objectives—the process itself would be valuable, particularly if it were based on a general consensus of child-centered philosophy—but that is not yet likely for all teachers.

The team of Science 5/13 project thus put forward their set of objectives (one of many pattern possibilities that are equally valid) as a series of thinking-pegs, by way of illustrating the way teachers might (if they chose) go about thinking out their own objectives. At worst, some teachers might agree to adopt the project's pattern of objectives, as one adopts a recipe, "to see how it works out" before changing the pattern to suit themselves. At best, the team hopes that individual teachers or groups of teachers will discard the project's objectives and formulate their own. A great deal of benefit comes from having the objectives written down. Reading them over is a constant spur to reconsidering them and is often a reminder of objectives that have been allowed to lapse. There is no doubt about the value of a stated pattern of objectives in planning work; far from restricting the work, reading the pattern of objectives opens it out. And working "with objectives in mind" helps one to keep direction in an area when it is often difficult to decide which way is best.

It is one thing for the project team to state their aims and objectives; it is, however, quite another for them to show how they propose to translate them into classroom practice. To write a course would ensure that subject matter was covered, but it would suggest a restriction of teachers' freedom to maneuver, and would be unlikely to stimulate children to seek out their own problems and solve them. Yet teachers need support and subject matter is of some importance: the difficulty lies in finding the compromise, the balance is different for different teachers.

Because the study of science was taken as the exploration of the environment in some of its aspects, the team agreed to produce units of work for teachers based on such a process and related to different areas of study such as were likely to be investigated by children. These units, were closely related to the pattern of objectives and were offered as support for the teacher when her pupils embarked on studies covered by the material of the unit. Further and most important, they were to be offered as illustrations of ways whereby the team proposed that teachers would be likely to achieve the objectives stated: as specific examples—if teachers chose to use them as such—of ways in which teachers might set about doing the same sort of thing for themselves. These units contain possible starting points, illustrations of classroom practice, and suggestions for materials and apparatus that it might be valuable to provide; and they contain a certain amount of background material to guide the teacher and provide her with references, without restricting her freedom to follow the path she chooses. To some extent the units were intended as maps of the area, rather than conducted tours through it.

These materials were to be tested in primary and secondary schools, evaluated as to the extent to which they aid the achievement of the objectives stated, and revised in the light of that evaluation before being published.

The two projects described in this chapter are not the only ones offering help to teachers of children in what Piaget calls *the concrete operational stage*—which is the one that precedes the stage of abstract reasoning; the range in mind also includes some part of the period of transition from the first stage to the second. The Oxford Junior Science Project was one such project, although somewhat limited in its resources. This project was devoted to the thesis that children might form an appropriate picture of their environment through well-formulated concepts of energy, structure, life, and chance. The Nuffield Foundation also sponsored as its three earliest projects separate ones on physics, chemistry, and biology aimed at providing material for pupils between the ages of eleven and sixteen. A fourth project was later set up in Combined Sciences for pupils between the ages of eleven and thirteen. It might well be that a teacher would be confused when faced with such profusion of detailed and varied advice as offered in all seven projects; but it would be far worse if she lacked a variety of considered advice from which to make her own choice.

From what has been said in this chapter, it should be clear that in Britain the onus for planning work in primary-school science is placed squarely on the class teacher and her headmaster. At present, she generally is not sufficiently well trained in science, and the means for helping her to become so are sketchy but will improve. But through her aid children can themselves learn about science and develop attitudes that later will stand them in good stead. If she is a good teacher, she will take her actual children as her starting point. With their guidance and her own planning she will put them in the way of gaining experiences that are valuable to them now and likely to be still more valuable later, when they seek to make patterns of their experiences and to extend them with the aid of the structure that their more mature minds will be able to perceive in the science they study.

10. Social and Environmental Studies

GEORGE BAINES

GEORGE BAINES *is Headmaster of the Eynsham County Primary School, in Oxfordshire. His teaching experience has embraced the whole age-range and includes youth work also. He has taught in urban schools and rural schools and has served as guest or visiting lecturer at a number of English colleges of education.*

One sunny morning toward the end of the Spring term I felt that life in school was a little flat and that interest was flagging. So I turned to my colleague, Wendy Thomson (there were just two of us in this small village school of Brize Norton, West Oxfordshire), and said "Let's go out, shall we?" A short discussion decided the plan and I telephoned for a bus which we could hire for the morning to take us into the countryside and back in time for lunch. Of course we were fortunate in working for a Local Education Authority like ours in Oxfordshire where heads of schools are trusted and encouraged to take initiative and run their own schools as they wish so that spontaneous journeys like this are possible.

All 47 children (aged 4+ to 11+) and their two teachers set off for a morning's ride into the Cotswold countryside via Burford to Bibury and returning through Eastleach and Shilton.

This expedition was thoroughly worthwhile in stimulating new interests and providing fresh impetus for new growth. Keeping a sharp lookout for any useful starting points in our completely unplanned or prepared itinerary we stopped whenever it seemed worthwhile. We walked in a spinney (copse, thicket), spongy with damp moss, fungi-ridden and rich with specimens of twigs, bark, and rotting logs infested with creature life. We watched a man driving a tractor and towing a drill as he drilled and sowed a field with seed. At Bibury the ducks were fed and counted, the river's depth measured and recorded, the speed of the water's flow measured, and ancient stone buildings studied. The journey was punctuated with these investigations and discoveries, and we returned to school loaded with specimens, stimulated with interest, and energized with excitement.

After lunch was cleared from the worktables and the resource areas were reprepared for use, everyone (for the most part willingly and earnestly) set about recording and communicating their particular interest derived from the experience.

Six-year-old Sarah had been the only one really curious about the stone squeeze-belly stile at Barnsley church, and she wanted to work at that. She started by drawing a picture of it from memory and from her crude on-the-spot sketches. More mature 10-year-old Mary had noticed and been caught by the differences in the towers of the twin churches at Eastleach and set about finding out more about different architectural styles. Michael (seven years old) carefully drew a picture of the lichen on a piece of twig, discovering a new world under his magnifying glass. Ian (seven and somewhat slow) examined and counted the wood lice in a log. Five-year-old Johnny painted a mallard, while the measurers of depth and flow of the river worked out their math problems. Deborah, although nearly 11, had been excited by the now rare sight of a man with a horse and cart in a field, whereas eight-year-old Gillian was absorbed in the humor of the pig that held us up by insisting on walking in the middle of the road.

The demands upon us as teachers were great and we had to draw cooperatively upon our collective resources in order to be adequate in the situation. But we had long since learned this technique, and even the unprepared journey did not worry us because we as persons had continued to grow and develop ourselves; we had become sharper and more sensitive to the richness of starting points found in the natural environment. Many of the scales had been chipped from our own eyes (we were again fortunate in that we were influenced, inspired, and succored by inspectors and advisers, such as Robin Tanner and Edith Moorhouse), and we were like the children—eager, delighted, receptive, perceptive. Because of greater length of life and experience we could engage and draw the children's attention to that which thrilled us. Professionally, this was how we saw our job: to guide, stimulate, share ourselves, establish right relationships; to make explicit what was implicit in the lives of the children; to provide opportunity, resources, and atmosphere for the natural, individual, development to come about.

For some time following that journey, the school was a busy place of endeavor, serene and gentle, as school should be when needs are being met adequately. All the resources were available at the same time for all the children. We had developed, planned, and organized the interior of our late nineteenth-century building so that we could work in this way. A time structure for the day had been replaced by a space structure—the school was a workshop for learning, allowing for child-initiated activities as well as those of the teachers. An attempt had been made to make the classroom at once inspiring, practical, demanding, and satisfying. By removing, changing, or realigning furniture, spaces had been contrived for a variety of activities and resources based upon children's needs and interests; and each space was made articulate according to its function. Thus the building could "speak" to the child and tell what was expected of him at school. We learned to do the right things in the right places, to maintain the order and discipline of the place, to live and work cooperatively as a community sharing facilities and a good, full life together.

Part of the idea was that although school was a contrived environment, we did not want it to be so fundamentally different from (or even alien to, as it could be for some) the natural home environment. The children were grouped vertically for similar reasons—the hierarchical age-pattern of family and social life was the norm. [Where but in schools are humans herded and boxed according to age or ability? No wonder school and what goes with it is so often rejected later since it bears but little relationship to real life!] However these were not the only reasons for so ordering the school or devising the curriculum. Basically, it stemmed from the recognition of the undoubted fact that all children are uniquely individual and different. To recognize such differences as there are and not arrange for their flowering is really to negate the idea of education. Individual needs and interest must be catered for as they arise, enthusiasms need to be fostered, and success encouraged or even contrived.

The fact of the individual differences was re-emphasized for me by the school's morning nature-hike by bus (such work has gone on in good schools since schools first began) when it was noticeable how very few incidents had engaged the attention of more than one child. The completed work from the journey, when displayed, showed a wide variety of interest, effort, and ability emphasizing differences and (for me) other important ideas educationally. One was that age need be no criteria as to the selection of material to be presented to children—all had enjoyed exactly the same expedition, but each had taken from it what he wanted and could at his own level. It was similar with their recording and communication of the experience. Another idea which became reinforced for me was that we must always keep the child in mind when speaking of "environment." For most of them that which engages their attention is something real and tangible, which they can literally hold in their hands. It is through the senses that the mind is fed. For the young child abstract and detached ideas are arid; dynamism comes from contact. Real activity is what matters, and this can be turned into experience (i.e. you are a different person as a result of it) through language which helps to formalize and abstract ideas. For me, learning can only be based on interest; and children are interested in their environment, especially and effectively their immediate one—the one to hand. School is part of the environment and through its building and organization, by its very nature it is a for-better-or-worse "teaching instrument," as the distinguished architects Mary and David Medd have so put it.

In our school we had tried to set up a community in and through which one learned to live, while still living fully as one learned. The basic question asked was, "What will it do for the child?" We knew that unless a child gained in all-round growth as a result of our efforts, we were wasting his time—which no one has the right to do.

Hence, the journey into neighboring, familiar surroundings where stimulation was available and possible for all; hence, the children being allowed to take from it what they could; and hence, the school and its provision for individual needs and interest with its emphasis upon learning rather than teaching. (These latter processes do not necessarily cohabit!)

I sometimes tell my colleagues in the very much larger school where I am now that our job is to "prescribe the environment of school, to release the children permissively into it, to observe and diagnose needs from their activities, and to draw upon all our professional resources to meet those needs." We need to make "connections" for them and make things explicit. We must be experts in human relationships; and we must be rich, growing, full human beings ourselves. Only then can we maximize the educational potential of every interest which engages the child.

How to make use of the opportunities and realizing the possibilities is quite a challenge when one uses the study of the environment as the integrating factor in promoting the acquisition of skills, growth, gaining in knowledge, formation of concepts, and the development of right attitudes.

For example, when we had stopped at the first spinney there were some for whom its damp darkness was uninviting, so they remained exploring its perimeter. This fact provided an opportunity for comparison between the contents in ground litter outside the tree-covered area and that under the trees.

At Bibury itself three boys had playfully contemplated pushing someone in the river, so I led them to consider its depth. Through the clear, trout-filled, running water we could see pebbles and plants on the bottom. Refraction of the light made it appear level and shallow, but could we trust our eyes? From the small arching footbridge (which set further problems) the boys lowered a heavy tool tied to the end of a piece of rope until it touched bottom. The watermark on the rope was measured and recorded. This procedure was repeated near both banks and in the middle of the stream. From the measurements obtained the boys were able to draw a sketch of what they had done and develop this into a block-graph recording and an actual drawing to scale of a vertical section through the river and its bed. Why it was deeper in the middle proved an interesting discussion and probably pointed to further investigation later. Here are four samples of their recording the river-measurement experience (Figures 10-1 and 10-2; and two written reports):

Measuring the Rate of Flow of the River at Bibury. What We Did.
We measured 22 yards, which is one chain. We measured from one set of steps to another set of steps. We went to find a stick and a feather. I then went down one set of steps and Philip gave me a

stick. Mr. Baines said "When I put my hand down put it in the water." Mr. Baines got up at the other set of steps and put his hand down and Mr. Baines and Ian took the time in seconds. The stick took 18 seconds and we did the same to a piece of paper and the piece of paper took 15 seconds. Again we did the same to a feather. The feather took 16 seconds. And then we went to find a twig, a spray of ivy and Philip put the twig and the spray of ivy together. They both took 16 seconds.

Melvyn Fitchett (10)

Speed of River Flowing at Bibury.

We added the three speeds together and divided it by three which came to 16 and one-ninth seconds so we called it 16 seconds. This means that the approximate speed of the water is 1 chain in 16 seconds.

There are 10 chains in a furlong and 8 furlongs in one mile therefore 80 chains equal 1 mile.

In miles per hour the water's speed is 80 × 16 equals 800 plus 480 equals 1280 seconds.

Divide by 60 to bring to minutes so that it takes 21 and one-third minutes to travel one mile. 21 and one-third minutes is approximately one third of 1 hour so the approximate speed is 3 miles per hour.

Philip Bellenger (8)

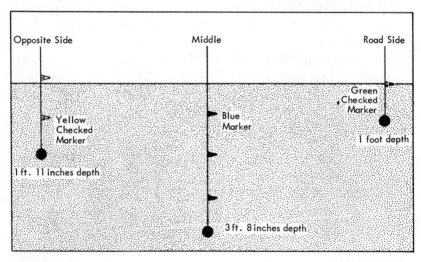

Bibury River depth. From a sketch showing how we measured the depth (by Melvyn).

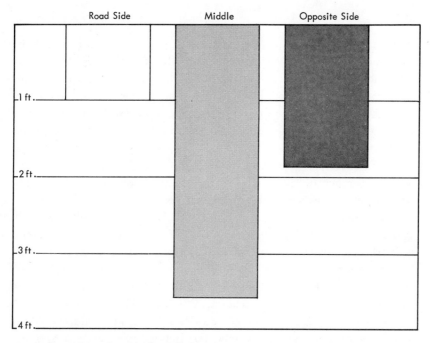

	Road Side	Middle	Opposite Side
1 ft.			
2 ft.			
3 ft.			
4 ft.			

A graph to show the depth of the water of the river at Bibury, as measured
from the bridge *(by Robert)*.

Several other boys enjoyed watching the swirling patterns on the
water's surface and thought that it moved in opposite directions at
the same time. By dropping a leaf onto the surface and then other
floating objects we saw that the flow was all in one direction. How
fast? A 22-yard chain was marked off on the bankside and different
kinds of floating objects were timed with a stopwatch over this distance. The calculations for conversion into miles per hour were tabu-
lated and recorded back at school. Some girls had noticed different
waterfowl and noted such differences as there were so that identification would be possible later back at school. Some five- and six-year-
olds were fascinated watching a waterfowl conducting his ablutions
on the bank, unconcerned with ogling eyes. For many of the youngest
children it was sufficient to be there and observe what the others
did, to hear their conversation and to begin to come to terms with
this larger environment. What they gained would emerge at a much
later time perhaps even unnoticed by anyone.

But to go on a journey wasn't a necessity, merely a novelty at
that time, as the immediate surroundings of the school provided
abundant material. I learned that that which society really values

is contained within the buildings—customs and traditions of its communities—and can be discerned by those that seek. Thus, one could avoid the pitfall of bookish, secondhand, memorization at this primary-school age, and keep in touch with fundamentals. History could be found in the craft and place, geography in the materials and farms, philosophy in the people; all were real, interesting, of moment, and in use.

A diversity of trees grew around the school and in the village, and we frequently returned to them. Identification, seasonal changes, growth habits, fruit formation, size, use, parasites, birds, dye sources, visual refreshment, contemplation, and language development all came out of studies of them. Quite a lot of written work (which I was pleased to call "creative writing") came from conversations over the orchard wall. Some of this writing shows evidence of the children drawing upon other experiences (notably movement and poetry) to aid them in their communication. We teachers shared poets with them; poets like Edward Thomas, Robert Frost, and Andrew Young whose descriptive poems we enjoyed. But we also made use of our own senses and language, our own feelings, and general knowledge so that subject divisions never arose and, when we were inadequate, we had to grow and find other sources for help.

Here are two poems about trees, written by our own poets at Brize Norton School:

The Blackthorn
Sharp, spiky, separated shapes shooting sideways.
Brand new buds sprinkled with snowflake petals.
A strong, sturdy stem with direct branchings off.
The tingling feeling of the ever moving bud,
as it opens out,
And yet another snowy blossom appears.

                                                     Jacqueline Sollis

The Old Apple Tree
The twisted tormented tree turning towards the sun,
Its branches all entangled like knots in a piece of string.
Some buds have burst,
Others are bursting like green butterflies settled on a twig.
The white blossom scattered here and there.

The trunk like a huge pipe sucking up sap
And sending it into thousands of branches.
Growing on grassy banks
Sloping its way towards the wall
Of the farmyard.

Verena Hunt

One source for the children were the local craftsmen and other inhabitants. From an old stonemason we borrowed a range of his tools and made an exhibition of them in the school. In this way we could hope to stimulate and provide starting points within the school building for those who came with nothing of their own. Exhibitions of this kind were always in evidence as well as those made by the children or by us out of the children's many and varied finds. Throughout the building were collections of stones, bones, feathers, shells, cones, and the host of other "to hand" things in which children are interested. We were carefully selective and kindly discouraged the cheap meretricious rubbish abandoned by our affluent mass-producing society, which persists in using good material badly or for unsuitable purposes. We were concerned with fundamentals and true values even though much of the children's trivia could have provided us with opportunities for learning. Our basic curricula were the "great world material" (this expression I had also learned from Robin Tanner)— those universal things of Earth that man has found and uses to serve him; stone, clay, wood, fibres, and more, and it was these that we encouraged the children to explore. From time to time, we would highlight one aspect of great world material in an exhibition while the other materials remained within the school environment. The mason's tools were drawing attention to stone again, a local building material and therefore an indigenous craft. This time, instead of just looking at stone, or buildings, or quarrying, we were studying the man who used the material. It never seemed right to introduce to children of this age material or information that was completely outside their experience. I had decided that to deepen their knowledge of what was there was preferable to broadening it to the secondhand, superficially. In this way I could encourage attitudes through which the children would broaden themselves as necessary and desired.

Individual items were taken from the exhibitions and the making of a simple folder or book was encouraged. In the first instance, making pictures was done using different media and techniques so that accurate observation was developed. Then accurate recording was sought through writing down precise description and measurements. When imaginative work and research findings from books and elsewhere were all recorded and added to the whole, a complete "integrated" record of the object was produced making a handsome book, of which a child could be proud.

Graham became very absorbed in the mason's tools and worked assiduously at his self-chosen task. He demonstrated hitherto unknown ability with his powers of observation, perseverance, accuracy, neatness, and thinking. His book about the tools became a reference source for other children—what better motivation for a book? His interest in the tools took us to our ancient Norman Church of St. Britius to find evidence of the craftsmen's work with such tools. The finely carved tympanum of the doorway arch inspired his lino-cut pattern which he block-printed as a cover for his book. Here is an excerpt from Graham's book, in which he has written about the stonemason's slat hammer:

The Slat Hammer

The slat hammer has a point at one end of the head, the other end is flat like an ordinary hammer. It has a long handle which is 13 inches long, the head is 7 inches. The slat hammer weights 1½ pounds. The head is black and brown in color. The handle is nearly twice as long as the head. The top slopes down as it gets thinner toward the tail end and tapers. The head end is octagonal. If you were to cut through the head end you would have a section with 8 sides. The tail-end has a flat base and flat sides but has a round top. If you cut through the tail-end it would be nearly round in section.

The slat hammer is used for making holes in the slats for the pegs to go through.

Graham Sollis

The church was another source to which we returned again and again with children of all ages, for all sorts of reasons. Visitors to the school were often taken to the church by the children and given a conducted tour. We trusted them and would leave them to pursue their studies on their own without fear of their misbehaving. Its Norman origin gave us many an excursion into history as did the village name of Brize Norton (from Brun's Norton or Brun's settlement to the

North, also of Norman origin). An effigy of a crusader in the church gave a fine historic starting point as well as the "woolsack" tombstones in the surrounding graveyard. But most often it was the building, the stone, and the man who used it which got us going.

I remember returning with a group after a visit when Peter (who has permanent aches from a horse-kicked-in head) said, "I'm glad I didn't have to build it." "Why?" "Think of carrying all that heavy stone. I'll bet that church is heavy." And so we were off: How heavy was the church? Let's weigh it! (By calculation of course.) That proved an almost insuperable task for us, which we never completed because it took so long and interest waned when broken by a holiday. But we did so much math. through it! To measure weight we needed a suitable unit, and since stones were all different in size and weight we built a cubic foot of stone in the schoolyard. (We were on the limestone so it was similar to the building stone and commonly found lying around in the soil.) Each separate stone was then weighed, and, by addition, the weight of this cubic foot was found. Verena suggested that since stones varied might not cubic feet?—so another, different one was built up and measured. The two total weights were different, which gave me an opportunity to introduce the idea of an average; and yet a third one was built and weighed. In this way they arrived at an approximate average weight of a cubic foot of stone. With this unit of measurement for weight they now needed to find the number of cubic feet in the walls of the building. Height finders were used, angles measured, curves calculated. Total walls were calculated and windows and arches subtracted; and although it was a difficult assignment the children stuck at it very well.

One day, a different group discovered a marked stone by a doorway which reminded them of a sundial. By experiment with a stick and the shadows, recording the results, and allowing for British Summer Time, they proved it to be a kind of sundial but only certain hours were marked. Subsequently, from books and teachers, they found this stone to be a dial showing times for Mass and the ringing of the Sanctus Bell. From this, quite a lot about ecclesiastical life and practice was learned.

One always had to be prepared for the unexpected as when the day came on which five-year-old Colin challenged God to speak! He was building (with wooden building blocks) Noah's Ark about which he had heard in the Church Sunday School when six-year-old Julie told him that it would need to be very much bigger. After a while he asked, "How did Noah know it was going to rain?" "God told him," was the unhesitating reply from Julie. A short pause then out he went through the French window, looked into the sky and called, "God, is it going to rain today?" Three times he asked and receiving no reply returned to report that "He's not there; so that's that." Was this a valid learning situation, and what use could be made of it? Just one of the challenges for which one has to be prepared!

Often it was much easier as when Tina (aged eight and tempestuous) stamped with rage as the pet hamster repeatedly leapt from her hands. "Oh! why doesn't he know I only want to love him?" she cried. "Do you really love him Tina? What would you want for him if you really loved him?" And so Tina could be led to grow in this aspect of life.

Five-year-old Colin came proudly one day to show an aeroplane he had sawed, hammered, and nailed together at the woodwork bench. We were adjacent to the large airbase at Brize Norton and I assumed this to be his model of the new Belfast transport plane. Most indignantly he said "No it's not! It's a swing-wing, vertical take-off aircraft!" And true enough, he had arranged for the wing to swing or rather pivot and had put three nails at the point of balance for lift-off. But did he know what "swing" meant? What extension of learning could I obtain from this situation? From a few questions it was apparent that the concept "swing" was still confused. Therefore I tried "vertical" and connected this word with movement within his experience: "Curl your body up near to the ground, keeping your weight upon your feet. Now begin to uncurl and stretch out into a tall narrow shape. Is your body now vertical or horizontal?" Colin asserted it was vertical and could show me vertical lines in the room. In a similar way we tried "horizontal" and established that. To consolidate all this I asked him to paint me a pattern with vertical and horizontal lines. Later, when he brought his pattern to show me I noticed that all the lines were in one direction and said, "But you have only painted . . ." He, smiling, turned his paper through half a circle and gleefully demonstrated his grasp of the concept.

Learning was derived not only from studying the countryside but also from individual play pursuits. Activities within and without the school were no longer separated, and I began to see the children as their own integrators of experience who could make connections for themselves. One might be unable to predict or prescribe when they would use their information, nor did one realize how much incidental learning took place until it emerged in a different interest area.

Once, after a session of movement of an expressive kind tending towards drama, an eight-year-old girl whose home could be described as difficult wrote about her experience in movement. We had been concentrating upon hands and feet and this had been extended to the imaginary handling of sand and walking on it, to the finding of shells and pebbles and romping in the sea. This girl had never been to the sea and had no real experience of the seaside. Yet her writing was vivid and clear; the movement experience had been real for her because she had drawn upon her school play/experiences with water, sand, shells, and pebbles which made the imagined beach most real. Here is her written record of a seaside experience, as gained from a Movement session.

At the Seaside.

At Movement we went to the seaside and we walked along the beach and found lots of pebbles and we jumped over the waves and I fell in.

We found a cave and I went inside and it was dark inside and I kept bumping my head. When I went in it was like a ghost.

We had a bucket and spade and made a sand castle and jumped it. We felt the sand with our fingers it felt ever so smooth.

We walked in the water and walked on the beach. Pebbles were there, they hurt my feet. I found a pink and white pebble, it was very small. I liked the colour best because pink and white look nice together.

Jennifer Davis (8)

Another occasion when the children showed us that what we were doing with them was having a cumulative effect and giving them personal resourcefulness came from a piece of dramatic play that they developed.

An exhibition had been built in school but this time instead of focusing upon a great world material its theme was color. Again, this was something we did from time to time and in so doing while restricting their coloring palette for a short time, we would heighten

their sensitivity to color and, perhaps, did a little toward their acquisition of good taste. For this particular exhibit we had concentrated on black and white and, because the children used it so much,
it was an unusually long time before we could change the display.
Here is a poem written by an 11-year-old girl as a development work,
starting from our exhibition of black and white:

> *The Moonlit Night.*
> *Dark sea water rushing madly,*
> *Splashing the silver sand.*
> *The waves black, sky thunderful.*
> *On the beach appears*
> *A man, solitary and small,*
> *Indistinct and silver,*
> *Walking heavily, angrily,*
> *Sweeping sand,*
> *Matching the mood of the sea.*
> *As the sea grows calm*
> *The figure diminishes,*
> *Disappearing into the black*
> *Unlit parts of night.*
> **Deborah Cockwill (11)**

The children made pictures, books and studies on a whole variety of
topics: "White foods," "White flowers," "Trees with black in their
names," and others; and one was "The Black Death." The play had
come about from the study of the plagues in history. The story was
of a family who lived in London at the time of the Great Plague.
The twins in this class acted as twins in the play, in which they
were to catch the disease and die of it. A great deal of historical and
geographical fact came into the play, but they were unhappy with
it because it ended with death. Just about this time the whole school
went on a journey to Bath where students of Dietrich Hanff at New-
ton Park College of Education acted as our hosts. The younger children explored the college and farm while the older ones visited the
famous crescents, (residential areas), abbey, Roman baths, and museums of this beautiful city. Incidentally, it was here that red-haired,
seven-year-old Michael, on alighting from the bus in Lansdown
Crescent remarked, "Ha! the middle ain't where the middle is!" To

our astonishment he was right; in a quick sweep with his "seeing" eyes he had noticed that the architect had countered the effect of the slope of the hill by offsetting the central colonnade. The time spent in Bath was both rewarding and revealing and proved a most enriching experience. However our players with the plague—clever things—found a way to resolve their death difficulty: The twins were taken to Bath for the healing waters! The feasibility of such a trip was examined and the journey planned. The family sailed by ship from London to Bristol and from there by coach and horses to Bath; solution carefully checked and a happy one.

While I was watching the enactment (not a performance) of the story on one privileged occasion, another amusing fragment of dialogue demonstrated the resources gained from incidental learning. When the stricken family were boarding the coach for Bath at Bristol dock the vessel's Captain decided to accompany them. Climbing up to the driver's seat he said, "Hello, I think we've met before, your name's Tchaikowsky isn't it?" And the answer shot back was: "Yes, and I know you, you're Moussorgsky, I like your music too"!

Not always did we have idyllic or romantic beginnings—there were other occasions. The building of a new bungalow near to the school was a good opportunity for finding out things. Road reconstruction, sewerage-pipe laying, visitors, feast days and festivals, news items, books, vehicles, weather, pets, meals were all used if the opportunity arose.

One morning several near-filthy children arrived at school carrying lumps of very rusty pieces of old iron. They had been foraging in the old burnt-out ruins of the village blacksmith's shop. The last old smith, Albert Print, had been a custodian of the school before he died, and we had one or two examples of both his useful and decorative ironwork around the building. The children had stumbled across a further supply, and we now developed a display of "rustics," as they came to be called. We had all sorts of bits and pieces, tools, scrollwork, spares for machines, and building items. This collection was to become a constant stimulation in the school; someone or other would be making a study of a "rusty" whenever visitors came. One six-year-old made her first successful simple book from a curly shape made of iron, and the poem she wrote about the "rusty" proved that she had really become familiar with the object of her study. Here it is:

The Curly Shape
A curly shape,
A curly shape,
Rusty, brown and yellow.

A little bit heavier than a packet of tea,
A bit smaller than my hand,
About an inch wide,
One third as thick,
When stretched out straight
Eight inches long.

Stiff and rough to feel,
Hard and cold to touch,
Not pretty to look at,
But pleasant to see.
It would decorate a gate,
But not on me.

Sarah Thomson (6)

Thus it went, with the immediate environment providing abundant opportunities for the pursuit of knowledge, techniques, skill, and enriched living. The children themselves provided the interest and set the pace with the teachers guiding, helping, extending, selecting, and deepening the experiences. Parents and spouses got involved too. Wendy's husband Tom Thomson was a great support and a blessing.

Of course not everyone is so privileged as to work in such an area with such children and parents, and I have not always done so either. But I used this same approach in the brick, railway, London over-spill town of Bletchley in North Buckinghamshire, where I once taught. There we used the railway a great deal, the factories and their products, the transporting traffic on the arterial roads, museum services, and the social services, such as gas, water, electricity, and postal. Here, too, hobbies were valuable (if developed), and all kinds of sports, games, and pastimes were used. As always, the starting point was the learner—if what one presents proves of no interest there is not much point in pursuing it. Formerly, we arbitrarily selected a list of topics considered suitable and desirable information for children to learn; but when we evaluated by testing, the results of what was "learned" were always sickeningly sobering. A teacher would be extremely fortunate if two thirds of the "facts" had been memorized at the end of the term—an extreme waste of the input energy and time.

At Bletchley I learned that one could always start with the place name. Again perhaps I was fortunate with a place name of Saxon origin (Blecca's leah, or the clearing in the forest made by Blecca). Part of the new town was an old town named Fenny Stratford, which was on the Roman road called Watling Street. Here also were a weekly cattle market and pits from which clay was dug for making bricks. This connurbation could be just as rich for children if one learned to open one's own eyes to the possibilities and kept to the fundamental idea of children in their own particular environment.

In this town (where things can be arid because of newness and sameness) it was a challenge to open a new school on a new housing estate. We tried local transport as a topic, using the railway, roads, and canal. We tried Romans and Saxons; we tried school journeys. But eventually, what was successful for me was looking in the window of the new general stores and choosing something to buy. The class went back to school, each with a fruit or a can of something, or whatever and began to investigate. Better still, though, was when we walked back to the shop later to measure our walk, and we began to collect wild plants on the way. From the curb and in between the paving stones we found twenty-seven varieties of plants, and that really got us started. Here, too, it was that which was "to hand" that seemed to capture their interest. There were always occasions when a letter was received from a relative abroad to stimulate one child; but usually the starting point was found by taking them back to seek into their own immediacy so that they gradually began to find and provide their own interesting starting points.

Currently, I am in a very new school with an exciting new building and over three hundred children of first-school age. Here the principles are the same: the recognition of differences, learning through the environment, active involvement in one's own learning, and school as a practical workshop while being a stimulating, satisfying place and community. It would seem that when learning is really individualized and personalized then it becomes most effective. To be individualized it must take heed of each child's needs, capacity, personality, and interests; to be personalized it must be relevant and enriching. By opening the children's eyes and minds in the school building through our contrived experiences, we are gradually turning them into the world outside, to which they are beginning to return with interest and motivation. Not all activities are experiences but school should be trying to make them so. It is a place for meeting new ones, widening others, and deepening all. My concern is for growth in people and for giving them an abundance of life, rather than measuring them and feeding them with information to be regurgitated later. Using the environment to this end, making school part of the whole, and school life merely a part of the continuum of a lifetime of learning is the only way I know of making life full and rich while all-round growth is sought.

But I must end with children. One day, in a home-bay, I came across quiet, dour, seven-year-old Robert sitting in the rocking chair gazing out of the window. This was a legitimate activity as far as I was concerned, but I wondered whether learning was going on. "Do you like it in here, Robert?" "Oh! yes, Mr. Baines, look at the trees— they're funny." "Why? What's odd about them?" "No shadows." And in the spring sunlight it did seem strange. "Oh! I see why. No leaves. Won't it be lovely when they have their leaves?" And I crept away so as not to destroy this hallowed moment.

On another occasion I received what I consider my greatest, flattering, reassurance. After a holiday by the sea a little girl returned with a present for me—her favourite pebble! I hope that I have been instrumental in bringing her and all the others to the knowledge of the universe contained in a grain of sand, because I believe that is what life is really about—it is to that to which I aspire. Here is a poem written by an 11-year-old girl at Brize Norton, which I feel sums up this new philosophy about using the environment in connection with primary-school studies:

The Wallflower's Story.
The soil grew stuffy,
And I was weak.
I thought to germinate,
I thought to grow.

Yet I thought of fearful frost,
Of wild winds and snow.

But the exciting experience
Of seeing the sun
I could not resist or retreat.
Until at last I took the temptation.
I was dazzled and dizzy.
My surroundings were bright and exhilarating.
I was mature and happy at last.

Mary Thomson (11)

11. | Movement, Music, Drama, and Art

JOHN ALLEN

JOHN ALLEN is Her Majesty's Inspector of Schools with national responsibility for drama. He has been a scriptwriter and producer for the Schools Broadcasting department of the BBC and was director of the Glyndebourne Children's Theatre. He is a member of the Young People's Theatre Panel and the Drama Schools Committee of the Arts Council of Great Britain and is on the Drama Advisory Panel of the British Council. He is also an author with several books to his credit.

Let us begin by looking at the kind of work in the arts that goes on in many primary schools in this country. We will take as an example an infant school in a borough due east of London. It is an unattractive building dating from the early years of this century. It consists of eight classes each with about 40 children drawn from a culturally im-poverished area. The classrooms were large and featureless until the present staff got to work on them. The passages have walls lined with tiles of a singularly unpleasant brownish-ginger color. The head teacher in her penetrating understanding of the children is typical of a very great number of infant school head teachers who share her energy and ability; in any case, she is at least a *prima inter pares*.

The head teacher and her staff are busy preparing the passages and classrooms before the children arrive (although there are other schools in the country where the children let themselves in and settle down to work before the staff arrive). They set out books invitingly, arrange the flowers, decorate the walls with the children's work, and prepare a great variety of materials on tables, desks, and the floor. In each classroom and broader hallway there is usually an attractively mounted display. This may be a nature table on which there is set out a variety of seeds, leaves, shells, bones, tree bark, and almost any natural object that the teacher can acquire or which a child has brought; or it may be a science display with mechanical oddments, screws, nuts, bolts, the gizzard of a gramophone, or the innards of a television set. The display may have an aesthetic emphasis and consist of many glass or pottery artifacts. It may be of textiles and fabrics of various textures, hung, folded, and draped; or the emphasis may be on color with everything displayed in tones of white, brown, or blue, for example. There might well be a display of musical instruments, but these would be for the children to use rather than simply to look at.

Each classroom is inevitably stamped with something of the teacher's personality and reflects her tastes and interests and what she feels to be the needs of the children. There may well be a play-corner marked off from the rest of the classroom with a couple of screens. In the rooms used by the younger children there are usually trays of sand with small shovels and wooden spoons and a large trough of water filled with buckets and containers of many different shapes and sizes; bricks on the floor, and clay on the tables. In another room there is a pile of empty cereal packets with jars of paste, scissors, and rolls of sticky paper. In another there are some lumps of kneaded clay; and in another there are miscellaneous piles of material, fabric, string, straw, and many other materials for making collages. In the large assembly hall the floor is completely covered with large sheets of paper with three or four pots of paint and two or three brushes of different thicknesses beside each.

The head teacher gives her staff considerable freedom in the planning of their rooms, but she is always available for advice and to discuss any suggestions they may make. Her criticisms and comments are always kindly but pertinent. Thus, although each classroom is highly individual the whole school tends to reflect their head teacher's educational ideas. This head/staff relationship is free and based on mutual respect and it helps to release the great creative energy that is found in schools of this kind.

The classrooms are ready and the children burst, explode, into the school. In a few minutes most of them are hard at work at the activity of their choice. The few who are undecided may be assisted by the teachers. Rapidly an atmosphere of concentration and animation develops; much chatter, but with a purposeful tone. Some children play alone, some in groups. No one is idle, no one is coerced. Here a group of boys in chefs' hats are making buns which they will ask the cook to put in the oven. Another group of boys are building a ship out of packing cases and decorating the rigging with flags. The floor of the hall is acrawl with children painting. Every corner of the school is in use, and if the weather is fine the playground is too.

After 30 to 40 minutes of this intense activity, some of the children run out of steam. But if the whole collections of drawings, paintings, collages, models, plays, dances, and musicmaking—if everything that the children had done in this short space of time could be recorded and brought together as the collective achievement of 300 East-end children during the first half hour of a weekday morning, we should have something to wonder at. This is the sort of thing that happens in many infant schools.

At this point the teachers, who have been busily moving round among the children, helping, advising, and discussing, may suggest continuing activities for those children who have finished their picture, collage, model, or game. They may suggest to one child that she write down what she has been doing. They may remind another that he might measure his model and record it in his number book. They may allow a group to go to the library and find a book that will tell them, for example, about ships' pennants. They may help a group of boys who had become Vikings and wanted to know what sort of helmets the Vikings wore to find a book with pictures of Viking helmets and then make some. The children who had been constructing geometric shapes out of wire and pipe cleaners and drinking straws were encouraged to find out the names of the shapes they had made and to try and draw some mathematical conclusions.

All this activity is based on the belief that children should be given opportunities to handle a wide range of materials and in working with them to discover their nature and their properties. In making a model out of clay or paper or cardboard a child learns something about the material and uses it to create something to his own satisfaction. In playing with water he may discover that a tall thin bottle may hold the same amount of water as a short fat one. When different colors of paint run into each other they make still further colors. Curious effects are achieved by twanging the strings of an instrument in different rhythms and combinations. The skill of the teacher lies in encouraging children to use as large a variety of materials as possible and in helping them to draw the appropriate conclusions and master the relevant concepts. It is in this aspect of their work that the experience of the head teacher is of the greatest value.

Concepts and conclusions may seem to imply an esoteric skill; but a great deal of successful teaching is done by the teacher who is ready to talk seriously to children and listen to what they have to say. This means, of course, the establishment of a warm personal relationship with the children. But it is also the beginning of what some may consider to be the most important skill a child has to learn, the use of words. For speech is not only our most articulate form of communication but an activity, as many people think, that is closely related to most kinds of thought processes. Thus, the manner in which a teacher talks to her children is a highly important aspect of the whole educational process.

Surprisingly, language is not always handled with confidence in English primary schools, although most teachers attach considerable importance to conversation and discussion. They read the children stories and encourage them to tell stories themselves. They introduce them to poetry and verse through nursery rhymes and material especially written for young people. And at the same time they help the children to learn to read and write, taking advantage of the activities already described which give the children something to write about. The child whose curiosity has been aroused and whose creative instincts have been quickened soon becomes determined both to record and express his feelings, ideas, and achievements on paper as well as to unravel the code which is the key to so much pleasure, knowledge, and excitement—the written language.

In our east London school great importance is attached to music. Every day, though at different hours, the children participate in it as an act of worship. They walk into the assembly hall with their friends and sit wherever they like on the floor while a teacher plays good music on the piano. Because the community is multiracial and multireligious, the assembly is nondenominational, and the head teacher uses it as an opportunity to introduce children to music and literature as well as religious and moral stories and ideas. The children sing with great sensitivity and sometimes act a play they have composed themselves. The school has recently declined in numbers, hence it enjoys

"Children are encouraged to work expressively so that they come to understand something of the nature and quality of movement."

the availability of two spare classrooms, one of which is used for music. The room is filled with a variety of percussive and melodic instruments that the children use creatively on their own or with the help of the teacher. At almost any time of the day small groups are to be found here, sometimes strumming instruments, sometimes playing individually, or, as they grow older, in groups.

The other spare room is used for drama and all kinds of dramatic play. A great variety of dressing-up clothes are neatly arranged on shelves round the walls—dresses washed and ironed, a variety of hats, caps, helmets, and headgear galore for both sexes. Groups of children use this room when they want more space for their games than is available in the classroom; privacy to tell each other stories, and sometimes to dance to the gramophone. It has been used for groups of children to dance to music composed and played by other children in the school.

Another important part of education in this school is movement. This usually takes place in the assembly hall. Sometimes the teacher

lays emphasis on helping the children to acquire agility and certain physical skills. Sometimes she will bring out gymnastic apparatus which the children can use in a great variety of ways, thus developing their confidence and ability to manage their bodies in different situations. Sometimes she encourages them to work expressively so that they come to understand something of the nature and quality of movement; what it is to move fast or slowly, lightly and heavily, with weight, strength, in straight or twisting lines, or with a sense of space. These qualities of movement sometimes give rise to ideas or feelings that the teacher can develop in terms of dance or drama.

We have given a picture of some of the work to be found in a typical infant school in order to establish the principle that the arts are firmly based within the curriculum of most English primary schools. Children become familiar with the arts and learn through the arts. They grow used to expressing themselves in a large variety of materials which they learn how to use. They experience an implicit connection between many of these activities. They learn something of what is meant by responding to the environment, which is a concept to which most infant teachers attach a great deal of importance. A lively environment is not only a matter of well-chosen pictures on the walls and flowers in pleasant vases throughout the school: it is the atmosphere created within each classroom in particular and within the school as a whole by the arrangement of the desks, the materials that are available for the children to use and the manner in which they use them. Atmosphere is the quality of conversation that goes on among the children and with their teachers; it is created by what the school sounds like and what it looks like, and how the children behave to staff, to visitors, and to each other. Thus, in their work and by their work the children help to create an atmosphere to which in turn they respond. An infant classroom often has the exhilaration of an artist's workshop or studio. Dressing-up clothes, musical instruments, lumps of clay, stones, curiously shaped pieces of wood, tools, nails, straw, cotton-reels, numerous fabrics are all laid out in a manner that demands they be used, or observed, responded to by some further act of creation. Thus, the environment of a school depends not wholly on its architecture (although architects are now designing schools in response to these ideas), but also on the perennial triumph of lively teachers with creative ideas over inadequate surroundings.

Teachers are now giving considerable thought to the relationship between all these activities. There is a kind of constant interaction between whatever it is that stimulates a child and demands to be expressed and the inner life on which depends the necessity for that statement. The teacher lurks in the wings, as it were, ready to help the child who needs help to find the appropriate form of expression for his image or idea. Sometimes the teacher finds that a child's skill in one subject can be extended to help him in subjects where he is weak. A child who appears to have little to talk about may reveal considerable vision in his paintings. Another can move extremely well and yet never mix with a group. Another likes manipulating numbers but is socially shy. A teacher watches a child paint a picture, then says to her, "That's a lovely painting: tell me about it." [Not "What is it?"] The child begins to talk and eventually asks the teacher to write beneath it: "The dragon is chasing the shadows of the birds and the road is deserted." What a remarkable relationship between a verbal and a visual image.

Movement

As children grow older, moving from infant to junior school and on to years of puberty, they acquire a surer understanding of the various arts and greater skill in their use. Let us therefore consider the arts as they are practiced in junior schools in some detail; and if we take movement first, it is because our bodies are the most obvious evidence of our existence and identity. Children need to move and perhaps the first task of any primary-school teacher is to ensure that the children have opportunities for plenty of exercise. The Plowden Report (paragraph 705) clearly summarizes the variety of physical education that is included under the word *movement:*

[Movement] may be concerned with agility, on the ground or on apparatus, with ball or athletic skill, or with expressive movement of dramatic or dance-like quality. In such work, exercises or techniques are unlikely to be taught; the aim is rather to develop each child's resources as fully as possible through exploratory stages and actions which will not be the same for any two children. When these ends are pursued successfully, the children are able to bring much more to any situation than that which is specifically asked of them; the results

transcend the limits of what can be prescribed or "produced," and lead to a greater realization of the high potential of young children.

A skillful teacher does not watch the movements and the physical ability of the children only during physical education lessons. He or she observes their physical behavior in all their work. The manner in which they hold and use pens or paintbrushes, knock in nails, saw wood, show a capacity for accurate construction, run about the playground—even eat and drink—all tell the perceptive observer much about their pupils' physical skills and capacities. In their movement lessons the teacher provides opportunities for the great variety of work already mentioned. Sometimes they turn to educational gymnastics which employs a wide range of equipment giving children opportunity to explore a wide variety of movement. Sometimes the children develop a dramatic quality in their work (this is discussed in detail later in this chapter). On other occasions, especially perhaps when the teacher has been using music as a stimulus, a dancelike quality develops and the children may explore many qualities of movement in space. Children may very well enjoy being introduced to some of the set patterns found in social, country, and national dances, but it is when they express an overflow of feeling, energy, or excitement in a great variety of patterns and movements that we see this high potential for physical expression to which the Plowden Report refers. Schools up and down the country that provide ample opportunities for all kinds of movement (and where as a result the children have acquired considerable resource) can demonstrate the astonishing beauty of movement that boys and girls of all ages achieve in dance, the skill they acquire in gymnastics and various forms of agility, and the expressiveness of their work in drama.

Music

Closely associated with movement is music, still associated in many people's minds with rather dull class singing for the majority of children and special coaching in instrumental playing for the more musically gifted. This gift for music seems to show itself earlier than other artistic skills, but when it is recognized, which is not always easy, the children are usually helped by visiting specialists. Happily an increas-

ing number of teachers are interested in providing a musical education
for all the children. At the very least they try to create opportunities
for children to listen to music. As already shown, the assembly at the
east London school was one example of such an opportunity. But many
teachers also want to listen to music with their children in the more
intimate atmosphere of their classroom. They encourage their children
to hum and sing tunes on "laaa." They sing nursery rhymes together;
the repertoire soon increases to include folk songs and simple canons.
Then, they may play games with words together, making rhythmic
patterns out of given names or the names of flowers or animals. These
patterns of rhythm and stress may then be pitched on one, two, or three
notes and almost without knowing what they have done the children
have composed a tune to their own words. This will give them confidence to make up their own rhymes and set them to music perhaps
to their own accompaniment.

An important aspect of musical education is making music with
instruments. In addition to the range of percussive instruments that
includes drums, tambourines, triangles, cymbals, and virtually anything
that can be struck there is now a variety of pitched percussive instruments: in some such as glockenspiel and chime bars the notes are
metallic; in others ranged around the xylophone they are wooden.

Another important development in musical education has evolved
from the work of Carl Orff in the extended use of the pentatonic scale,
that is, the sound patterns that can be made by the black notes on the
piano, which have the remarkable quality of producing a pleasing
harmonic effect in whatever combination they are played. Many schools
are now provided with a collection of musical instruments, percussive
and melodic, which the children can play on their own or under the
guidance of their teacher.

On such a basis as this, progress can be rapid. The children may
move from the pentatonic scale to use of the modal and diatonic scales,
of which the C-major scale on the piano is the obvious example. Virtually the whole world of music is now available to them. Around the age
of eight, many of them will derive great pleasure from the recorder, or
one of the four members of the recorder family (soprano, alto, tenor,
and bass). Some will become interested in notation and the technique
of writing and reading music. Some years ago, when music like the
other arts was seeking to escape from excessive formality, there was
a revulsion against any form of notation except for the most gifted chil-

dren; but it is now agreed that by giving names to the various pitches with which children who have had some kind of musical education are familiar, they can learn the "solfa" ladder without difficulty and become skillful in the use of notation. This skill enables them to write down the tunes they composed with much the same pleasure as they take, in other aspects of their work, in the writing down or recording of their thoughts and observations in words. Any musician would wish to add that musically gifted children of primary-school age are at the best age to begin learning various orchestral instruments. It is by no means uncommon to find a small orchestra among the older children in junior schools.

Since music is largely composed of sounds listened to by the ear it has much in common with language which is an organization of sounds made by the voice and utilizes similar elements of stress, tempo, and pitch. The close relationship of music and speech has been noted by teachers of foreign languages who find that children with an ear for pitch master new rhythms of speech rapidly. The skills of reading and writing are discussed elsewhere in this book, but it would be surprising if the authors of these chapters did not emphasize the importance of children becoming accustomed to expressing themselves in words and of acquiring a love of words for their own sake before being required to spend too much time on writing. The fact that many nursery rhymes have become a part of the very substance of English literary culture is not by reason any intellectual statement they make but because of their exquisitely felicitous expression of sharp simple images in a variety of meters. It is difficult to think of any body of poetry that contains such varied rhythmic vitality, often coupled with such wonderfully appropriate tunes. One has only to spend a few minutes recalling such songs as "There Was a Lady Loved a Swine," "Hickory Dickory Dock," "The Grand Old Duke of York," "I Had a Little Nut Tree," and "Lavender's Blue" to realize again this exquisite combination of words, meter, and tune.

Some teachers argue that an ability to handle words is found only among the academically more able children; and it is true that the "bright ones" indulge in a constant play with words, and in some schools they cultivate a kind of semantic mythology among themselves. But this does not absolve teachers from helping the less able to speak clearly, a faculty on which depends to some extent the preservation of a social democracy. Thus, the cultivation of a feeling for words is one thing, and much fascinating work is done by means of rhymes, jingles, poetry, and the use of music and language in a variety of contexts, but it is on their meaning that the ultimate validity of words depends and many teachers feel strongly that the impulse behind a vigorous use of language is to have something to talk about. This is one of the fundamental ways in which they make use of what we have called *the environment of the school,* i.e. the study of the neighborhood, visits to places of interest, and so on. After a walk in the country a small boy wrote:

And a mist came down and separated autumn from winter.

His teacher felt fully justified in believing that here was a perfect synthesis between experience and its expression in words.

Some readers may note that this chapter does not say enough about the nature of children's imaginative development. This apparent reticence about an important subject was deliberate—to avoid the expression (much too often used) that we must "stimulate the children's imagination," as if a dose of music or art had the stimulating potency of a "pep" pill. Every child and every adult enjoys his own life of fantasy and we draw on it as we draw on our various skills and resources for our own purposes. But the imagination is something more substantial. It is not a dreamworld but an achievement. A moment of imaginative insight or an act of imaginative creation is the result of putting certain known factors together; ideas, some notes of music, verbal images, or methods of handling a lump of clay. Sometimes under the impulse of who knows what aesthetic or intuitive or intellectual impulse we become aware of a new structure, a new relationship, a new experience expressed in abstract or artifact. Many teachers believe that we draw the best imaginative writing from children not by setting them so-called imaginative subjects such as "A Journey to the Moon" but simply by helping them to use words in a significant manner. An extremely imaginative poem was written by a child on the unpromising subject of a dead hedgehog, discovered in a field beside the school. But the story has further interest; for when the girl was asked when she wrote in prose and when in poetry she replied, "When I want to describe a thing I write in prose, and when I want to write what I feel about it I write poetry." This girl had gone far in understanding the use of language. But a boy passing by overheard the remark and added con-

temptuously, "Coo, I buried it." The process was perhaps summed up
by an Australian psychologist who described the imagination as a
process of going from the known to the unknown. This seems to be a
useful signpost for work in art as well as science.

Drama

A dramatic element enters into the activities of children when there
is a quality of personal involvement in a situation or when there is a
kind of identification with a character. This, however, is nothing new
but, as we have seen, a natural aspect of children's play which is a
basic element of what takes place in an infant school. But children do
not play less as they grow older; they play in different ways, just as
adults have their own forms of play. Sometimes we play in a recrea-
tional spirit. But even this cannot be divorced from some kind of
satisfaction in achievement. A boy plays about with a ball; hands roam
over the notes of the piano; a pencil doodles over a piece of paper;
and all the while a part of our mind is involved in the control of the
ball, the arrangement of the notes, the significance of the lines on the
paper. Children often use dramatic qualities in their play because an
identification with people from the world they know enables them to
extend their own experiences. They are putting known factors together
to explore the unknown. Therefore many teachers try to preserve this
quality of play in the junior as well as the infant school for it enables
children to explore the nature of a material, whether or not they wish
to make something with that material or use it significantly. In dramatic play children have become accustomed to dressing up and involving themselves in dramatic situations. In infant schools many
educational advantages accrue, one of which is the facility with which
many children talk in an imaginative situation of their own contriving.
But it is in the nature of drama to involve a number of activities. Movement, language, the visual arts, indeed almost every activity of the
children is incorporated at one time or another in their drama or dramatic play. It follows therefore that if the children have had opportunity to develop their resources in movement, language, music and
the other activities, they bring very considerable skill and imaginative
wealth to their drama. Conversely, their work in drama can contribute
to their understanding of the component subjects by supplying situa-

tions in which they can develop their skills in speech, movement, and all kinds of artistic expression.

It is difficult to separate the distinctive field of drama from the arts and activities of which it is compounded. Teachers find it difficult to argue (if it must be argued) that drama is a separate discipline from movement, English, music, or the visual arts. Its uniqueness probably lies in the field of human relationships. Drama provides children with an opportunity to discover something of their own personality through exploring that of others in spatial terms, in an imaginative setting. It is an aid to conceptual thinking and it provides experience in conflict and tension.

These claims cannot be substantiated in the way that an essay on art can refer to reproductions or one on music to records and tapes. Even on film and television it is very difficult to catch the totality of a dramatic experience. There is therefore a tendency to justify drama through the quality of the language and the writing to which it can give rise; undoubtedly, in terms of imaginative stimulus and personal involvement drama can do a very great deal to help children whether intellectually gifted or not to express themselves both in spoken and written words. An example of this was written by a boy of ten; he was of extremely low intellectual ability and it was difficult to decipher what he had written in his book. Following a long and superbly realized improvisation (in which the whole class had participated) about a plague in a Derbyshire village in the late seventeenth century, he wrote this passage:

I am in the village and I have got the plague. I wear charms round my neck to protect me. I went to church and said my prayers. I went to Margaret the witch and she gave me potions and spells and I put signs on my door but I have the plague. I lie in bed with the door of my house locked and a red cross painted on the door. Lord have mercy on us!

The environment of a child's life does not always stop at the school or the town or village in which he lives. It is the task of education to enlarge the frontiers of children's experience in time and space and understanding. In 1964 the schools of England were filled with projects on Shakespeare. In 1966 we saw innumerable reenactments of the Norman Conquest. Here is the opening of an epic written by an able boy of nine years to accompany an improvisation on this event:

> *Edward the Confessor, almost dead,*
> *Asks for Harold from his deathbed,*
> *He calls for his friend's son*
> *In great anticipation.*
> *At last arrives Goodwin's relation,*
> *"You will be," the Confessor said,*
> *"King of England when I am dead."*
> *The old king slept in Harold's hand,*
> *He sighed, "Soon you'll be king of this fair land."*

But we must refer again to the relationship between the arts. It is one thing to stimulate children and give them an understanding of the potentials of the various arts; but it is also important to help them select the art, or the form of expression, in which an impulse can best be expressed. This is why it is poor educational practice to develop the arts in isolation from each other. The children may listen to a story and want to act it. But some may prefer to paint a picture of some single episode. Others may wish to compose some music for a dance that came into the story. And each of these activities may lead to others. In a good school there is a constant interflow of ideas between all subjects and activities, so that false distinctions between play and work, the arts and sciences, intelligence and imagination, are broken down.

Understandably enough it is in the nature of specialists to see their own subject as the possible center of the whole curriculum. It is true, no doubt, that music, drama, English, art, or movement—and why not biology and science?—could all provide a kind of node from which other disciplines could dive off; doubtless it would be possible to find English schools in which every possible variation and relationship of curriculum planning is being explored. But the problem for the average head teacher and in turn for every classroom teacher is what to select in order to help the children to establish relationships, to see that their educational diet is balanced. No one suggests that even the subjects that have been treated in this chapter can all be developed to the full. Time does not allow. But a teacher who knows the contribution that each activity is making to the total education of the children does not find it impossible over the year to provide them with experience in most of the valid disciplines, independently and in relation to each other. The visitor very quickly learns to detect, on entering a school for the first time, the educational ethos or ambiance of the school made up of the sounds the children make, the manner in which they move about the school, the quality of the pictures on the walls, even the choice of cup out of which a visitor is invited to take coffee.

Art

One of the happiest educational developments in recent years has been the blurring of distinctions between art and craft and between visual activity in general and the other subjects. Although the hegemony of painting and sculpture is still preserved to a certain extent in the academic preservation of that curious term "fine art," there is little tendency in primary schools to suggest that a greater or finer sensibility is required to paint a picture than to make a vessel out of clay. A teacher recently went so far as to suggest that there is little distinction between pottery and cooking for both involve the handling of some natural material, treating it, and then heating it.

Recent developments in the visual arts have been based on the realization of how many materials (apart from traditional ones) can be used for artistic purposes: paper, wood, straw, rush, willow, string, clay, dough, lumps of salt, many metals, and new synthetic materials such as polystyrene, and a great variety within each kind. Each material responds to a certain kind of handling.

How lucky are the children who live in country schools where some of these materials can be gathered from hedges and fields in the neighborhood. One thinks of schools in the Cotswolds where the children gather wool from the fields, spin it, dye it, weave it, possibly dye it again, mostly with materials they have gathered themselves. Thus they learn the significance of shape, texture, color, pattern. They realize how color alone can be explored in terms of many different media and the way in which many colored pigments are compounded of flowers and fruits that may be growing around the school. Then they must explore and use the tools appropriate to the different media and materials: pens, brushes, pencils, stubs of wood, twists of paper, tips of the fingers, feathers, hammers, chisels, saws, and the rest. I observed an extremely impressive lesson when the teacher took off one of his shoes and passed it around the class, asking the children to examine closely and critically the materials with which it was made and the shape, construction, design, and its social and personal appropriateness. There was hardly an object of clothing which the children did not then submit to similar scrutiny. Another splendid project was seen in a country school where the children were engaged in weighing the local church (See Chapter 10). This involved historical research and complex mathematical calculations. Was this art, architecture, mathematics, geology, history, English? And does it matter? Another school in the north of England was developing a project based on the wild flowers that were growing near the school. Why did these particular flowers grow there and not others? What was singular about these flowers? Why were they of that particular shape and design? Was their color significant? What sort of soil were they growing in? And once again a whole class of children became involved in a project in which the frontiers between biology, history, geology, geography, art, and language became virtually indistinguishable.

Children in urban schools are similarly encouraged to open their eyes to their neighborhood. There may be very few aesthetic qualities in the streets around the school; even so, there is much of interest in an industrial area and our senses must be quickened, even if they reject what they respond to.

The Educative Value of Teaching the Arts

What are we trying to do in helping children to be literate in the arts? Is it enough that they should leave their primary schools able to compose a piece of music, or paint a pleasant picture, or take part in an improvised play, or weave a piece of cloth? In one sense, yes; each achievement is its own reward. In another, no. A child lives as a member of a social group in a certain physical environment. He has to learn to develop relationships, to come to terms with people and things. His relationship with his parents and his brothers and sisters helps him in time to cope with strangers. The bed in which he sleeps, the carpet on which he crawls, the chair in which he sits, the food he is given to eat are early experiences in a lifelong process of accommodating himself to aspects of the environment that are over familiar, or terrifyingly strange. A child has to learn to accept the elements, changes of temperature, rain and wind. He must learn to acquire a sense of time, of distance, of perspective. All these experiences involve an ordering of the mind and the development of a kind of sensory memory based on personal experience. A child needs to handle an object, to learn about it with his finger tips or his lips or tongue before he knows it. Then he can judge other objects that appear to have similar qualities from this reservoir of tactile experience.

Yet, as we have emphasized in this chapter, it is not merely a matter of an aesthetic response to the elements in our environment. Mankind has a will and a capacity for mastery. Thus we handle things and look at them and smell them and, like Adam, give them names, and reproduce them in our own creative terms. Our own communicative and expressive language develops. To recognize a lump of clay as clay or wood as wood does not go far as an educative experience. But when we shape the clay or wood to our purposes, as we shape sounds to our language, we develop ourselves in the process of developing a relationship with our environment.

So it is with people. Children paint pictures of their parents. They identify themselves with their parents in their play. When they work and play in groups they are learning to live with other people; and in literature and drama they are extending these relationships. A good primary school offers children seven years of growth and discovery punctuated by glowing moments of satisfaction in achievement.

12. | Modern Languages

N. R. MULCAHY

N. R. MULCAHY, M.A. (Oxon.), M.Ed. (Illinois), Her Majesty's Inspector of Schools, London, was seconded to the Schools Council where for the past seven years she has been organizing the Pilot scheme for French. Previously she taught in primary and secondary schools in England and also worked in Kenya, Australia, and the United States of America.

General Description of the Nuffield Experimental Scheme

Unlike all the other subjects discussed in this book, French is not merely a new approach, but is an entirely new subject as far as the vast majority of primary schools in this country are concerned. It might therefore be as well to consider at the outset what are the main aims of the Pilot scheme in French and what it hopes to achieve.

First, it should be stressed that the scheme's aim is not to establish whether or not it is possible to teach French successfully in primary schools. Obviously it is possible, as had already been proved by limited experiments carried out under favorable conditions. The Pilot scheme was designed to ascertain on what conditions it would be feasible to contemplate the general introduction of a modern language into the primary-school curriculum in terms of the consequences for the pupil, the school, and the teacher. The main questions to which it seeks answers are

1. Is any substantial gain in mastery of a foreign language achieved by beginning to teach it at eight instead of eleven?

236

2. Do other aspects of educational and general intellectual development gain or suffer from the introduction of a foreign language in the primary school?
3. What are the organizational, teaching, and other problems presented by such experiment?
4. Are there levels of ability below which the teaching of a foreign language is of dubious value?
5. What methods, incentives, and motivations are most effective in fostering learning of a foreign language?

As far as the organization of the Pilot scheme is concerned, there are three main agents involved at the national level:

1. The Schools Council, an independent body composed of representatives from the Department of Education and Science, the Local Education Authorities, and the Teachers' Associations, with the latter in the majority on the governing Council itself and on all its committees. The Council—working mainly through its administrative officers and Her Majesty's Inspectors of Schools—is directly responsible for the scheme's administration, finances, teacher training, and educational and linguistic developments in the schools.
2. The Nuffield Foundation, an independent charitable Trust, which has set up its own considerable organization for the production and testing of materials to be used in the schools.
3. The National Foundation for Educational Research, another independent body, financed partly from national and partly from local resources. This body is carrying out an assessment of the Pilot scheme over a ten-year period, with major and minor reports appearing in alternate years.

Because the aim of the Pilot scheme is to ascertain the conditions necessary for success if the introduction of French in the primary schools is to become part of national policy, the scheme has not been weighted towards success; on the contrary, difficult conditions have been deliberately included. The areas selected represent as true a cross section of the whole country as it was possible to find: socio-economically favored/deprived areas; areas with a good/poor supply of teachers; rural/urban areas; new housing estates on city outskirts and old city-centered, slum-clearance areas; old/new buildings; experienced/inexperienced teachers; an even geographical distribution covering the whole country. All these factors have been taken into account and are included within the sample of 13 areas, 125 schools, and approximately 6,000 children aged eight to ten years, in each of the three years.

Teacher Education

Administratively, the Pilot scheme was ready to be launched in the schools in September 1963; but an adequate supply of fully prepared teachers was considered to be of such overriding importance that the entire year of 1963–64 was devoted to their training. The teacher-training program is the keystone of the whole structure and as such deserves looking at in some detail.

The program was organized in two stages (local, then national) and comprised two main areas: language and method.

In each location the Local Education Authority set up its own training program within guidelines drawn up by the Schools Council to ensure comparable standards being reached throughout the country. The courses were designed solely to improve the linguistic competence of the teachers, most of whom had had very little contact with the language since leaving their own grammar (high) schools some ten, twenty, or even thirty years previously.

LANGUAGE

The emphasis was on accurate oral fluency, coupled with correct pronunciation and intonation, these being regarded as the most essential linguistic qualifications for teachers of young children. The written word was not entirely neglected but was mainly directed towards increasing the teachers' own enjoyment of the language, especially through reading. Each class was based on a language laboratory and, wherever possible, native speakers were used for monitoring purposes. The basic course in all cases was audio-visual. It was supplemented by small conversation groups, acting of playlets, discussions, lecturettes, and debates—all with the emphasis on the spoken word and in all of which the teacher-trainees were expected to play an active part.

By these means it was hoped to ensure that at the end of the year's training course most would have reached the standard required to proceed to the national course; that is, they would be able to understand a lecture given by a native speaker at normal speed on a topic of everyday interest. Naturally, the time taken to reach this standard varied, depending on the individual teacher's previous experience of the language, his linguistic aptitude, and the number of hours devoted to study. Consequently, no time limit was set, each teacher progressing from the local to the national course when he, his tutor, and later a specially constructed test decided he was ready.

Because of this wide variety of local conditions, Authorities differed greatly about the arrangements they were able to make for these courses. In one very favored area it was possible to release the teachers from their schools for one whole day a week, while substitute teachers took over their classes. But the more general pattern was for teachers to be released from their schools a couple of hours early, and this combined with a few hours of their own time furnished the three to four hours (once or twice a week) required for the language course.

Once a teacher had reached the required standard at his local course, he had a choice of four national courses to which to proceed for a further three months' intensive training. The two largest of these were held in France, in Paris and Besançon; and all the teachers were strongly advised to attend one of these. For those whose domestic commitments prevented them from so doing, two similar courses were established in England, one in the North and one in the South.

The purpose of these courses was similar to those held locally, but they were much more intensive and of a higher standard. Further, their scope was extended to embrace a more formal study of the language, including grammar and translation but with the main emphasis still on the spoken word. An additional advantage of the course in France was that it enabled teachers, many of whom had never been there previously, to become acquainted with French life and customs and so be in a better position to satisfy their pupils' curiosity about everyday events in France.

Both the local and national courses were solely concerned with improving the teachers' command of the language. There still remained the question of method, which had to be tackled if the teachers were to be given the opportunity of putting their newly acquired linguistic fluency to good use in the classroom.

METHOD

Three residential courses in method, each lasting ten days, were held in various parts of England so as to enable all the 150 teachers concerned to attend. The courses were staffed by members of Her Majesty's Inspectorate whose chief object was to introduce the teachers who had no previous experience of teaching a foreign language to audio-visual methods and techniques suitable for young children. All the main audio-visual courses on the market were demonstrated and their relative advantages and disadvantages debated in small discussion groups. Moreover, the practical application of these courses in the classroom demands familiarity with audio-visual equipment and dexterity in its use; therefore, opportunities for this were also provided, as the use of such equipment is not standard practice in most of our primary classrooms.

Having completed this local and national training in language and method, the teachers launched the Pilot scheme in their classrooms at the beginning of the new school year in September 1964.

CONTENT

All the teachers in the Pilot scheme are free to use whatever materials they wish, though in fact about 80 per cent are using the Nuffield course *En Avant*.

En Avant was originally designed as a five-year course to cover three years in the primary school (ages 8 through 10) and two years in the secondary school (ages 11 and 12), but it has since been extended to cover the full span of compulsory secondary education till the age of 16.

The course is an audio-visual course that is intended for use with large classes and by teachers who are not specialists in the French language. The content of the course has been chosen with particular regard to its usefulness in everyday situations and is based on interests likely to be appropriate to each age-group.

The *En Avant* course has three main aims:

1. To teach the pupils to understand, speak, read and write French rather than to teach them *about* French.
2. To provide a simple introduction to French life.
3. To contribute to the pupils' general educational experience.

The course seeks to develop the various language skills in the following order:

Stage 1. Listening, understanding, repeating, speaking. (4 terms)
Stage 2. Reading. (2 terms)
Stage 3. Writing. (3 terms)

Although these skills are interrelated, each presents particular problems to the learner, and it is considered important that the child should not be expected to undertake them all simultaneously. This progression from an oral acquisition of material to a written use of it is mirrored in each lesson unit throughout the course; all material is mastered orally before it is either read or written.

The course attempts to present the teaching points systematically, step by step, and in the early stages it is more interested in securing fluent control of a comparatively small number of structures than a large vocabulary. The emphasis is always on a gradual and programed progression, with constant practice and development of what has been learned, and also with periodic revision lessons in addition to the "internal" revision which is a part of every lesson.

Stage 1

Stage 1 consists of 40 units, each unit providing about one week's work at the rate of five 35-minute periods per week.

The visual presentation in this stage takes the form of a flannelgraph and figurines. In the early stages where ideas are simple and unsophisticated, it is felt that the flannelgraph is the most effective teaching aid as it is flexible and uncomplicated and the children are able to take an active part by using it themselves. Flash cards depicting animals are also used in counting and doing simple arithmetic; and there are flash cards to illustrate verbs of action, weather, road signs, and adjectives.

The audio aid consists of tapes recorded in Paris by professional actors, both adults and children.

Introducing apparatus as a class activity.

CONTENT OF THE LESSON UNITS

Each unit is divided into several sections, which are presented in the following order:

1. Presentation of sentence patterns.
2. Development of sentence patterns.
3. Presentation of vocabulary.
4. Development of vocabulary.
5. Situation.
6. Activity.
7. Exercises.

As far as possible, new patterns are introduced with known vocabulary, and new vocabulary is introduced in known sentence patterns. In order to help the pupil to acquire automatic control over these patterns as quickly as possible, simple exercises of the language-laboratory type have been recorded on tape and form part of the development of many of the units.

The focal point of each unit is (5), the situation. These are short playlets that can be acted by the children, and each one provides suitable situational context for the teaching points of the course. In the early units of the course, simplified dialogues have also been recorded in order that children who find difficulty in improvising and adapting the situations can take part in simple conversations. The situations and games also provide a means of introducing additional words and phrases likely to be of use and of interest to children.

Games, songs, and other activities are important features of the course. They are introduced partly to provide interest and variety but also because they give the pupil a further opportunity to put language into action. The songs include some which have been specially written for the course, employing only the sentence patterns and vocabulary previously taught.

Stage 2

Stage 2 introduces reading while continuing to develop the oral aspects of the language. It includes materials designed to introduce the children to reading through recognition of the French words with which they are completely familiar in the oral form.

Reading is introduced through sentences, never through isolated words out of context.

The sentences for reading are presented on stout card strips for display at the front of the class, large enough to be visible from all parts of an average classroom.

The sentence on each reading card is taken from the situation of the same unit. These sentences are recorded on tape, and there is a space for repetition. The cards are displayed, together with the appropriate picture poster on the special display stand, which is provided.

Stage 3

Stage 3 concentrates on writing in French, using these methods:

1. The introduction of writing.
2. Further development of the reading process, moving from the recognition stage to true reading.

3. Teaching in French as well as teaching French.
4. The introduction of a limited number of new sentence patterns and vocabulary items to be taught actively, for the extension of the children's passive vocabulary.

READING

The same method of introducing reading used in Stage 2 is continued and developed, that is, children see only material with which they are orally familiar. They are now presented with a connected passage rather than with individual sentences. The passage for reading is a shortened and simplified version of the story, usually recorded in two versions on the tape, i.e. unspaced and spaced. The reading habit is reinforced by a reader and supplementary readers which can be used by individual children or in groups.

WRITING

So far, the less able children have been shielded from the effects of competition with children more adept in the written situation; therefore it is essential to keep them from feeling a sense of unease and insecurity when writing is introduced. Sentences are therefore short and simple at this stage, and the teacher is urged to give generous help and praise, as in Stage 1 and Stage 2. At first, all written exercises are preceded by oral practice.

Various Stages in Writing

COPY WRITING

1. Copying short sentences from the text *after* first hearing the recording of the sentence.
2. Copying short sentences from the text *before* hearing the recording of the sentence.

MEMORY WRITING

1. Writing a short sentence, one word of which is covered, after first having read the complete sentence from the text. The complete sentence is read out as the children write.
2. As in 1, but with more than one word covered.

DICTATION

1. The text is displayed and the children read a selected sentence, both as a class and individually. The sentence is then covered and the children are invited to write it down. As they write the teacher repeats the sentence as often as is necessary, without using an unnatural intonation or emphasis and without isolating single words.
2. A sentence is displayed with visual support, and the children read it silently. After a suitable length of time has elapsed, the sentence is covered and the children are invited to write it down.
3. A visual is displayed and the teacher reads the sentence associated with it. The sentence is not on display and the children write it down unseen. The teacher repeats the sentence as often as he feels necessary while retaining correct intonation and phrasing.

A careful progression from short simple sentences to longer ones is maintained.

WORKBOOKS

The workbooks contain only material that is familiar to the children in both its oral and written forms. Before attempting any written work, each activity is presented orally as a class activity. At the completion of each activity, opportunity is afforded the children for reading out what they have written.

The written work is carefully graded so that all children may feel a sense of progress and achievement. This work is presented as an interesting and amusing activity in the hope that the less academic children will not feel that they are being introduced to a more formal type of presentation, which would take all the pleasure and interest out of learning French. They are encouraged to *want* to write and therefore the content of what they write must always be meaningful, never automatic.

Because the workbooks will be the personal property of each child, it is hoped that the children will be encouraged to take a special pride in the presentation of their work. They should regard their own work as being a contribution to the booklet and as supplying the finishing touch and take great pains in working correctly and neatly.

Voilà le père de Roger.
Qu'est-ce qu'il fait dans la vie?
....
....

Ecris la bonne phrase dans la
bonne case.

Il est fermier.
Il est boucher.
Elle est hôtesse de l'air.
Il est boulanger.
Elle est concierge.
Il est garçon de café.
Il est facteur.
Il est pêcheur.

Voilà la soeur de Marie.
Qu'est-ce qu'elle fait dans la vie?
....

Voilà un homme.
Qu'est-ce qu'il fait dans la vie?
....
....

Voilà un homme.
Qu'est-ce qu'il fait dans la vie?
....
....

Voilà un homme.
Qu'est-ce qu'il fait dans la vie
....
....

Voilà un homme.
Qu'est-ce qu'il fait dans la vie!
....
....

Voilà un homme.
Qu'est-ce qu'il fait dans la vie?
....
....

Voilà une femme.
Qu'est-ce qu'elle fait dans la vie
....
....

"Workbooks contain only material that is familiar to the children."

246

Introduction to French Life

Background information about France and French life is given with each unit. This consists of a short passage in English describing some feature of France or French life that has some bearing on one or more of the sections of the unit. The situations and dialogues also illustrate the habits and customs of French people.

General Educational Experience

It is considered of great importance that the course should contribute to the child's general educational experience, both by developing his personality and by widening his knowledge of the world around him. Therefore, much of the subject matter of the units—particularly in the later stages—and many of the activities that form an integral

Integrating French and geography.

part of the course are designed to link up with other subjects in the curriculum.

For the teachers there are detailed notes on how to make use of the course, though it is emphasized that these suggestions are intended for their guidance and not as overriding instructions, which would prevent them from using their own methods of presentation and development. By design, the inexperienced teacher will find them helpful and instructive, and the experienced teacher will regard them as an attempt to give practical help in a method of teaching which, though enjoyable, is nonetheless very exacting.

The first draft of Stage 1 of the French course was tried out from January to July in 1964, in fifty volunteer schools. These schools contributed greatly to the success of the experiment by sending in their criticisms and suggestions, many of which were incorporated in the revised draft of the course. It is felt to be one of the strengths of the course that it has been written with active teacher cooperation and participation.

In the Classroom

One of the fundamental principles of the Pilot scheme is that French should be taught to all members of the age-group concerned, regardless of the children's level of ability. This principle has been adopted for two main reasons: firstly, we in this country simply do not know for certain whether there is a level of ability below which it is inadvisable to teach our children French. All we have are theories, because there is no previous practical experience from which reliable conclusions might be drawn. The Pilot scheme provides the possibility of this practical experience and is therefore too good an opportunity to miss. Secondly, at a time when we in this country are moving more and more away from formal, structured class teaching, it was felt that it might be a step backwards to introduce this program at the primary level where, up to now, children have learned mostly by individual or group methods and only rarely by being taught as a whole class. The emphasis has been on individual experience and discovery rather than on class teaching; and it is here that a great difficulty arises with the teaching of French.

By the very nature of language a child cannot discover it for himself; he has to have the right pattern established for him by others. Moreover in the early stage at least, this requires passive listening on his part rather than the active doing, to which he is accustomed in other classroom activities. Thus, French would seem to be pulling against the mainstream of current educational thought in this country as to the ways in which young children learn best; and it was mainly for this reason that many enlightened educators were against the introduction of French into the primary school. They feared a return to the bad old ways, with the emphasis on the teacher teaching rather than on the child learning, especially when to add to their mistrust it appeared that books (as a possible source of contamination of the purity of the spoken word) were likely to be banned in French, while being strongly encouraged as an independent source of information in all other subjects.

In order to help bridge the gap and reconcile what at first seemed to many educators as two irreconcilables, much emphasis has been placed on the development of group work, with the greatly increased scope it gives children to take an active part in their own learning. At first sight, in a good classroom where group and individual work are being encouraged, a typical French lesson is indistinguishable from any other, because the barriers between passive listening and active doing have largely been broken down. It is true that the lesson nearly always starts with class teaching because this is the only really feasible method of introducing a new structure or vocabulary; the children must first hear the new item, understand its meaning and be able to repeat it correctly before they are able to do anything with it. But once this stage has been reached—and this need not take long if the new item has been carefully selected and is skillfully presented—then the children are let loose on a wide variety of activities, one of which at least will incorporate further practice in the newly acquired item.

Suddenly to let 40 children loose in a room full of "games" and to expect them to speak French is to invite disaster. The games will certainly be played with enthusiasm, but in English; therefore, with their whole point lost. To get the children to play games in French, it is essential that at least one member of each group know exactly what is to be done with each piece of equipment (although this does not preclude the children's own improvisation if they so wish, and indeed this is actively encouraged). This same member must also have a complete command of the limited language necessary for engaging in the activity. To ensure that both these conditions are met the teacher almost invariably introduces the new activity as a class— not a group or individual—activity, because this gives her the opportunity of quickly spotting the children whose interest and not necessarily their intelligence allows them to master the situation quickly. When the class breaks up into groups, these key children are appointed the group leaders for that particular activity; and so the teacher can be reasonably confident that the framework is sound. Secure in his knowledge and anxious to display it the leader allows little backsliding from other members. How quite delightful it is to hear a demure little girl saying firmly to a much larger boy "Non, ce n'est pas ça, répétez." Of course, the leaders are changed for the different activities, and by careful choice of material the teacher sees to it that even the least able has the chance to shine. To make certain that all runs smoothly she herself moves unobtrusively from group to group joining in and taking her turn at being questioned and "taught" with the rest of the group.

These activities in small groups give even the shyest and least able children tremendous confidence and satisfaction. They know they can handle the situation competently, they love the kudos of being able to speak French and are often far more exacting than the teacher in the standards they set for one another.

In the very early stages within the first few weeks of commencing French, these group activities (games) are very limited in scope because the children naturally have such a small stock of knowledge on which to draw. The game may comprise nothing more than brightly colored cards with various objects painted on them. All the children vie with each other to see who can acquire the biggest pile of cards in two minutes and thus be declared the winner. The group leader points and asks "Qu'est-ce que c'est?" to which the other children reply in turn "C'est un camion; C'est une balle." Such a card should be designed for the practice of recently acquired vocabulary or to revise that learned earlier; emphasis should be placed not only on getting the word right but also on its gender (a great stumbling block for English-speaking children) together with accurate pronunciation, any lapses being corrected by the group leader and the correction repeated by the child concerned. This is a pleasant way of going through those formerly dreaded vocabulary lists.

Language reading cards.

Not only are practically all the materials used for these activities chosen by the teacher specifically in the light of the needs of that particular class, but they are also made by her and attractively presented in bright colors, varnished over for gloss and cleanliness. This occupation is a time-consuming one, and teachers in England like those elsewhere are hard pressed for time. It is very important therefore that each piece of equipment should serve several purposes and be capable of adaptation at many levels. For example, at a later stage the vocabulary cards described could be used to practice the structure: "De quelle couleur est le camion; la balle"; and so forth, and the corresponding agreement of the adjective: "vert, verte; gris, grise." Needless to say such grammatical terms as *adjectival agreement* are never mentioned; the children learn, not laboriously by memorizing rules as most of us did, but by repeated use of the correct form in natural situations. At a still later stage, the same cards could be used for the new structure "Où est le camion; la balle?" and practice of the prepositions "sur, dans, derrière," the group leader varying the position of each card as he puts the question, while still using the same cards. Finally, no question at all might be asked;

each child draws a card from the pack face downwards and then says anything he knows about the one he has drawn; for example: "Voici une balle verte. Elle est grande. Elle est sur la table." If another child can add a correct statement about the card he becomes the owner and the card has to be passed to him. The game grows in excitement as each child feverishly searches for something to add in order to regain his original card or acquire that of his neighbor.

In this last stage, each child speaks on his own initiative and not merely in reply to a question. This stage is particularly important and one too often neglected in the traditional language classroom where a correct answer to a question is regarded as the height of achievement. But in fact this is not how we talk to one another; if everyone were to wait for the stimulus of a question nobody would ever speak. But so often we are content to train our pupils in this highly artificial convention and then wonder why they are incapable of speech.

One of the most gifted teachers of primary French in this country uses this spontaneous expression by the children as the basis of her whole method, and the results are astounding. She has no course materials as she prefers to devise her own with the requirements of each particular class in mind; she uses no audio-visual aids because she considers that they come between her and the children. Instead, she relies on the natural instinct of every normal child anxious to express himself in words and communicate his hopes, joys, and fears with other people. In her classes children are encouraged to break in whenever they feel inclined, making observations and asking questions, relevant or irrelevant, whenever the fancy takes them. At first it may seem like pandemonium and one wonders how the children will ever learn anything as they are always so busy talking; it is only on reflection that one realizes how carefully they must have listened in order to be able to say so much and with such excellent pronunciation and intonation.

The process is started in the very first lesson with simple exclamations in which every child, no matter what his ability, can join with equal facility. "Quelle catastrophe!" soon becomes a general favorite as "Madame" obligingly engineers situations in which the expression can be used appropriately. Perhaps she drops what she is holding; "inadvertently" sweeps something off the table; "accidentally" trips over something on the floor while the children roar with delight "Quelle catastrophe!" A handful of such exclamations ("quelle chance, quel dommage, d'accord") cover practically every situation that is ever likely to arise in the classroom and can be trotted out at all stages when a child is at a loss for other words; they also give even the least able child the opportunity to join in (at a simple level) with his companions, no matter how complicated the linguistic pattern has become.

But of course as the children gain confidence they soon begin to discern new structures and vocabulary in the constant flow of carefully selected but always completely natural French to which they are exposed, and these they then make their own. Usually, it is one of the brighter children who first reproduces the new pattern, say, "Est-ce que je peux?" But when the others see what rewards it brings: "Madame, Est-ce que je peux jouer? (chanter? danser? manger?)" they are quick to repeat it themselves so as to obtain the same desired results. (Madame's answer is of course always: "Oui, certainement, vouz pouvez.") It is this constant building on the children's interests, which forms the basis of this method, that keeps the children alert and determined to take part. Their curiosity: Madame's question, "Qu'est-ce qu'il y a dans le sac? Devinez!" never fails to elicit a rapid review of all their vocabulary as the children fire off the name of every object they can think of. Their inquisitiveness: An object guessed becomes temporarily the property of the child who guessed correctly. Their restless energy: Game succeeds game and with it structure succeeds structure in quick succession. Their desire to be physically active: They catch each object thrown to them; run round the room collecting objects from other children; perform some action, and so forth. All this may sound like Bedlam let loose, but it is amazing how in the hands of a skillful teacher this apparent chaos produces a rich linguistic harvest with the children busily going about their activities in the normal way—the only difference being that they are speaking French not English.

The environment must however be controlled with this end always in view, i.e. only those games and activities are presented for which the teacher knows the children already possess the necessary vocabulary and structures. It is useless presenting the children with a game of Bingo (a great favorite) if they do not know their numbers and how to add them together in French. But once they have learnt them as a class activity, by bouncing and throwing balls and counting in unison the number of bounces or throws, they can then be exposed to more individual cardboard or wood games. At this stage, it may well happen that the children are so anxious to talk that the teacher cannot get a word in and is therefore unable to present the new material that she has prepared for the lesson. In such cases she may be driven to saying: "Mais taisez-vous, mes enfants! Moi aussi, je veux parler." But what a triumph that she has actually got to ask the children to stop talking French. Surely a healthier situation than the long drawn-out pauses with which we are more accustomed in the language room when a pupil anxiously searches his memory for the correct tense, verb ending, gender, and adjectival agreement before he can utter the simplest sentence.

French in an Integrated Curriculum

In the first instance, in order to launch French as a new subject in the primary curriculum, it had to enjoy certain privileges; for example,

Integrating French and history.

specially selected teachers who were given extended leave of absence to attend training courses. But now that the Pilot scheme is in its fifth year, greater efforts are being made to consider it as just another aspect of a unified curriculum rather than as a special subject requiring special treatment. The aim is that wherever possible French should be taught by the regular class teacher and not by a specialist, either from within or without the school. This prevents dislocation of the timetable to suit the requirements of the visiting specialist and also gives the class teacher the opportunity of allowing French to flow over into other activities and not be confined to its own watertight compartment. This treatment of French on exactly the same footing as other subjects is important if the children are to learn to see all their work as a harmonious whole with subjects intermingling and interacting to their mutual advantage.

For this reason French is, on occasion, used as the means of communication—for that is what it really is—when the children are engaged on other activities such as art, handicrafts, physical education, organized games, and so on.

Just as French contributes to other activities so do other activities contribute to French. For example, in needlework the children might make French regional costumes for their dolls or for themselves and, if this study of costume is extended in time as well as space, it can be linked with history in a review of period costumes throughout the ages. They might then be so pleased with their efforts that they decide to mount their exhibition, perhaps for a parents' Open Day or for permanent display and admiration in their classroom. This involves the use of tools, wood, and other materials and might be undertaken as part of their work in handicrafts. So in this case French, history, needlework and handicrafts are combined to enable a single project, arising from the children's own interests, to be carried out.

Other less ambitious and more obvious combinations that one frequently finds are: with music—French songs; with dancing—French dances; with needlework—costumes, wall friezes (as illustrated: *La Vie en France*); with geography—a study of the part of France the class will be visiting on their school journey; with history—the many dramatic episodes from the long interwoven history of England and France, sometimes as seen by a French observer of the time. The burning of Joan of Arc, for example, looks rather different from this point of view and is thus a salutary exercise which may perhaps lead to a better international understanding among the rising generation.

Children study places in France they will visit on a school journey.

How One Headmaster Introduced French into His School [1]

Let me quote an extract drawn from a Headmaster's account of how he introduced French into his school and how he sought to integrate it with the rest of the curriculum, because it is of particular interest as demonstrating practice rather than theory.

By examining the syllabus in English and mathematics we discovered that a great deal of subject matter (previously accepted as essential) could very well be left out. The amount of time saved by the cutting of such unnecessary subject matter was sufficient to introduce a new subject, in this case French. This was achieved with no upheaval to timetables, such as shortening of lessons or working extra minutes here, there, and everywhere.

As a result of specialization by the French teacher (the school has only one French teacher) it became necessary for other teachers to

[1] G. Cox, Pontygof County Primary School, Ebbw Vale, Manmouthshire, Wales.

become involved in teaching her class. There were two courses open to me: either have the relieving teachers teach whatever subjects appeared on the timetable or let them teach subjects in which they had a particular interest and specialized knowledge. I resolved to adopt the second course because I felt the teachers would be happier and more enthusiastic about teaching their specialized subjects and as a result the children would benefit. The results have certainly proved this, but the greatest effect has been the complete involvement by the staff in all aspects of teaching methods and subject matter contained in the syllabus throughout the school. There is certainly a much greater feeling of cooperation, and teachers who for many years confined their efforts to the top of the school, have developed a much better appreciation of what happens at the lower end since they now make a substantial contribution themselves.

My staff and I decided that the integration of French should be carried out slowly and care should be taken not to overburden the curriculum with things French. Thus, only a limited number of items were introduced when and where it was felt necessary and appropriate.

The selection was also limited because it was felt that where it would be an easy matter to expand at a later date, an initially complicated scheme might lead to overorganization and create other difficulties. Moreover there was a lack of suitable material, especially reference books and illustrated materials. It was decided that art, craft, needlework, geography, history and music were particularly suitable subjects with which to launch our scheme and could without difficulty absorb something French.

GEOGRAPHY

Here, I favor the use of assignment cards and children working in groups. A sample card illustrates the kind of work done. The children can work on the assignments at any spare moment during the day.

HISTORY

In this case the scheme was confined to French history as it related to British history: the Norman Conquest, Joan of Arc, D-Day landings, among others.

Both the history and geography were correlated with art, craft

An assignment card.

and needlework and with our visit to France: Bayeaux and Arromanches-les-Bains, with its Museum of the Normandy landings.

ART AND CRAFT

In these areas children were involved with the production of pictures, charts, models, scrapbooks, dolls, illustrated maps. The dolls to date have been produced in two forms: regional costume (geography) and period costume (history). Three girls made themselves costumes, and at the recent showing of our French teaching film to the parents the girls wore their costumes and distributed programs.

For schools that are interested in pottery I would suggest that figures such as dolls can be produced very simply in clay. These can be fired and glazed in various colors. The children get a great deal of enjoyment and the production is fast and simple. In addition, mosaic, tiled interpretations of the Bayeaux tapestry could be produced, but we have not attempted this yet.

The use of puppets in teaching French is well known and these can be produced in craft lessons very simply indeed with the clothes made in needlework lessons.

Puppets are used to teach French.

MUSIC

The teaching of French songs as part of the French lesson did not appeal to me because music teaching has in recent years become more involved and includes the use of various instruments. I felt time taken in a French lesson to produce a worth-while production using orchestration would be better spent in other meaningful activities. Therefore I asked for the cooperation of another teacher to take charge of the singing, while the French teacher taught the words and I orchestrated the music. I should like to recommend three books of French songs which I have used: Mon premier livre de Chansons—this book is beautifully produced, contains the piano parts and also two very helpful records of all the songs in the books. The singing of the songs by French children is delightful and would be a great *help to nonmusical teachers of French. The other two books are:* Chantons un peu *which contains piano parts with English and French words for thirty songs and* Jeunesse qui chante—*a small book containing five hundred songs with music. Only the melody is written for the piano but it does not take long for the teacher of Music to write the full score.*

But in many schools French is confined neither to a set period a day nor to other aspects of the curriculum; it flows out beyond all these and takes many shapes as extracurricular activities, depending on the tastes and wishes of the staff and children concerned.

Very popular are the French clubs. These, along with other clubs, take place immediately after school at about four o'clock and are open to any child who wishes to attend. Because of the wide range of linguistic competence a wide range of activities has to be offered in order to provide something worthwhile for all. Some children might decide to make large wall-books with colorful pictures and a few simple sentences underneath to serve as an introduction to reading; others might paint murals illustrating various aspects of French life, for example, a typical French house, school, policeman, or market which can be used for oral work; others might model the fruits and vegetables and other objects for the shops that are to be found in nearly every classroom; others might make the puppets in which they so greatly delight and which are often the best means of getting the shy or introverted child to take part in an oral lesson.

Instead of making things other children will be doing things. For example, playing a French ball game; dancing a French folk dance; shopping in a French shop; making up their own playlets and then rehearsing them before presenting them to the whole group. Others will be quietly going about some play of their own unconnected with any group, perhaps reading a French book or simply looking at its illustrations; listening to French records; looking at a postcard album of France or just watching the others until they find some activity in which they would like to take part.

The main purpose of these clubs is not to teach, as such, but to provide a focal point where all the children in whom a love of France has been kindled in the classroom may come together to share their enthusiasm and give expression to it in forms of their own choosing.

How One Class Teacher Used Model-Making as a Stimulus [2]

The following note on model-making by a class teacher of French may serve as a more detailed illustration.

Model making is a very good way of stimulating the children to find out details of the French way of life. Boys of the 10+ age-group love making models and many of them purchase kits to work on at home, which involve an enormous amount of detail. The desire to put authentic detail into their models at school encourages them to delve into the French scene: What cars should they put into a French street scene, Simca, Peugeot, Renault, Citroen? What do the buildings look like? the railway trains? street signs? and a host of other details. All these lead the children to find out about France and the French.

Subjects found suitable for model making and which give children some information about the French way of life are: The caves of Lascaux; winter sports; a fishing village in Brittany; a château in a wine-making region; cross-channel car ferries; a French harbor; French railway station; French airport; village. Other topics have proved interesting: French cars and where they are manufactured; the perfume industry of Grasse; the Tour de France; French stamps and pictorial postmarks.

MODEL OF A CAVE AT LASCAUX

The story of the discovery of the cave at Lascaux with its wonderful palaeolithic paintings always seems to hold the interest and fire the imagination of the children, particularly as it was discovered by a group of French boys out rabbiting.

Both the method of color by the use of ochres and soot and the wonderfully simple yet effective outlines and shapes of the animals appeal to the children. One of the paintings depicts a man dressed up in the skin and antlers of a deer, and it is assumed it was painted because the artist thought it would give him power over the animals when he went hunting. The ideas of magic and mystery continue to fascinate the children, and the fact that the artist worked with only

[2] Mr. Saunders, Glenbrook Junior Boys' School, Wigman Road, Nottingham.

the light of a stone lamp in the depth of the cave adds to the eeriness.

The simplicity of the cave pictures makes them ideal for the children to copy and so relive the part of the artist.

The model was made of every conceivable type of household packet stuck together, with a little half-inch mesh wire netting to help to form the roof, the whole being generously covered with small irregular shaped pieces of well-pasted newspaper and then painted with ordinary school powder-paint.

The written work was drawn from a mixture of taped broadcasts, the information in the BBC pamphlets, school reference books, and reference books obtained by the children from the Public Library.

On the annual school outing, the children who made the model also visited Regent's Park Zoo where there are excellent reproductions of these cave paintings in one of the tunnels leading from one part of the Zoo to the other.

Another very popular focal point of interest is the French table at school lunch. This is presided over by the teacher of French and all children have the opportunity of sitting at it in turn. The menu is printed in French wherever possible. [Some English dishes defy translation, e.g. Toad-in-the-Hole?] It is handed around and discussed, choices are made and orders given to the "garçon" who fetches the food from the hatch. Conversation can be on any subject of the children's choosing within their linguistic competence, but the opportunity is also taken to teach them in a natural setting the names of all the utensils and food as well as how to ask for what they need. This prepares them for at least one aspect of another extracurricular activity which is the highlight of the whole of their three years of French—the school journey to France.

A School Visit to France

This trip takes many forms depending largely on local circumstances. In one remote village school where some of the children had never even visited their county town some 12 miles away parents would have been aghast at the thought of their treasures setting out on the unknown terrors of the Continent. To reassure them and gain their support the Headmaster invited them to accompany her on a flying weekend visit which she was making to explore the possibilities at the proposed destination. So delighted were they with this novel experience that they determined that all the children should have the chance of going the following year. In order that nobody should be excluded for financial reasons the school organized a fête in the vicarage garden to which the whole village came and which realized sufficient money to send all the ten-year-olds free of charge.

Other school journeys are more ambitious, being organized by the Local Education Authority, not by individual schools, and involving all the schools in the area that wish to participate. Under this scheme there is a continuous exchange of staff and children throughout the whole of the summer term. At the beginning of the term a group of 30 English children with their teachers fly by chartered plane to a camp school in France; 30 French children and their teachers use the same plane to bring them to England on its return flight. In both camps the children are grouped with another 30 children of the same age; thus, each camp simultaneously has a group of 30 English and 30 French children with a mixed staff of French and English teachers. The morning is devoted to lessons and whenever possible, for example, singing, physical education, miming, art, and the rest. The children are taught in groups of mixed nationality, English being spoken in England and French in France. Where such a procedure might lead to confusion, as in the case of mathematics, the children are taught separately by their own teachers; although an English teacher teaches the French children their English lesson while the French teacher teaches the English children for their French lesson. At first this may lead to the children being a little tongue-tied while they grow accustomed to their new teacher and especially his perhaps different (and more authentic) accent; but their shyness soon wears off, and the children enjoy being taught the foreign language by a real Frenchman or Englishman. By mutual consent the French and English teachers often stay in each other's rooms while the language lessons are in progress as they find this very valuable experience both from the point of view of language and of method.

The rest of the day is devoted to more general activities in which the nationality groups are always equally mixed: swimming, tracking, organized games, matches, excursions to places of interest, shopping expeditions, sing-songs, camp fires, among others. By the end of the week, most of the children have made friends among children of the other nationality and at the weekend each child living locally invites a foreign child to his home to spend the weekend with his family; likewise, the teachers are invited by their opposite numbers. This personal choosing of guests by the children avoids the clash of temperaments and tastes one can get when the choice is an arbitary one made by adults. It also helps to make the foreign child really welcome as he knows he has been specially invited. In the few cases where children do not get spontaneously invited, the teachers make unobtrusive arrangements to bring this about.

Every child thus gets the chance to spend two weekends with a foreign family whose own child has invited him personally. This experience gives him a splendid opportunity of verifying all he has been told about French family life in his three years at school and also provides him with the invaluable experience at the age of ten of learning to adapt to foreign habits and to take them in his stride as something quite natural, not strange or ridiculous. Besides, by being isolated from his fellow nationals he is forced to use his foreign language all day to make himself understood and thus learns to use it as a normal means of communication and not as something confined to a classroom. In some camps the foreign children do the daily camp shopping for the meals. This makes real all that well-rehearsed but contrived shopping to which they have grown accustomed in school; it is a real triumph for them when they arrive back at camp with the items they were commissioned to buy. Naturally, in such cases there is an arrangement with the local shopkeeper that he will take back items purchased in error.

On this question of the children's ability to use the language in real life situations in a foreign country, an extract taken verbatim from a Headmaster's account of his school journey is interesting:

Our fears concerning language problems proved unfounded. The children were confident in dealing with situations in the shops and hotel and appeared to be surprised that they could be understood. The town people were very helpful indeed and were delighted that the children were attempting to speak French. As one would expect many barriers were broken down. The children and the people they frequently came into contact with had a delightful experience which they will never forget.

A teacher from another area reported that the shopkeepers in Poitiers were so impressed by the children's French that they offered the teachers free ice creams to compensate for all the hard work they had obviously done during the preceding three years. The proof of the pudding is certainly in the eating.

13. Helping Teachers Make the Transition from the "Old" to the "New"

DAVID PRYKE

DAVID PRYKE is Assistant Headmaster of St. Leonard's Junior School, Bridgnorth, Shropshire, and is working at the present time on an experiment into the possibilities of Team Teaching with junior children. He has a Diploma in Education with special reference to young children from the University of Newcastle Upon Tyne.

At this point in time, change seems to be society's most stable feature; as never before, educational systems are being forced to consider the direct relevance of what they do and how they do it against a background of constant and apparently accelerating change. Formerly, the basic purpose of education was to transmit the culture to the developing generation, but this goal is not totally adequate now. Change dictates that what is passed on must have relevance to the world of today and of the future. What seems of value now may be worthless half a century hence.

Relevance to purpose and need is becoming the test of value within the primary school, and ever increasing demands are being placed upon teachers as they seek to give full effect to their work. Colleges of Education are producing teachers with a considerable depth of personal study in a child-centered approach to education that is doing much to give fuller meaning to the new concept, as evidenced in preceding chapters. These teachers are part of the "new." To say they know nothing of the "old" may be incorrect, for perhaps it is true to say that development in education in Britain has always come through a blending of the best of the new ideas with the best of what is current, or has gone before. However, teachers with some years' experience, whose training was completely of the "old" may and do find themselves at a disadvantage when confronted with, say, the "new mathematics." They feel inadequate and unable to cope, being limited by their own training. It is this large group of teachers who need most help in making the transition to more recent developments.

What has given us an "old-new" situation? The strongest feature may be the removal of the teacher from the center of the stage (the teacher as instructor) and his replacement by the child (the active learner). It is somewhat paradoxical that the removal of the teacher from a purely instructional role has made the job more taxing, requiring more personal knowledge and skill than ever before. Even those whose training is as little as ten years old find it difficult to know when not to intervene in the learning situation. To answer in depth some of the questions that the learning situation creates, one can search one's personal knowledge to the limit.

Education influences society and is in turn influenced by it, and a pattern of change can be seen evolving from the beginnings of universal education to the present day. The Church has always figured large in formal education and as an institution outside the family probably has greatest experience in providing such education. Voluntary effort gave general formal education its birth, early in the nineteenth century. The Industrial Revolution changed man's whole habit of life and social outlook and made compulsory education necessary, and from this point there has been no regression. The state was slow to become directly involved in general provision for education and even then was insistent that this education should be "sound and cheap," being sure that education could be accomplished fully by the time the child reached ten years of age. Also, teachers had only to have a minimum of training, if any. They were required to restrict through discipline and to teach how to read, how to write, and how to manipulate simple numbers. Apart from producing what seemed to be desirable results, no more was considered necessary. To try and condense the details of this evolution and to deal with it adequately would be a digression. Nevertheless, it is a far cry from the beginnings to this point in time, when increasing amounts of money are sought to keep pace with development, when demands to extend the duration of compulsory education are everywhere, and when teachers must consider "the whole child." Severe discipline and the punishments attendant on it are in question, and the desirability of the voice of the Church and religious teaching within education is being argued.

For teachers then, there has been call from the start to look forward; to question the appropriateness of material, method, and technique. This has always been done and often under great difficulty, particularly in the early days and even to times just prior to the Second World War. With the ending of the Second World War there came a desire to look again at everything attendant on life. Education was seen as the key perhaps to a better world. There was an increased demand for the best possible education for all. Now we find that society itself is in a state of transition, particularly in that the very standards and values upon which society is built are being put into question. In higher education the value of some courses as planned at the moment is being questioned by the students themselves.

Where are the primary school and the primary teacher within this total picture? The primary school contains children between the ages of five and 11+, and very often particularly in areas of concentrated population these children may be divided into infants of five to seven years in infant schools and juniors of seven to 11+ in separate junior schools. This may be laboring a point, but it seems worth doing because it is from practice in many infant schools that the change from "old to new" has begun to evolve. Currently, this change is in process of development in junior schools and is beginning to be considered— perhaps with some suspicion—in secondary schools. Remembering then that practice with very young children is quite advanced and that with slightly older children it is coming to full development, it can perhaps be said that the British primary school is a very stimulating place in which to work, because the whole conception of its purpose is growing. Primary-school teachers find that as demands on them are constantly increasing, they are having to rethink many accepted educational ideas regarding their work, and they are having to re-educate many parents as the value of present developments in the primary school is proved. It may be worth adding at this point that parents are making much use of opportunities of coming into schools to look at the work going on and talk about it. This now seems to be essential, because the better the liaison between home and school and the more sympathetic in outlook each is with the other, the more effective the education of the child is likely to be. How far do parents become involved? The tradition is that school and home are separate and "never the twain shall meet." If a parent came to school it would often be in a recalcitrant mood, a mood usually deriving from lack of communication created by parental exclusion from school. Perhaps teachers of some experience still regard parents in school with suspicion—the teacher comes under the prying eye. This need not be so. Numbers of parents are very appreciative of what is going on, and they respect the right of the professional educator to conduct the school. They do not interfere with policy and practice and it is right that they should not.

Why must the transition be made from "old to new?" The placing of the child in the center of the stage has already been mentioned; and the point may be: Why is this so? Two things seem to dictate why it is so and these have arisen with the one inextricably connected to the other.

1. During the last twenty years society has turned to education to solve its major ills, and the demand has come for equal opportunity for all children. Necessary in the transition, then, is helping teachers think through society's demands as they appear now.
2. Research is giving increased knowledge of how children learn. This knowledge is having to be considered, in order to make the process of education more effective. Teachers need time to become acquainted with recent child-development study.

Thus firstly, in the transition teachers must try to predict the future into which children will grow. To have to do this is new, because heretofore the future of the child when his schooldays ended was likely to follow a definite pattern. He would get a job and this would occupy him for the whole of his working days. Not so now, for such is the rate of change that very many children in school at the moment will have to change their jobs maybe several times in a lifetime. Somehow then we must educate children to be adaptable, so that re-education is possible for them as they grow older. The speed of socio-economic change is so great, however, that prediction of the future is almost impossible. There are indications that there will be more wealth and more leisure, although the greatest increase in leisure time seems likely to fall to those whose work is of a purely mechanical and repetitive nature. Consumer choice will increase and majorities will be dominant in decision; the rights of the individual may be eroded even further. Communities will increase in size, and skill in living harmoniously together will be required. This seems to suggest that children will require rich opportunity in school for:

1. Development as individuals in the society of school.
2. Thinking for themselves.
3. Adaptability.

To make these opportunities possible, much new thinking on the part of educators is necessary.

Secondly, and a great influence in the transition, is the increasing availability of knowledge about children and their development. Teachers are becoming more and more influenced by the work of Jean Piaget and the valuable guide he gives concerning the ways in which children learn. The stages of intellectual development that Piaget sees are being followed through by teachers and seem to be reasonably accurate guides, when viewed from the point of developmental age. Method and organization within the classroom are changing therefore, and the period of childhood up to age 12 or 13 is being viewed not merely as a step in the direction of adulthood but also as having a complete value in itself. The thesis of Rousseau that "nature would have them children before they are men" is being given some regard, and three facts about children's learning are now well established:

1. Young children learn by actively participating in their learning.
2. They learn by talking and discussing.
3. They learn through play.

Demands from society and new knowledge from research are forcing teachers at all levels to reconsider the effectiveness of the "old," and it may perhaps be fair to say that at this moment development of ideas is going ahead with increasing purpose. There appears to be a tendency in education to deal with new concepts in one of two ways: either to regard them with great suspicion and be reluctant to have anything to do with them at all, or, to seize them joyfully, forget everything that has gone before and herald them as a panacea. The latter may have happened with "new math." It has been well said that "nothing moves in this world that is not Greek in origin," and the word *new* may be rather misplaced in its attachment to mathematics. It may always be true to say that the greatest progress comes when a blend of traditional and new is being sought in the development of educational ideas; and this seems to be happening now.

Three considerations arise as teachers seek to make their work more responsive to need:

1. Children in society as children.
2. The curriculum.
3. The timetable.

As these three points are considered new methods and organization are evolving, and the crucial problem arising in the transition seems to be how best to help teachers who are already trained. Time is needed to talk about fresh ideas, to try them out, and to compare results. Colleges of Education have less of a problem, because students are not hampered by previous training. Colleges can start in the right place with a "tabula rasa"! This does not mean that there is no call on them to rethink ideas, but time and opportunity are on their side.

As the concept of education extends and deepens it becomes essential for teachers to appraise these three considerations: children in society as children, the curriculum, and the timetable. Only by getting the first point in its correct perspective will it be possible for the other two to evolve. (In this chapter, as some development is given to the three points, however, the first is considered last.)

The Curriculum

Until recent years, curriculum and content were of paramount importance. This was basic academic tradition. Now comes the idea: "Here are children and this curriculum should suit their needs, as far as can be seen."; rather than, "Here is the curriculum and children will fit it." The curriculum in any British school has always been the direct responsibility of the head of the school and development of it has been appropriate therefore to the particular conditions of each school. This still appertains and it is hoped will continue to do so, because it is one of the strengths of the system. As far as young children are concerned, knowing more about how children learn is making teachers reconsider the demands placed on the curriculum. The old idea of curriculum was:

> *Ram it in. Ram it in.*
> *Children's heads are hollow.*

But today, four points reach a little beyond this maxim and demonstrate the change of emphasis:

1. The curriculum should enable the child to get to know himself and his possibilities.
2. It should provide opportunity for him to think for himself.
3. It should enable him to make his personal contribution as someone who has need to grow intellectually, physically, spiritually, emotionally, morally, and aesthetically.
4. It should allow him to undertand (as fully as he is able) the world as he comes to know it.

These demands that the curriculum should be broader and deeper than ever before seem to indicate that one of the essential requirements in helping teachers make the transition from old to new is to find an answer to the question: How can planning be made more effective?

The Timetable

There is the need for a wider dissemination of knowledge about how children learn. So far, this knowledge seems to indicate that above all else there must be flexibility in timetabling the work of young children; and flexibility seems desirable on three counts:

1. Learning takes place at varying speeds and this is determined by the development level reached by the individual.

2. Children learn in various ways, including talking, discussing, doing, listening. Some may require time when they can shut off and do nothing.
3. Interests are varied and last for longer or shorter periods, so we must beware of stopping activity while interest abounds, or flogging it when it has declined.

A new conception of timetabling seems to be called for to cope with this need for flexibility. For teachers whose training is traditional, the timetable gives purpose and security. For teachers with little experience, rigid guidelines give confidence. An integrated day seems to be the answer but how can teachers best be helped into this transition?

Children in Society as Children

What about school as a society of people? Characteristic of the old was the belief that school was a place of work and the effectiveness of the work was revealed in the examination. In order to work pupils sat in one place in silence and followed strict instructions from the teacher. Children were of distinct types; even now, some children have their educational destiny decided at the age of five complete with label A or B or C. For some teachers at work today (perhaps for many) this is the story of their own school life, and it should not be cast aside too lightly, for time was when education was regarded as a painful business, for "the limbs of Satan." Furthermore, only the privileged few could have the type of secondary education likely to lead to increased opportunity later; accordingly, these few were sorted out as early as possible. It is interesting that many of the affluent middle class in England still regard selection of their child for education in a grammar school as a symbol of status.

In putting these things right in the light of what is known of children now and what is foreseen as the demands of the future, a whole system is being asked to change. How can teachers be helped through this?

The class of about 40 and its teacher has been the basis of organization within the primary school since its inception. Sometimes this has led to class teachers becoming confined by the four walls of the classroom, guarding their autonomy and planning and evaluating programs for their own class. The class is still basic to the organization of many primary schools, and the most recent recommendations say this should be so; but there is beginning to be a movement away from this, as open plan schools are developed. The demands of social development, curriculum, and timetable are making it more desirable that teachers within a school should cooperate to a greater degree, because this can make programs more effective. One positive way of helping in the transition to new practice in sizable schools is to encourage teachers to consider working as part of a team, rather than as individuals in isolation. It must be remembered, of course, that some teachers work most effectively as individuals, so enforcement into a team form of organization is not desirable as general practice. When considering teachers in any context the great limitation is always their scarcity, but team work in school can make possible what is to a degree "retraining" without requiring replacement teachers. One way of beginning team teaching is to work across one age-group and create a situation in which, say, three teachers work with upward of a hundred children. Whether there is a horizontal or vertical distribution of responsibility within the team will depend on enthusiasm and experience, but the certain thing about team organization is that it can fulfill all the requirements of the "new," and can confront teachers with all the problems which need rethinking in the light of present-day knowledge and demands.

What can working in a team give to teachers? Working in a team creates a situation in which teachers must cooperate and this opens up considerable possibilities in the wider deployment of talents and the helping of inadequacies. In addition, team organization brings a larger group of children together as a unit, and thus again greater demand is put on individuals to cooperate; the range of required social skill and responsibility is increased. It appears that a society like ours is becoming ever more crowded and will depend increasingly on cooperation. For this reason, a move away from competition may be good, because a more effective sense of social responsibility is likely to be created in a cooperative rather than a competitive atmosphere.

Teamwork with an enthusiastic leader and a large group produces planning, talk, and argument that force the consideration of new ideas stemming from increased knowledge of children and efforts to predict the future society into which they are entering. Such talk and discussion plus the questioning of one's own practice is throwing various ideas into question. For example: Should children be "streamed"? Is there any argument to favor grouping children by ability? As far as primary-school children are concerned, the answer to this question seems to be, no. But "streaming" is still in vogue and history dictates that this is so, because equal opportunity for secondary education is a comparatively recent development. In this respect the system still harks back to the days when selection for a limited number of places for secondary education was necessary, and the sooner the "right children" could be found the better. This does not mean that the need for selection no longer arises. The time will inevitably come when selection for this or that course, or this or that specialization must be made. Unless the finest brains are developed to the fullness of their capacity, our survival as a nation may be in peril. Or is this type of thinking insufficiently forward looking? Are the issues bigger than this?

As teachers are being faced more squarely with the problems of what they do, there comes a realization that the more we can allow a child to be treated as an individual with something to offer the community in which he finds himself as a child, the more useful he may become as an adult. The more a child can be allowed to use direct experience the better he will learn how to learn. The more he can take part in organizing the community in which he finds himself at school, the more he can be faced with tackling problems, making decisions, and helping others; and the more adaptable he may become to changes he encounters later.

The teacher is being bombarded with the child and the needs of the child; and the teacher who is trained and working with the child every day is often being called on to do the impossible. He is asked to work, to keep abreast of developments, to deepen personal knowledge and interests, to be as much an individual as it seems desirable for the child to be. Team organization can at least help to deepen the professional side through discussion and argument.

Then comes the question of how much of a specialist does the teacher need to be? Specialist knowledge in a variety of fields is vital. Now the important question seems to be how is a specialist best employed? The answer does not seem to be in the type of specialization of old, when an entire group of children was taught by the specialist for a certain period of time. Rather what seems to be required is the use of the specialist at any time when children require his specialist knowledge. The specialist will be more and more required as the amount of knowledge increases; and beside this, no one teacher can cope in sufficient depth with all the demands for knowledge as children grow older. One effective method of using the specialist can be in the form of a "consultant." In this way, the depth of knowledge and enthusiasm of the specialist can be wisely used to the benefit, not only of children, but of fellow members of staff. For children up to and even beyond the age of 12 the greatest asset that a teacher can have is great width of experience in many fields plus a depth of knowledge that some children and fellow teachers can call upon to satisfy a particular level in their personal development. Use of specialist teaching should not create a situation in which subject matter is taught for its own sake. It should always serve the needs of the child. Neither should specialization in one area of knowledge lead to rejection of another area. It does not seem desirable in an age calling for adaptability to allow children of 12 to shut out any area of experience before wide exploration of it has been made possible. Sending the child with the need to the teacher seems more realistic than sending the teacher to all children at the same time, as in the days of "isolated specialism."

Specialization is now modified as a result of knowing more about children. New entrants to the profession are benefiting from more child study; established members can extend their knowledge from working in a team of teachers. Teamwork takes up a great amount of time and this is not always easy to find, but ancillary help can ease difficulties. "Teachers' aides" are not yet beyond suspicion, but this type of assistance from interested people outside the profession seems to have great possibilities. There are as yet difficulties, and answering them is not easy, but perhaps useful gains will come as answers are found. Much more can be given by the trained professional if time-consuming tasks are removed—tasks such as preparation of materials and routine supervision. College of Education students might be incorporated for certain periods of time in a team set-up. Working a step forward from the ancillary, they could derive benefit from being with children and working with groups of children, even sitting in on planning sessions. The group is still a feature of the new approach. Although the provision of individual attention is always sought, time and numbers militate against this; and the answer becomes the group to suit the need. This solution seems easier within team organization. To return to the point of students working with a team of teachers: this is merely a thought, but one that might merit further exploration. What is more than mere thought is the fact that inexperienced teachers can benefit from joining a team; because help and advice are more readily available and isolation in a classroom less likely, thus many initial fears are removed.

Effective as teamwork can be in helping teachers develop new ideas in primary education, great demands are put on time and energy if teamwork is employed. Assessment and evaluation can absorb much time after the normal hours of school. And how far are assessment and evaluation possible in an individual approach to learning anyway? When in session the teacher is having to give more and more physical and mental energy. With a pardon for the cliché, the function of the teacher is still to teach, and a balance between the complete teacher-centered and the complete child-centered approach has to be found. Interest in full development of individuals is asking for more than this. A retired teacher of some distinction is noted as saying that because of the demands of today, teaching thirty years ago was a "piece of cake." This may be so, and research seems to indicate that there was less call then to sit down and attempt to find solutions to problems such as corporal punishment or the teaching of religion, to mention just two.

As has already been indicated, many children in school now will be called upon to retrain for employment perhaps several times during their lifetime. To some extent there is a call for teachers to do this now; and in the future, teachers no less than anyone else seem likely to be involved in regular retraining. How can this be done? Where will the time come from? As school staffing is, little can be done in term time. There are evenings, weekends, holidays. But teachers get tired and they also have lives to live. Perhaps this is going beyond my thesis in this chapter. The whole problem of keeping up to date with developments as yet defies a completely satisfactory solution, but positive efforts to keep teachers *au fait* with developing educational thought has been made for many years through "in-service training courses." The quantity of these is increasing, with provision being made by Local Authorities which employ teachers and by the Department of Education and Science. The depth of study into which these courses go and the period of time over which they extend vary considerably. They may vary from an evening course in a local school, to a year of full-time study in a University Institute of Education.

The fact that teachers are in no way obligated to attend courses of any kind after the completion of a required period of professional training seems at once good and bad. It seems good because it preserves a certain autonomy of which teachers are rightly proud, giving the right to choose. It is interesting because of this that applications for many retraining courses far exceed available places and (perhaps doubly interesting) that many courses take place at times beyond those in which schools are in session. It seems bad, and particularly so at this point in time, because it fails to recognize the speed of educational change. Teachers need to make contact with the latest ideas and the theory which is influencing what appears to be more positive practice. Theory and practice are completely complementary; the adage "an ounce of practice is worth a ton of theory" merits little consideration. What seems impossible is the ability to create time for teachers to be able to stand back from the job in the classroom and survey what is going on in wider fields of influence at times other than their own. Some courses provide for this, but only those that extend over a period of time such as a term or more. Many of the valuable evening or weekend courses, or those covering a week, occur when teachers are at their most tired and least receptive. Willingness to increase educational efficiency is related to conditions of work, salary, recognition of effort, as well as professional responsibility and sense of vocation. It would appear that consideration must come soon for a situation in which teacher retraining can take place and this retraining may have to be obligatory. After a span of five years, it seems, previous training may be only partially effective and something will be required to bring individual teachers up to date with progress in theory and practice. Knowing the demands that the staffs of primary schools face in seeking to develop the "whole child," often in classes which are far too large, in rooms which lend themselves but poorly to optimum working demands, then it seems worth stating that serious consideration must be made by someone on the effects of the school on teachers as well as on children. No attempt will be made here to suggest a solution to the problem. It may be pointless to state that more teachers are needed.

What courses seek to do seems right. They present new ideas, provoke thought and discussion, increase knowledge, and make it possible for expertise to develop. They permit study in depth of a particular interest, or of education generally. They bring together teachers, advisers, and inspectors and assist in developing a relationship among them that is most conducive to the production and implementation of new ideas. Retraining courses now need space and time in which to be developed to the greater benefit of more teachers and should be regarded as much a part of professional commitment as the job of teaching itself.

In calling for a situation in which there is a more general dissemination of ideas in the change from old to new, there may be a risk of ignoring the fact that advance often comes from the development of ideas by individuals. Many headmasters of vision have brought about radical change within the confines of a particular school. To take the practice of these individuals and look at it in detail may be of little value, because to generalize their ideas is often impossible. This is so because their method may well be completely personal and applied to a very particular situation, along with colleagues who are in total sympathy with it. To consider their work can have some value in that it may have aspects that can be developed to suit particular needs. It would be unwise to dismiss any progressive work out of hand.

Change within a school can be effected in what seem to be two possible ways and both these rely on the fact that headmasters have great autonomy and freedom of action—privileges which should be closely guarded. The head of a school can find himself with a staff that is completely at one with his ideas, and he can introduce change of method quickly and with some direction. In such a situation his guidance and conviction and encouragement serve to influence his staff and lead to its seeing the purpose behind what goes on. Educational aims are agreed and understood. Secondly, the head of a school may find his staff contains an individual or a nucleus of individuals who seek to develop ideas that seem to have validity in their situation. He allows the development of these ideas, seeking at the same time a spreading outwards to the rest of the staff, by encouraging them to look at what is happening and to talk about what they see. Both these situations can produce work that is progressive, forward looking, perhaps even ahead of its time. It can also encourage the overdevelopment of a particular personal whim or fancy, and it is rather the concern of this writer to be as completely objective as possible and seek help in transition, which is of more general application.

As has been said of late, there has been an increased supply of courses for teachers, and these are proving invaluable in helping the development of new methods and ideas. Some opportunity is being given to teachers to organize things for themselves through the medium of the Teachers' Center. These centers seem to be in anything from an embryonic stage to a complete development stage, and argument is strong as to what they should provide. What seems to be the idea behind them? As I see it, the employing Authority provides a building in a particular area (be this a city or a town and its surrounding district) in which teachers can meet socially and professionally to talk and work, at times to suit themselves. Supposing a building is available —and provision is sometimes difficult—then equipment will be provided as required. The Center is organized and run by teachers, some of whom form an elected committee with a chairman. Action comes through this elected body and all teachers are at liberty to suggest what organization and activity should be. Ideally, the Center should be available to teachers at all times and should have the services of a "warden" or someone in charge; and it is conceived as providing for the needs of teachers from every section of education. In this way activities can involve cooperation between teachers in primary, secondary, and further education.

The well-organized Teachers' Center has a great potential to help teachers cope with new educational demands, and much good could arise from the cooperative working of teachers in primary and secondary schools. Active contact between these types of schools may often be very small, but it is increasing and must increase as changes in the traditional academic approach to secondary education become insufficient and methods used with older primary school children are seen to be worth extending to the early years in the secondary school. Centers provide a real opportunity for teachers to help themselves—not that they have never done this before. Total concern for education has always been shown by the teachers' professional organizations and help has always been available for them. The Center puts help right on the spot and can make available the skill of local teachers for the benefit of colleagues, as well as using outside help to answer the problems and needs of an area. Books in a growing library can be of much value and the possibilities for the use of apparatus can be discussed and tried before being employed. It seems that the Teachers' Center will stand or fall on the strength and enthusiasm of its chairman and committee, and much responsibility is theirs for making the Center a stimulating place. How far a Center can be used during the time that schools are in session seems open to question, but its use ought to be possible in times other than the teachers' own.

The Teachers' Center may bring into closer contact teachers from primary and secondary schools; and to reiterate, the changes arising as the primary school develops are beginning to influence practice in the early years of secondary education. Signs indicate, however, that the primary school, as we conceive it now, may itself have its development arrested. The name *primary school* may disappear, but the methods and practices that have emerged and are still emerging from it will strengthen in what will be called *middle schools.*

The concept of the middle school arises in part from consideration of research into child development and the light this throws on the ways in which children learn. The indication is that children between eight and 13 years possess great similarity in method of learning; and so extension of the best primary school practice may be worth considering. Transfer to the secondary system may be profitably deferred. Educational provision for young children is now being thought of in terms of *first schools* for children aged five to eight (or nine) and *middle schools* for those aged eight to 12 (or nine to 13). There are arguments in favor of both the proposed age-ranges for middle schools, although perhaps the nine to 13 grouping has more in its favor. First and middle schools do already exist in various stages of growth, but the setup of first schools, middle schools and *comprehensive schools* is by no means general practice yet. It may not be for some time. It may never be. No further transition may be imminent, as close examination is made of learning within the age range eight to 13. The primary school as we know it may not complete its emergence, but what is fairly certain is that its methods will have much influence on middle schools. First schools will take the best of current infant-school practice and use and develop this, and because of what has gone before, their birth will be comparatively painless. Middle schools may have problems. Research into the ways in which children learn makes it difficult to deny that eight to 13 covers a period in development during which a definite pattern of learning can be seen. Formal thinking is slowly becoming a possibility, but learning through concrete things is yet of crucial importance to understanding.

Teachers are now having to think through or even formulate the philosophy of the middle school and this will be made easier to some degree through courses and discussions—always remembering that a time arrives when talking becomes unproductive and positive action alone provides results. The middle school should be above all else an entirely new conception, something more than either an extended junior school or a diluted secondary school. It seems that the best practice of the junior school should become its great criterion. Teachers who staff it will need sympathy for this practice, and the place within it of the specialist teacher will need to be thought out carefully. It appears that the initial idea of establishing middle schools did not come from teachers. What an opportunity this could be for teachers to make themselves heard concerning the planning, building, and equipping of these schools. Or will this be yet another instance of development on a "shoe-string budget"; much good intention but little purpose?

How do teachers see the middle school? Perhaps many have neither the time nor the opportunity to consider the theory underlying it and the practice it seems to demand. Considering that its success will depend on the foresight, personal knowledge, and expertise of the teachers who staff it, what opportunity will be provided for teachers to make the transition?

14. An American Reaction

VINCENT R. ROGERS

VINCENT R. ROGERS *is Head of the Department of Elementary Education and Professor of Education at the University of Connecticut. He is a former Fulbright Scholar, author of* The Social Studies in English Education *(Heinemann, 1968), co-author of the* Social Science Seminar Series *(Charles E. Merrill, 1965), editor of* A Sourcebook For Social Studies *(Macmillan, 1969), and the author of numerous articles on education in England and the United States of America. He has been active in the curriculum-reform movement of the 1960's in the United States and has recently become involved in educational projects in Africa and Italy.*

There is a particularly poignant moment in Arthur Miller's *Death of a Salesman* in which Willy Loman confronts Bernard, a childhood friend of his son Biff. Bernard is now a successful lawyer; Biff is unemployed, unhappy—a failure. Willy pleads with Bernard to tell him "the secret," that is, how did *he* do it? How did he make it, while Biff simply gave up and fell out of the race?

Sometimes I think that teachers can be compared with Willy—particularly in their attitudes toward educational change and innovation. They are looking for some magical new kit, some packet, some profound new insight that (once possessed or grasped) will send them

283

happily on their way to a promised land of successful, effortless teaching.

Whatever their perspectives, the chapters of this book do dispel the notion that there might be some easy way to achieve good education for children. There is no magic formula, no secret, no commercially produced package or program that (if one assiduously follows the "teachers' guide") will produce instant success. On the contrary, as all good teachers know almost instinctively we learn that teaching is hard, demanding, compelling *work*. It takes time to know children; it takes time to work with them, to create learning opportunities and materials; it takes time to learn enough about the environment to be able to utilize it as a challenging curricular source for children; it takes time to think, to read, to visit, to discuss, to seek, to grow, and to continue to grow.

Our authors also tell us, however, that given time, energy, talent, and commitment a new kind of teaching is possible for many teachers, and—more importantly—a new kind of *learning* is possible for most children.

Perhaps it is a mistake to use the word "new." Students of education undoubtedly are aware that many of the ideas expressed in this book have been stated before in other times and other places. Rather than quarrel about the uniqueness of the message—or engage in perhaps fruitless debate about its origins, I would prefer to say that at this moment in time for the vast majority of the world's teachers the kind of education described in this book is indeed a new and challenging thing. Perhaps its uniqueness lies not so much in its originality as in its successful adaptation on a large scale in the public or state-supported schools of an entire nation. In other words, although we may well have *said* it before, I don't think we have ever really *done* it before; this seems to me to be the genius of British primary education today.

If, then, these ideas are not necessarily new to American and other educators, how do we explain their successful implementation in Britain? Why have the British made this kind of education work to a degree unprecedented in educational history? What is unique about the British experience that may help explain their ability to do that which most of us have only talked about?

Tentative Hypotheses for the Success of British Primary Schools

This book began with a statement of the philosophy supporting it; most books do, just as most American schools have some statement of their educational goals buried in their curriculum guides or in other official publications. However, the major difference between what is happening in Britain and what has happened here is that in Britain this philosophy appears to be both understood and taken seriously by a large number of teachers and headmasters.

STAFF COOPERATION TOWARD GOALS

Occasionally, I have talked with a principal who expressed a well-thought-through rationale or philosophical underpinning for what he wants to do in his school. It is exceedingly rare (in my experience) that one is able to leave the principal's office, visit classrooms, talk to teachers and children and find any real consistency of educational thought among the members of a school faculty or staff. The truly striking thing about the new British primary schools is that one *does* find such consistency in many of them. Headmaster and staff seem to be pulling in the same direction, supporting each other, understanding each other, moving the whole educational enterprise toward an agreed upon goal. When this happens one can expect meaningful, observable change to take place; and it does.

QUALITY AND BACKGROUND OF TEACHERS

Another possible explanation for British success may lie in the quality of the individual teacher. [Obviously, this must be a highly subjective analysis; I have no scientific data to support my hunches.] Nevertheless, if the reader will simply browse through Vernon Hale's chapter (Chapter 7), which deals with creative writing, one cannot help but be impressed with the resources that he had at his command. He utilized the music of Stravinsky, poems and novels by modern writers, as well as the works of a 16th-century geographer. In addition, he used some of his own poems as points of departure or stimuli for his children. Mr. Hale is an unusual man—but after visiting British primary schools for a year, I came to the conclusion that there were many more teachers like him teaching in such schools than there were in American elementary schools.

In other words, I found a broadness of educational background among many British primary teachers that enabled them to enrich and stimulate their children in a way I have rarely seen here. Their intellectual and cultural *répertoire* was more varied, more provocative. This background makes a profound difference in one's effectiveness as a teacher, and I cannot ignore it as one possible explanation for at least part of the British success.

This observation opens up a Pandora's box of questions relating to the nature of teacher education in Britain and in the United States as well as questions concerning secondary education in both countries. Obviously, this book is not the place to pursue them, but my observations do suggest that an intensive, systematic, comparative study of teacher education might be exceedingly timely and valuable.

CREATIVITY IN USE OF TEACHING MATERIALS

A third hypothesis, which is certainly related to the others, concerns the conception British teachers and headmasters have of appropriate and useful teaching materials for children. Perhaps because of lack of funds or other reasons British teachers seem to rely far more on their own wit and creativity in gathering all kinds of teaching materials that will help fill specific educational gaps for the individual child in a given school.

One often gets the impression in an American school that if the duplicating machine were to break down for a week, some teachers would be quite desperate for something to give their children to do. The usual diet of fill-ins, matchings, and color-ins would be unavailable; what, then, does one do? How does one teach without packaged exercises and workbooks, without a basal reading series, without 30 social studies textbooks for the whole class, or without the magical, guaranteed successful, cannot-do-without You-Name-It Company's phonics (or other) program?

In a good British primary school one sees everything used as a stimulus for observation and creative work in art and writings, from a real pheasant's head to a display of wine bottles. One sees teacher-made devices and gadgets of all kinds used to facilitate the learning of science or mathematics. Somehow or other, if the school doesn't provide it, many British teachers seem to have not only the ability but also the willingness to make it or create it. They see this as part of their job, part of their responsibility to children. I do not think this spirit exists to anything like a similar degree in America.

THE PRIME IMPORTANCE OF THE INSTRUCTIONAL PROGRAM

A fourth explanation may lie in the deep concern most British head-masters have for their schools' instructional programs. Nothing matters more to the headmaster of the kind of primary school we have described in this book than the children, what and how they are taught, and what and how they learn. Indeed, virtually all British headmasters continue to teach on a part-time basis. I submit that this is not true in the vast majority of American schools, and that our principals do not perceive themselves as curricular or methodological leaders. Rather, they find themselves caught up in a whole host of problems ranging from bus scheduling to the staffing and running of the school cafeteria; problems that must be dealt with, and soon; problems that should be settled by secretarial help or an assistant; problems that encourage a principal to put off concern for the really crucial questions with which he, above all, should be involved.

Obviously, these are generalizations that cannot be expected to hold in all cases; there are exceptions of all kinds and degrees in both British and American schools. Nevertheless, I think it fair to say that such differences do exist, and that they in turn help the outsider to understand not only what is happening in Britain, but why it is happening as well.

GOVERNMENT SUPPORT FOR "THE NEW EDUCATION"

A final point that may also have an observable effect on the direction taken in the emerging British primary school is the weight of what might be called official sanction and support for "the new education." While headmasters and teachers jealously guard their collective right to develop the sort of education that is perceived as right for their children, the position taken by the Department of Education and Science in Curzon Street in London (formerly, The Ministry of Education) and by many Local Education Authorities is highly supportive of the kind of primary school described in this book. Indeed, the recently published Plowden Report [1] on primary education in Britain may be

---

[1] *Children and Their Primary Schools: A Report of the Central Advisory Council for Education* (London: Her Majesty's Stationery Office, 1966).

conceived of as a mandate for the British primary school to move with all deliberate speed in this direction.

Salient Features of the Educational Revolution

So much, then, for explanations for the emergence of a new kind of primary education in Britain. Perhaps it would be useful at this time to outline in more specific terms the nature of this new education as seen by one American observer. Whereas the preceding chapters describe in considerable detail the sorts of things that are happening in British classrooms, in this chapter I propose to sum up the salient features of this educational revolution in somewhat broader terms, discussing both advantages and disadvantages of their approach.

EXCITEMENT, CHALLENGE, POSSIBILITIES

To begin with, it seems as if the new British primary school is committed to the notion that children should live more fully and more richly *now*, rather than at some ill-defined time in the distant future. Education, then, is not preparation for life; rather, education *is* life with all of its excitement, challenge, and possibilities. One hastens to add that this idea is not new. What is new is that this is happening here and now in perhaps 20 to 30 per cent of the primary schools in Britain.

FLEXIBLE CURRICULUM

In order to achieve this goal, British teachers and headmasters conceive of the curriculum as a series of starting or jumping-off places. An idea, a question, an observation—child's or teacher's—acts as a stone thrown into the middle of a quiet pond. The ripples begin, one idea leads to another, and a study is under way. In contrast, American educators seem far more concerned from a curricular point of view with identifying and then covering in some particular order or sequence a series of ideas, concepts, generalizations, or skills that (theoretically) form the backbone of the curriculum in any area—which we shall discuss in greater detail later. However, it seems worth mentioning that there appears to be very little content that is regarded as "basic" and "essential" in the eyes of the English teacher or headmaster. While he tries to understand the nature of the broad academic fields in which he works, he tends to see them largely as possibilities rather than as prescriptions. He tries to challenge and stimulate within a broad framework of cultural and societal significance, but he does not pre-plan to the extent that beginnings, middles and ends are clearly laid out in six-week study "units." The curriculum then emerges through the mutual interests and explorations of children and their teachers working together; occasionally in large groups, sometimes in small groups, and often as individuals.

INTERRELATED STUDIES

Another characteristic of the emerging British primary school that is closely related to the preceding point has to do with the eagerness of teachers to cut across subject-matter lines in their handling of any study that may evolve in their classrooms. Art, music, history, poetry—all are brought to bear on a given problem or topic, and it is often difficult to tell whether children are studying history or geography, art or science. This freedom tends to give a wholeness to learning that must be lacking in more compartmentalized curricula, and it helps support and build the image of the school as a place where lifelike questions may be investigated as opposed to questions that may appear to be narrowly academic.

UNOBTRUSIVE TEACHING

A fourth observation has to do with the British teachers' concern for *learning* as opposed to teaching. Rarely will one find such a teacher standing in front of the room teaching a "class" lesson. Rather, one gets the impression that the teacher is largely a stage-setter, a stimulator, who encourages and guides but who does *not* appear to direct. It is often difficult to find the teacher when one first walks into a typical classroom, since he/she is likely to be working with a child here and a child there, moving around the room among the children.

EMPHASIS ON THE THINKING PROCESS

Having said all of this, a fifth conclusion is inescapable, i.e. the significance of *process* over *product* in the education of a child. There seems little doubt that British teachers are greatly concerned with *how* a child learns: the kinds of questions he asks and the ways in which he goes about resolving them. Over the long haul, British teachers believe that these attitudes toward learning will prove to be infinitely more valuable than will the subject matter dealt with in the development of such skills.

FREEDOM AND RESPONSIBILITY OF CHILDREN

Similarly, British teachers seem greatly concerned about the development of real independence and responsibility in children—often to a far greater extent than American teachers do. In the best of British primary schools, a degree of individual freedom, flexibility, and responsibility exists in a way that is virtually unknown in most American elementary schools. Teachers do not hang over their children, supervising them in every conceivable activity: on the playground, in the halls, aboard buses, and (even) in the washrooms. All of this is done, of course, in a calculated way, recognizing that such qualities as independence and reliability need to be "practiced" as well as spoken about.

TEACHERS' RESPECT FOR CHILDREN'S IDEAS

Finally, one might say that the teachers who work with children in the kinds of schools described in this book seem to care deeply, perhaps passionately, about *children*. Children are to be taken seriously, not laughed at or ridiculed in the staff room. Children are to be watched, children are to be listened to, children are to learn from; children are the essential ingredients in the teaching/learning process; children make one's job exciting, challenging, rewarding, and truly professional. This point cannot possibly be exaggerated, and in a day-to-day practical way it underlies the intellectual or abstract educational philosophy that is more commonly used to describe this very real revolution in education.

The Educational Picture in America

As one reads about these exciting developments in British schools, one cannot help but wonder why such ideas have never really caught on here on the scale they have in Britain. Of course, there is much talk about creativity, the needs of children, the importance of taking responsibility for one's own learning, and so forth. Indeed, bits and pieces of the educational processes described in the preceding chapters do exist all over America. Rather, the complete expression of and commitment to a set of educational ideals seems to be missing here.

Now let us examine some possible reasons for American reluctance to move in somewhat similar directions. One must say at the beginning of such an analysis that a number of American teachers, writers, and teachers-turned-writers *are* deeply involved in a movement to bring a looser, more relevant, more child-centered, and experienced-based kind of education to American children. One thinks immediately of Jonathan Kozol, Herbert Kohl, James Herndon, and John Holt. These educators exemplify the turned-on, deeply concerned teacher, who—on the basis of his experiences in classrooms—has something to say about American education. In addition, journalists like Joseph Featherstone and Charles Silberman are also joining the crusade; and even as influential a group as the Educational Development Center in Cambridge, Massachusetts (the base for Jerome Bruner's curricular operations) has come heavily under the influence of the British primary school.

OUTSIDE PRESSURES

Because of the pressures brought to bear by this new breed of educational criticism, changes are being made in some public schools; and a few private schools have been founded here and there that are more completely faithful to the educational point of view described in this book. Nevertheless in all fairness, it must be said that these are more like scattered rumblings than part of an organized, well-directed, and advancing movement.

"SPUTNIK": 1957

Perhaps one reason for American failure to move more rapidly in this direction can be traced to the curricular and methodological impact of the launching of the Russian "Sputnik" in 1957. Of course, this event was perceived as an educational humiliation, and all the curricular developments that followed it during the next decade gave a push to a kind of education vastly different from the movement that was already underway in Britain.

To illustrate, one might visualize the basic sources of the school curriculum as three points of a triangle. One angle might be labeled "the child," a second angle "the disciplines," and the third, "society." In other words (and in, no doubt, an oversimplified, polarized way), one might develop a curriculum that emphasized the needs of the child. Or, one might focus on the academic disciplines themselves, drawing content and experiences from the disciplines and attempting to fit the child to that curriculum. One might look at neither the child nor the disciplines but, rather, carefully analyze the needs of current society and attempt to build a curriculum dedicated to the resolution of today's problems.

EMPHASIS ON DISCIPLINES

Obviously, the elementary schools of both Britain and the United States do not align themselves solely with *one* angle of the curricular triangle described. Nor is the triangle ever static, because considerable movement is usually taking place within it. On the other hand, it seems quite fair to say that whereas the British primary school *is* concerned with the demands of the disciplines and the needs of society, it can be found (in our hypothetical triangle) a good deal closer to "the child" than the American elementary school can. On the contrary, the thrust of educational activity during the last decade in America—indeed, what we have come to call "the curricular revolution of the sixties"—has moved us steadily and relentlessly toward the "disciplines" angle.

It is no news to American or British educators that the search for "structure," for "basic concepts and generalizations" in mathematics, science, social studies, literature, and other fields has dominated curricular activity in the United States during the years following Sputnik. Quite logically, this search has lead to an emphasis on separate subjects rather than on the integration or wholeness of the curriculum; it has led to further support for a traditional educational disease, which we will call "the covering syndrome," i.e. one *must* deal with certain "basic" ideas, topics, and problems in a given sequence or else one is clearly derelict in one's duty; therefore, one must avoid those diversions, those side-tracking situations that, while they *do* interfere with "coverage" and sequence, often lead to relevant and exciting learning for children.

RELIANCE OF TEACHERS' MANUALS

In an attempt to be as faithful as possible to what we perceive as the "work-ways" or methods of the various disciplines, American educators have spent a great deal of time and energy in organizing the new curricula so that children will not merely memorize and repeat concepts and generalizations as they themselves memorized and repeated the much despised "facts" of the old curricula. Therefore we talk a great deal about inquiry and discovery approaches to learning. A careful examination of the materials and methods that comprise many of the new curriculum projects and packages reveals (with some exceptions) that the kinds of questions raised, the problems studied, the discoveries or generalizations arrived at are rarely the children's. We try valiantly; we smile, entreat, and cajole. Some of the youngsters are caught up in it some of the time—perhaps an unusually challenging topic catches their fancy, or perhaps an unusually dynamic teacher draws them out through the force of his personality. More often than not however, we end up with something Vincent Glennon has described as "sneaky telling." We know where we're going; we know what the questions should be, what the "big ideas" are, and the conclusions one *should,* if one follows the teachers' manual, come away with.

Perhaps, in the final analysis, this is the best way to teach. Perhaps we cannot afford the luxury of exploring children's questions in whichever direction they may take us. Certainly there is little evidence which demonstrates empirically that the less-structured, more child-centered British teacher is producing a better product than is the tighter, more rigid American teacher. At the moment, the best evidence I can offer is simply watching children at work and at play over extended periods of time in schools. If their reactions, their activity, their art, music, poetry, and their attitudes toward teachers and toward school are valid criteria, I must confess that it seems as if we have a great deal to learn from the British.

MECHANICAL PANACEAS VERSUS INDIVIDUALIZATION

Perhaps another reason for our reluctance to move in the same direction as the British has to do with our comparative affluence, our ability and tendency to develop, pay for, and be entranced by mechanical panaceas, or what we have come to call "educational hardware." In both countries "to individualize" is regarded as a good thing. Increasing numbers of conferences and workshops are devoted to this theme in America, yet American teachers seem not to have learned the lesson that is grasped so well by many British primary teachers, i.e. one individualizes, as Philip Jackson [2] put it, by:

. . . *injecting humor into a lesson when a student seems to need it, and quickly becoming serious when he is ready to settle down to work; it means thinking of examples that are uniquely relevant to the student's*

[2] P. W. Jackson, *The Teacher and The Machine: Observations on the Impact of Educational Technology* (mimeographed, University of Chicago, 1966).

previous experience and offering them at just the right time; it means feeling concerned over whether or not a student is progressing, and communicating that concern in a way that will be helpful; it means offering appropriate praise . . . because the student's performance is deserving of human admiration; it means, in short, responding as an individual to an individual.

This conception is much, much more than allowing for differences in speed when moving through some particular program; it is more than telling children (automatically, if politely) that "You are wrong, please turn to page 15 for another explanation."

In other words, one individualizes by watching and listening to *children.* Of course, mechanical aids are useful, but there is no substitute for the concept of individualization expressed so ably by Jackson. Many American teachers have been seduced by the promise of technology and the brave new world ahead; their less affluent British counterparts, who are economic realists if nothing else, know that individualization will come to their children only if they (the teachers) make a concerted effort to individualize under classroom conditions that are not likely to change radically soon. So they collect, construct, beg, borrow, and (who knows?) steal materials of all kinds to provide the kind of learning environment they know is good—and they often do so for classes of 40 children, or more. Most British teachers are willing to agree (with Mort Sahl) that "the future lies ahead." They are not, then, banking on an educational promised land that may lie just around the corner; they are addressing themselves to solving the individualization problem in terms of their own intelligence and energy—*now.*

DISMAL STATE OF AESTHETICS

A third reason for the clearly observable differences one sees when visiting a "new" British primary school and a typical American elementary school has to do with what must be called the dismal state aesthetics—art, music, and particularly, movement—finds itself in in American schools. Even for our very young children many schools have music and art teachers that conduct 20-minute, weekly lessons that become *the* art or music program. Aesthetics generally takes a back seat to the more academic components of the curriculum, and it is not held to be either important or seriously educative by many teachers.

Perhaps this is a problem inherent in American culture rather than a school problem. Surely it would be rare indeed to see an American teacher seriously encourage children to use their bodies as a mode of expression. It would be even more rare to find the teacher herself joining the children and participating in the creation of a dance pattern. (Perhaps a new generation of teachers, reared on the less inhibited use of their bodies that has developed with the universal acceptance of "rock," will see possibilities in movement that their predecessors did not.)

In any event, things aesthetic are considered effete; they are not valued in the same way that reading and mathematics are. In my judgment, aesthetics plays an infinitely more important role in the education of British children than in America, and the hesitancy of American teachers to utilize these means of reaching children surely results in a major difference between primary education in Britain and in America.

THE KINDERGARTEN/PRIMARY GRADE DICHOTOMY

Another curious factor that gets in the way of American movement toward the more free-wheeling, less-structured British primary school may lie in an educational dichotomy that has puzzled me for many years. In Britain, children are treated as individuals from the moment they enter school at the age of five until they leave the primary school. For example, teachers of "reception classes" (five-year-olds) move children into reading, if the child seems ready to read. Similarly, a *six-* year-old child (a typical American first grader) is not pushed, hounded, and bullied into reading when he reaches that magical age—ready or not. In other words, I think we have created a very unreal and unwise division between what learning ought to be for five-year-olds and what it ought to be for sixes. One might call this the kindergarten/primary grade dichotomy. Traditionally, we usually find a far greater degree of freedom, child-centeredness, and looseness in our kindergartens than at any other level in the elementary school. Many American children begin their education enjoying learning, being happy in school, and contented with themselves. For many of these children, however, first grade becomes a cruel awakening. No more time now for learning as fun; now we must "work" (ready or not); now we must put away dress-up clothes, blocks, and spur-of-the-moment curricular explorations.

In a good British primary school, this dichotomy does not exist. A child comes to school initially to learn, and to learn at his own pace. This point of view is carried out continuously through the primary years.

Until the education of American five-year-olds is not seen as something generically different from the education of six-year-olds, it is hard to see how a continuous pattern of educational progress similar to that described in this book can be widely adopted in America.

THE COMPETITIVE ACADEMIC RACE

Finally, we might make mention of one other factor that may play a role in discouraging the adoption on a large scale of the sort of primary school we have been describing. I refer to the relative freedom that British teachers and headmasters have to develop the kinds of educational programs that they as professionals deem right—with minimum concern for outside pressure groups. Conversely, American teachers and principals are subject to tremendous pressures from parents and others; and no state-supported school can casually ignore them. This means that some changes will be easier to bring about than others; that what the lay public conceives of as "good" education may be adopted in the schools more readily than other changes. At this point in time, the American lay public seems to see good education as a hard-driving, highly competitive academic race; educational innovations fitting that image stand a better chance of acceptance than do other innovations.

In Britain, which has traditionally had an exceedingly competitive education system, the movement towards drastic change in the education of young children originated and was carried out largely by professionals and sometimes *against* the wishes of parents. This is not to say that British teachers and headmasters can do as they please, when they please with British children. It does mean, however, that they are more independent of and more protected from outside pressures of all kinds; and, I repeat, the lack of this condition in the United States may have something to do with the reluctance of American educators to adopt similar approaches on a wide scale in this country.

Criticism of British Primary Schooling

Having examined what is and what is not, and why this may be so, we turn now to criticism. This will, of course, be difficult, because during the first pages of this chapter I have not attempted to hide my considerable admiration for what I see happening in the modern British primary school. Nevertheless, what seems good can no doubt become better, and perhaps some of the questions raised during these remaining pages may serve to further that purpose.

NEED FOR SYSTEMATIC EVALUATION

The first point is really not a criticism of classroom practices at all. Rather, it is a plea for more systematic evaluation of the achievements of the schools described in this book. Those of us fortunate enough to have visited a good British primary school recognize almost intuitively that what we are seeing is mostly right, mostly effective, mostly sound. On the other hand, many educators have a way of asking questions that cannot be answered adequately by referring to one's personal observations. How, in fact, do children in such schools perform on various objective measures when compared to children who have had quite a different sort of school experience? Obviously, academic achievement is not the basic goal of such schools, but since it is not, what effects do these schools have on children's attitudes towards school, teachers, and peers? How does this experience affect their approach to learning, the problem-solving strategies they adopt, their persistence, their curiosity?

The nondisciple deserves answers to these questions and to many more. Obviously, one cannot wait until all the data are in, since children have a way of appearing, growing, learning, and developing *now*. Decisions about ways of teaching children and organizing schools have to be made on the basis of the best evidence that is currently available. Nevertheless, every attempt should be made to provide more objective evidence whenever possible. This, it seems, would greatly strengthen the eloquent arguments presented by the contributors to this book and by others who are similarly convinced that they have, indeed, found a "better way."

THE SCHOOL WORLD VERSUS THE WORLD OF SOCIAL REALITY

A more direct criticism is exemplified, perhaps, by a description of an afternoon spent in what was in many ways a fascinating primary school in rural Leicestershire. During the entire afternoon the children were free to carry out projects that were of interest to them. There was a great deal of arts and crafts activity—carpentry, weaving, block printing, and so on. The children were obviously well behaved, busy, and interested in their work. Yet I could not help but feel that this happy, involved group of children were somehow existing in the middle of what we all know to be a terribly complex, rapidly changing world— divorced from its reality, protected from its problems, and uninvolved in its conflicts and dilemmas.

Somehow, the "real" world that children explore in such schools is often a rather limited version of reality. It is a real world of fields, streams, trees, rocks, stones, flowers, birds and insects, if it is a country school. If it is a city school, it is a real world of traffic patterns, nearby shops, local museums and libraries, parks and gardens. The "real world" is often conceived of as that part of the world which is nearby; more precisely, that which can be seen, felt, smelled, touched, or listened to.

One might suggest then, that after all there are limits to how far one can go with personal, concrete experience as *the* essential teaching technique. Children can study only a small part of the world by direct observation and experience, and one must question the hours spent in making, building, and *physically* "doing"; hours that could, conceivably, be used in other ways as well. One wonders, for example, if in studying the woollen industry the process of making wool does not get treated all out of proportion to some of the related economic, social, and, in fact, even political problems that might be implied in such a study—granting, of course, that much of this "activity" would be intellectual rather than physical, vicarious more than direct.

One might argue, of course, that this is the job of the *secondary* school; that primary children are concerned with the properties, origins, uses and manufacture of wool, and not with related economic, social or political problems. Surely the gathering of in-depth experiences is crucial to the learning of primary children; whether such experience gathering precludes consideration of the types of questions mentioned above is, however, an unresolved pedagogical issue at this time.

In any event, if one largely limits the objects to one's study to those found only in the local environment, it is difficult to see how the school can play a significant role in helping children understand the broader world in which they live. Conflict exists about Rhodesia and about the immigrant-settled sections of British cities such as Wolverhampton and

Bradford. These problems are important to all British children—not only to those living in areas directly affected by such conflict. The fact that they do not always lend themselves to direct or "concrete" experience does not render them any the less important.

The real world of social conflict exists, and no school, no teacher, no syllabus will ever completely isolate children from it. Yet the schools' responsibility would seem to include some attempts at increasing children's awareness of the inadequacies and inequalities that exist in both their local and their wider environments. Failing this, children will muddle through, picking up ideas and attitudes wherever they find them and becoming more and more aware (perhaps through harsh personal experience) about the conflict that exists between the school world and the world of social reality.

THE FREE APPROACH NOT UNIVERSALLY APPROPRIATE TO ALL DISCIPLINES

Another area of criticism might be devoted to what some people have called the "messing about" syndrome. Simply stated, do children need more "closure" to their work in order to make it intellectually (as well as physically, socially, and emotionally) satisfying to them? Do some of the activities described in the preceding chapters call for more of a beginning, middle, and end?

Quite clearly, teachers of foreign languages and mathematics have had to do considerably more stretching than have those interested in creative writing to make their area of interest "fit" the model presented in this book. Rather than apologize for not fitting entirely into the mold, however, might it not be more honest (and in the long run more helpful) if we flatly admitted that some areas call more desperately than others do for the approaches outlined in the preceding chapters?

Let me hasten to add that I am quite willing to be shown that I am wrong and that relatively free approaches are uniformly good. Nevertheless, within the framework of a philosophy devoted to an understanding of the individual and a commitment to exploration and active participation on the part of the child, I think it might be possible to experiment with a greater variety of teaching procedures and forms of school or class organization than have been described or suggested here.

INSUFFICIENT ATTENTION TO BROADER CONCEPTS
OF UNDERSTANDING

Similarly, one might question the degree of curricular egalitarianism that exists in the emerging British primary school. Obviously, only the simplest of societies can hope to teach its children "all they need to know." Therefore, it has become increasingly important to ask, what knowledge is of the most worth to *our* society at this particular moment in time? Which ideas will help the nonspecialist citizen to understand the world in which he lives? Which ideas are fundamental enough to have transfer value, i.e. which ideas will help one to better understand a unique phenomenon that has not been formally studied before?

My British colleagues will immediately argue (with John Holt) that only the *child* can know what knowledge, what information, what understanding, is important and necessary to him. Identifying significant ideas seems to smack of predigested academic conclusions that have little relevance to children's interests or needs. I would agree. I would indeed argue further that this appears to be the major weakness in many of the American curriculum projects that were developed during the Brunnerian revolution of the 1960's.

However, this does not negate the argument that there *are* some things worth knowing; that some ideas help to order and explain our lives and the lives of others, while other ideas do not. It seems to me that the great weakness one observes in both British and American schools is the lack of knowledge about and understanding of such ideas among *teachers*.

It would be foolish indeed to suggest that a discipline like anthropology has developed no ideas that are really worth teaching to children; no concepts that help to order, classify, and explain the social world in which we find ourselves. The real value, the ultimate utility of such ideas, however, lies *not* in the creation of prepackaged "teacher-proof" curricula; rather, it is the classroom teacher who must grasp them and utilize them at the apropriate moment. In other words, "structure" belongs in the minds of teachers.

If teachers grasp some of the insights of physical and social science, for example, they will be able to help children see the generalized significance of events or phenomena that interest them. Similarly, they will be able to help children to ask questions that go beyond the merely descriptive; they will be able to see possibilities that may well have escaped them in the past. This is not to suggest that many British and American teachers are not already doing this; they are. I have already alluded to the considerable competence British teachers have in what we might broadly define as the humanities. Nevertheless, it seems to me that British teachers might be able to help children extract more significant learnings from the various projects and studies they engage in, if they were willing to examine the notion of structure in its broadest and most useful sense—particularly in the social, physical, and biological sciences. This has been done in mathematics; and I think most American observers would be quick to single out this area as an unusually effective component of the British primary-school curriculum.

One might mention other arguments, other "weaknesses"; these, however, seem to me to be among the most fruitful to discuss, and perhaps, among the questions most likely to be raised by American educators.

Conclusions

In Chapter 11, on movement, music, drama, and art, the thoughts of an eight-year-old boy at the onset of winter were used as an illustration of the synthesis between experience and expression in words. The reader may recall his words:

And a mist came down and separated autumn from winter.

Those who saw John Osborne's *The Entertainer* will remember the scene in which Archie Rice acknowledges to himself that he is, in fact, a talentless failure. He recalls a night in Canada when he heard a Negro entertainer sing with great sensitivity and beauty—"a pure and natural noise," he called it. "If I'd done one thing as good as that in my whole life, I'd have been all right," he says.

If most of us could get from our children one bit of writing as good as what that eight-year-old boy wrote, I guess we would be all right as teachers.

There is so much that seems magnificently "right" in the British primary schools I know that I hesitate to conclude this chapter on a critical note. At their best, these schools are nothing short of superb. They do, in fact, offer "another way" to those of us who are willing to listen and examine our own practices—however agonizing such a reappraisal might be.

INDEX

America
  educational picture in, 290 *ff.*
American criticism of British primary
    schooling, 296–301
  free approach not universally appro-
      priate to all disciplines, 299
  insufficient attention to broader con-
      cepts of understanding, 300–301
  need for systematic evaluation, 297
  school world versus the world of
      social reality, 297–98
American elementary schools compared
    to British primary schools, 290 *ff.*
  competitive academic race, 296
  dismal state of aesthetics, 294–95
  emphasis on disciplines, 292
  kindergarten/primary grade dichot-
      omy, 295–96
  mechanical panaceas versus individ-
      ualization, 293–94
  reliance on teachers' manuals, 292–93
American observations on success of
    British primary schools, 283–301
  salient features of the educational
      revolution, 288–90
    emphasis on the thinking process,
        289
    flexible curriculum, 288–89
    freedom and responsibility of chil-
        dren, 290
    interrelated studies, 289
    teachers' respect for children's
        ideas, 290

American observations (*Cont.*)
  salient features (*Cont.*)
    unobtrusive teaching, 289
  tentative hypotheses, 285–88
    creativity in use of teaching ma-
        terials, 286–87
    government support for the "new
        education," 287–88
    prime importance of the instruc-
        tional program, 287
    quality and background of teach-
        ers, 285–86
    staff cooperation toward goals, 285
Art
  in the infant school, 219–20
  in the junior school, 230–33
Arts in the primary school, 218–35
  educative value of, 234–35
Association for Science Education, 192

Books
  library areas in the classroom, 12–13,
      51
  use of, for pleasure and information,
      102–103
British Association for the Advancement
    of Science, 192
British primary school. *See also* Primary
    school
  American criticism of. *See* American
      criticism of British primary
      schooling
  American observations on success of.

303